Other Books and Series by Jeff Bowen

Applications for Enrollment of Chickasaw Newborn Act of 1905 Volumes I thru VII

Cherokee Intermarried White 1906 Volume I thru X

Applications for Enrollment of Creek Newborn Act of 1905 Volume I, II & III

Visit our website at www.nativestudy.com to learn more about these and other books and series by Jeff Bowen

APPLICATIONS FOR ENROLLMENT OF CREEK NEWBORN ACT OF 1905
VOLUME IV

TRANSCRIBED BY
JEFF BOWEN
NATIVE STUDY
Gallipolis, Ohio
USA

Other Books and Series by Jeff Bowen

1901-1907 Native American Census Seneca, Eastern Shawnee, Miami, Modoc, Ottawa, Peoria, Quapaw, and Wyandotte Indians (Under Seneca School, Indian Territory)

1932 Census of The Standing Rock Sioux Reservation with Births And Deaths 1924-1932

Census of The Blackfeet, Montana, 1897- 1901 Expanded Edition

Eastern Cherokee by Blood, 1906-1910, Volumes I thru XIII

Choctaw of Mississippi Indian Census 1929-1932 with Births and Deaths 1924-1931 Volume I
Choctaw of Mississippi Indian Census 1933, 1934 & 1937, Supplemental Rolls to 1934 & 1935 with Births and Deaths 1932-1938, and Marriages 1936-1938 Volume II

Eastern Cherokee Census Cherokee, North Carolina 1930-1939 Census 1930-1931 with Births And Deaths 1924-1931 Taken By Agent L. W. Page Volume I
Eastern Cherokee Census Cherokee, North Carolina 1930-1939 Census 1932-1933 with Births And Deaths 1930-1932 Taken By Agent R. L. Spalsbury Volume II
Eastern Cherokee Census Cherokee, North Carolina 1930-1939 Census 1934-1937 with Births and Deaths 1925-1938 and Marriages 1936 & 1938 Taken by Agents R. L. Spalsbury And Harold W. Foght Volume III

Seminole of Florida Indian Census, 1930-1940 with Birth and Death Records, 1930-1938

Texas Cherokees 1820-1839 A Document For Litigation 1921

Choctaw By Blood Enrollment Cards 1898-1914 Volumes I thru XVII

Starr Roll 1894 (Cherokee Payment Rolls) Districts: Canadian, Cooweescoowee, and Delaware Volume One
Starr Roll 1894 (Cherokee Payment Rolls) Districts: Flint, Going Snake, and Illinois Volume Two
Starr Roll 1894 (Cherokee Payment Rolls) Districts: Saline, Sequoyah, and Tahlequah; Including Orphan Roll Volume Three

Cherokee Intruder Cases Dockets of Hearings 1901-1909 Volumes I & II

Indian Wills, 1911-1921 Records of the Bureau of Indian Affairs Books One thru Seven;
Native American Wills & Probate Records 1911-1921

Other Books and Series by Jeff Bowen

Turtle Mountain Reservation Chippewa Indians 1932 Census with Births & Deaths, 1924-1932

Chickasaw By Blood Enrollment Cards 1898-1914 Volume I thru V

Cherokee Descendants East An Index to the Guion Miller Applications Volume I
Cherokee Descendants West An Index to the Guion Miller Applications Volume II (A-M)
Cherokee Descendants West An Index to the Guion Miller Applications Volume III (N-Z)

Applications for Enrollment of Seminole Newborn Freedmen, Act of 1905

Eastern Cherokee Census, Cherokee, North Carolina, 1915-1922, Taken by Agent James E. Henderson Volume I (1915-1916)
       Volume II (1917-1918)
       Volume III (1919-1920)
       Volume IV (1921-1922)

Complete Delaware Roll of 1898

Eastern Cherokee Census, Cherokee, North Carolina, 1923-1929, Taken by Agent James E. Henderson Volume I (1923-1924)
       Volume II (1925-1926)
       Volume III (1927-1929)

Applications for Enrollment of Seminole Newborn Act of 1905 Volumes I & II

North Carolina Eastern Cherokee Indian Census 1898-1899, 1904, 1906, 1909-1912, 1914 Revised and Expanded Edition

1932 Hopi and Navajo Native American Census with Birth & Death Rolls (1925-1931) Volume 1 - Hopi
1932 Hopi and Navajo Native American Census with Birth & Death Rolls (1930-1932) Volume 2 - Navajo

Western Navajo Reservation Navajo, Hopi and Paiute 1933 Census with Birth & Death Rolls 1925-1933

Cherokee Citizenship Commission Dockets 1880-1884 and 1887-1889 Volumes I thru V

Copyright © 2011
by Jeff Bowen

ALL RIGHTS RESERVED
No part of this publication may be reproduced
or used in any form or manner whatsoever
without previous written permission from the
copyright holder or publisher.

Originally published:
Baltimore, Maryland
2011

Reprinted by:

Native Study LLC
Gallipolis, OH
www.nativestudy.com
2020

Library of Congress Control Number: 2020917992

ISBN: 978-1-64968-083-9

Made in the United States of America.

This series is dedicated to the descendants of the
Creek newborn listed in these applications.

DEPARTMENT OF THE INTERIOR.

Commissioner to the Five Civilized Tribes.

NOTICE.

Opening of Land Office at Wewoka,
IN THE SEMINOLE NATION, INDIAN TERRITORY.

Notice is hereby given that on Monday, September 4, 1905, the Commissioner to the Five Civilized Tribes will establish a land office at Wewoka, in the Seminole Nation, Indian Territory, for the purpose of allowing citizens and freedmen of the Seminole Nation to select allotments of land for their minor children enrolled under the Act of Congress approved March 3, 1905 (33 Stat. L 1060), and for the further purpose of allowing citizens and freedmen of the Seminole Nation, whose allotments are incomplete, to select additional land in order to bring the value of their allotments up to the standard of $309.09, as nearly as may be practicable.

Each child whose enrollment in accordance with the Act of March 3, 1905, has been duly approved by the Secretary of the Interior, is entitled to receive an allotment of forty acres without regard to the character or value of the land selected.

Selection of allotments for minor children must be made by their citizen or freedmen parents or by a duly appointed guardian, or curator, or by a duly appointed administrator.

TAMS BIXBY,
Commissioner.

Muskogee, Indian Territory,
July 29, 1905.

This particular notice makes mention of the Act of 1905. The Creek and Seminole were closely related tribes. Both tribes' notices were like similar in nature.

DEPARTMENT OF THE INTERIOR,
Commission to the Five Civilized Tribes.

Closing of Citizenship Rolls

OF THE MUSKOGEE OR CREEK NATION.

WHEREAS, on June 13, 1904, the Secretary of the Interior, under the authority in him vested by the provisions of the act of Congress approved March 3, 1901, (31 Stat., 1058) ordered that September 1, 1904, be and the same is hereby fixed as the time when the rolls of the Muskogee or Creek Nation shall be closed:

Notice is hereby given that the Commission to the Five Civilized Tribes will, at its office in Muskogee, Indian Territory, up to and inclusive of September 1, 1904, receive applications for the enrollment of citizens and freedmen of the Muskogee or Creek Nation, and that after that date the application of no person whomsoever for enrollment as a citizen or freedman of said nation will be received by the Commission.

Commission to the Five Civilized Tribes,
TAMS BIXBY, Chairman,
T. B. NEEDLES,
C. R. BRECKINRIDGE,
Commissioners.

Muskogee, Indian Territory,
June 25, 1904.

A notice like this was printed in newspapers and posted throughout Indian Territory.

INTRODUCTION

This series concerns Applications for Enrollment of Creek Newborn, National Archive film M-1301 (Act of 1905), as described in the National Archives publication *American Indians*. It falls under the heading Applications for Enrollment of the Commission to the Five Civilized Tribes, 1898-1914, M-1301 and is transcribed from microfilm rolls 414-419. This shows the application forms filled out by individuals applying for enrollment in the Five Civilized Tribes under the Dawes Commission. These applications contain additional information that wasn't abstracted to the census cards that you find in series M-1186. This particular roll (Creek by Birth) contains its own series of numbers separate from M-1186. To find each party's roll number you would have to reference M-1186. On July 25, 1898, there was an Indian Territory Division created in the Office of the Department of Interior. This division was created because of the increased work caused by what was called the Curtis Act, named after Senator Charles Curtis. Basically, this law stated that the tribal rolls needed to be descriptive and pointed out that each tribal roll was without description and had to be redone. At this point there was such a struggle among the Creeks to accept that the Government was going to change their way of life, again, that their leaders were refusing to cooperate in handing over their census information. The Commission had found that enrolling the Creeks was a difficult task not only because the Creek feared what was coming but also because their tribal structure was consistent with being a confederacy with forty-four different bands whose tribesmen lived in different towns of which each had a king that was supposed to keep track of their citizenry. The Commission reported that there was very little evidence of any census that existed and what there was had been kept carelessly. There were attempts and tribal conflicts along the way, but the Curtis Act would make it so they had to do it again no matter what effort from the past. In 1899, Agent Wesley Smith educated Washington to the fact that it was difficult to verify Creek eligibility. The acts passed by the Creeks themselves concerning enrollment since 1893 had been strewn amongst the archives of the Creek Council in Muskogee, I.T., and there was no provision ever approved for the printing of the those enrollments. There was confusion and difficulty let alone the fact that surnames were practically unknown among the Creek. But there was no confusion on March 9, 1905, when the Commission stated they would come to seven towns in the Creek Nation and accept applications that had to be made on a standardized blank form and contain a notarized affidavit from the mother and the attending doctor or midwife. A few by mail, but most of them were offered to a field party led by Commissioner Needles. The Commission took in applications for 2,410 children by the deadline of midnight, May 2, 1905.

This series contains applications and correspondence from 1,171 of those claimants. Realizing there were over 2,400 applicants originally, it is understood that not all were accepted. Also included are names of doctors, lawyers, mid-wives, and others who attended to the Creek Nation before and during this time in history.

Jeff Bowen
Gallipolis, Ohio
NativeStudy.com

Applications for Enrollment of Creek Newborn
Act of 1905 Volume IV

BIRTH AFFIDAVIT.

DEPARTMENT OF THE INTERIOR.
COMMISSION TO THE FIVE CIVILIZED TRIBES.

IN RE APPLICATION FOR ENROLLMENT, as a citizen of the CREEK Nation, of Legus Rogers, born on the 11 day of Feb , 1901

Name of Father:	John Rogers	a citizen of the	U.S.	Nation.
Name of Mother:	Melvina Rogers	a citizen of the	Creek	Nation.

Postoffice   Gibson Station

AFFIDAVIT OF MOTHER.

UNITED STATES OF AMERICA, Indian Territory,
WESTERN DISTRICT.

I, Melvina Rogers , on oath state that I am 22 years of age and a citizen by blood , of the Creek Nation; that I am the lawful wife of John Rogers , who is a citizen, by ----- of the U. S. Nation; that a male child was born to me on 11 day of Feb. , 1901 , that said child has been named Lecus[sic] Rogers , and is now living. (child with husband in Guthrie Okla. since June 1904.)

                            Her
                        Melvina x Rogers
Witnesses To Mark: mark
  { JY Miller
    EC Griesel

Subscribed and sworn to before me this 16 day of March , 1905.

                        Edw C Griesel
                            Notary Public.

BIRTH AFFIDAVIT.

DEPARTMENT OF THE INTERIOR.
COMMISSION TO THE FIVE CIVILIZED TRIBES.

IN RE APPLICATION FOR ENROLLMENT, as a citizen of the CREEK Nation, of Louie Rogers, born on the ----- day of June , 1903

Name of Father:	John Rogers	a citizen of the	U.S.	Nation.
Name of Mother:	Melvina "	a citizen of the	Creek	Nation.

Postoffice   Gibson Station

Applications for Enrollment of Creek Newborn
Act of 1905   Volume IV

AFFIDAVIT OF MOTHER.

UNITED STATES OF AMERICA, Indian Territory, ⎫
   WESTERN   DISTRICT. ⎭

    I, Melvina Rogers , on oath state that I am 22 years of age and a citizen by blood , of the Creek   Nation; that I am the lawful wife of John Rogers , who is a citizen, by ----- of the U. S. Nation; that a male child was born to me on ----- day of June , 1903 , that said child has been named Louie Rogers , and ~~is now living~~. died 8 days after birth

                                            Her
                                  Melvina x Rogers
Witnesses To Mark: mark
   { J McDermott
     EC Griesel

    Subscribed and sworn to before me this 16 day of March , 1905.

                                       Edw C Griesel
                                            Notary Public.

NC 251   JLD
                        DEPARTMENT OF THE INTERIOR,
              COMMISSIONER TO THE FIVE CIVILIZED TRIBES.
                            . . . .

    In the matter of the application for the enrollment of Louie Rogers, deceased, as a citizen by blood of the Creek Nation.
                            . . . .

                        STATEMENT AND ORDER.

    The record in this case shows that on March 16, 1905, application was made, in affidavit form, for the enrollment of Louie Rogers, deceased, as a citizen by blood of the Creek Nation, under the provisions of the act of Congress approved March 3, 1905.

    It appears that the affidavit filed in this matter that said Louie Rogers, deceased, was born in June, 1903, and died eight days after birth.

    The act of Congress approved March 3, 1905, (33 Stats., 1048), provides:

"That the Commission to the Five Civilized Tribes is authorized for sixty days after the date of the approval of this act to receive and consider applications for enrollment, of children, <u>born subsequent to May twenty-fifth, nineteen hundred and one, and prior to March fourth, nineteen hundred and five, and living on said latter date, to citizens of the</u> Creek tribe of Indians whose enrollment has been approved by the Secretary of the Interior prior to the approval of this act; and to enroll and make allotments to such children."

Applications for Enrollment of Creek Newborn
Act of 1905   Volume IV

It is, therefore, ordered that the application for the enrollment of Louie Rogers, deceased, as a citizen by blood of the Creek Nation be, and the same is, hereby dismissed.

Tams Bixby Commissioner.

Muskogee, Indian Territory.
JAN 4 – 1907

BA- 581 & 584B.

DEPARTMENT OF THE INTERIOR,
COMMISSION TO THE FIVE CIVILIZED TRIBES.
MUSKOGEE, INDIAN TERRITORY, MARCH 16, 1905.
-oo0oo-

In the matter of the application for the enrollment of Cooper Davis and Ollie Davis, both deceased, as citizens ~~by blood~~ of the Creek Nation.

LUCY THOMAS, being duly sworn, testified as follows:

EXAMINATION BY COMMISSION:
Q What is your name? A Lucy Thomas.
Q How old are you? A 19.
Q What is your postoffice address? A Muskogee.
Q Are you the wife of Eli Davis? A No, sir.
Q Who is the father of Cooper Davis and Ollie Davis? A Eli Davis.
Q And you are not married to him? A No.

Eli Davis is identified on Creek Freedmen Card, Field Number 1927, and his name is contained in the partial list of Creed[sic] Freedmen, approved by the Secretary of the Interior March 28, 1902, Roll Number 6056.

Q When was Ollie Davis born? A April 7th.
Q What year? A 1901.
Q Is Ollie Davis living? A No.
Q When did he die? A June 22nd.
Q What year? A I disremember.
Q Was it last year? A No.
Q Was it year before last? A Yes, I think so.
Q Was it in 1903? A I do not know; he has been dead a little less than three years.
Q When was Cooper Davis born? A I don't know.
Q Was e born the same year in which he died? A Yes.
Q Was he born in 1903? A I think so.
Q Is he living? A No.
Q When did he die? A I disremember.
Q Did he die last year? A Yes, sir.
Q Was the early part of last year that he died? A Yes.

Applications for Enrollment of Creek Newborn
Act of 1905 Volume IV

Q How long did he live? A Eleven months.
Q He has been dead about one year has he? A Yes, sir.
Q Are you sure the dates are right? A Yes, sir.

Zera Ellen Parrish, being sworn on her oath states that as a stenographer to the Commission to the Five Civilized Tribes she reported the above case and that this is a full, true and correct transcript of her stenographic notes in same.

Zera Ellen Parrish

Subscribed and sworn to before me this 18 day of March, 1905.

Edw C Griesel
Notary Public.

NC 252   JLD

DEPARTMENT OF THE INTERIOR,
COMMISSIONER TO THE FIVE CIVILIZED TRIBES.

In the matter of the application for the enrollment of Cooper Davis, deceased, as a citizen by blood of the Creek Nation.

....

STATEMENT AND ORDER.

The record in this case shows that on March 16, 1905, application was made, in affidavit form, supplemented by sworn testimony, for the enrollment of Cooper Davis, deceased, as a citizen by blood of the Creek Nation, under the provisions of the act of Congress approved March 3, 1905.

It appears from the evidence filed in this matter that said Cooper Davis, deceased, was born April 14, 1903, and died on or about March 14, 1904.

The Act of Congress approved March 3, 1905, (33 Stats., 1048), provides:

"That the Commission to the Five Civilized Tribes is authorized for sixty days after the date of the approval of this act to receive and consider applications for enrollment, of children, <u>born subsequent to May twenty-fifth, nineteen hundred and one, and prior to March fourth, nineteen hundred and five, and living on said latter date</u>, to citizens of the Creek tribe of Indians whose enrollment has been approved by the Secretary of the Interior prior to the approval of this act; and to enroll and make allotments to such children."

It is, therefore, ordered that the application for the enrollment of said Cooper Davis, deceased, as a citizen by blood of the Creek Nation, be, and the same is, hereby dismissed.

Tams Bixby Commissioner.

Muskogee, Indian Territory.
JAN 15 1907

Applications for Enrollment of Creek Newborn
Act of 1905 Volume IV

BIRTH AFFIDAVIT.

DEPARTMENT OF THE INTERIOR.
COMMISSION TO THE FIVE CIVILIZED TRIBES.

IN RE APPLICATION FOR ENROLLMENT, as a citizen of the CREEK Nation, of Cooper Davis, born on the 14 day of April, 1903

Name of Father:	Eli Davis	a citizen of the	Creek	Nation.
Name of Mother:	Lucy Thomas	a citizen of the	U. S.	Nation.

Postoffice   Muskogee

AFFIDAVIT OF MOTHER.

UNITED STATES OF AMERICA, Indian Territory,
WESTERN DISTRICT.

I, Lucy Thomas, on oath state that I am 19 years of age and a citizen by -----, of the U. S. Nation; that I am ~~the lawful wife of~~ not married to Eli Davis, who is a citizen, by blood of the Creek Nation; that a male child was born to me on 14 day of April, 1903, that said child has been named Cooper Davis, and ~~is now living~~. died 11 months after birth.

Lucy Thomas

Witnesses To Mark:

Subscribed and sworn to before me this 16 day of March, 1905.

Edw C Griesel
Notary Public.

REFER IN REPLY TO THE FOLLOWING:

NC 252.

DEPARTMENT OF THE INTERIOR,
COMMISSIONER TO THE FIVE CIVILIZED TRIBES.

Muskogee, Indian Territory, January 16, 1907.

Eli Davis,
General Delivery,
Muskogee, Indian Territory.

Dear Sir:

Applications for Enrollment of Creek Newborn
Act of 1905   Volume IV

There is herewith inclosed[sic] one copy of the Statement and Order of the Commissioner to the Five Civilized Tribes, dated January 15, 1907, dismissing the application made by you for the enrollment of your minor child, Cooper Davis, as a citizen of the Creek Nation.

Respectfully,

Tams Bixby Commissioner.

BIRTH AFFIDAVIT.

DEPARTMENT OF THE INTERIOR,
COMMISSION TO THE FIVE CIVILIZED TRIBES.

IN RE Application for Enrollment, as a citizen of the Creek Nation, of ~~Indians~~ Phillip Tiger, born on the 12" day of February, 1902

Name of Father: James Tiger   a citizen of the Naw Creek Nation.
Name of Mother: Nancy Tiger   a citizen of the   Creek   Nation.

Post-Office: Coweta Ind. Ter.

AFFIDAVIT OF MOTHER.

UNITED STATES OF AMERICA, }
   Indian Territory.
Western Judicial   District.

I, Nancy Tiger, on oath state that I am about 33 years of age and a citizen by blood, of the Creek Nation; that I am the lawful wife of James Tiger, who is a citizen, by blood of the Creek Nation; that a male child was born to me on 12" day of February, 1902, that said child has been named Phillip Tiger, and is now living.

                                her
                           Nancy x Tiger
WITNESSES TO MARK: mark
   { R. M. Easley
    Ned Kelley

Subscribed and sworn to before me this 14 *day of* March, 1905.

My Com Expires   W.A. Brigham
Oct. 28" 1906.   *Notary Public.*

Applications for Enrollment of Creek Newborn
Act of 1905 Volume IV

AFFIDAVIT OF ATTENDING PHYSICIAN OR MID-WIFE.

UNITED STATES OF AMERICA,
    Indian Territory.
Western Judicial   District.

I, Lily Tiger , a Midwife , on oath state that I attended on Mrs. Nancy Tiger , wife of James Tiger on the 12" day of February , 1902 ; that there was born to her on said date a male child; that said child is now living and is said to have been named Phillip Tiger   her
                                                                   Lily x Tiger

WITNESSES TO MARK: mark
{ R. M. Easley
  Ned Kelley

Subscribed and sworn to before me this 14 *day of* March, 1905.

My Com Expires   W.A. Brigham
Oct. 28" 1906.   *Notary Public.*

BIRTH AFFIDAVIT.

DEPARTMENT OF THE INTERIOR.
COMMISSION TO THE FIVE CIVILIZED TRIBES.

IN RE APPLICATION FOR ENROLLMENT, as a citizen of the Creek Nation, of Joanna Tiger, born on the 11 day of March , 1904

Name of Father: James Tiger   a citizen of the   Creek   Nation.
Name of Mother: Nancy "   a citizen of the   Creek   Nation.

                              Postoffice   Coweta, Ind. Ter.

AFFIDAVIT OF MOTHER.

UNITED STATES OF AMERICA, Indian Territory,
Western Judicial   DISTRICT.

I, Nancy Tiger , on oath state that I am about 33 years of age and a citizen by blood , of the Creek Nation; that I am the lawful wife of James Tiger , who is a citizen, by blood of the Creek Nation; that a female child was born to me on 11" day of March , 1904 , that said child has been named Joanna Tiger; died on the 11th day of Mch 1905 , and was living March 4, 1905.   her
                                            Nancy x Tiger
                                                 mark

Applications for Enrollment of Creek Newborn
Act of 1905   Volume IV

Witnesses To Mark:
  { G.W. Farris
   Ned Kelley

    Subscribed and sworn to before me this 14 day of March, 1905.

My Com Expires   W.A. Brigham
Oct. 28" 1906.   Notary Public.

United States of America
  Indian Territory
Western Judicial District   SS

    I James Tiger on oath say; I am about 33 years of age I am the lawful husband of Nancy Tiger that there was born to us a female child on the 11 day of March 1904 and was named Joanna Tiger that said child died on the 11 day of March 1905 that at the time of the birth of said child no one was in attendance on my wife except myself; that Yanah Lynch a neighbor came to my house the next morning and washed and dressed the child and washed and assisted my wife.

                                         Jas Tiger

Subscribed and sworn to before me this 14 day of March 1905
My term expires Oct 28 1906   W A Brigham
                                Notary Public

United States of America
Indian Territory
Western Judicial District

                     Ned Kelly and Jasper Sarty on their oaths say that they attended at the burial of Joanna Tiger infant child of James and Nancy Tiger on the 11 day of March 1905 and that said child died on that date

                                         Ned Kelley
                                         Jasper Sarty

My term expires Oct 28 1906
Subscribed and sworn to before me this 14 day of March 1905
                                         WA Brigham
                                         Notary Public

Cr. NC 254.

                               Muskogee, Indian Territory, June 9, 1905.

Nancy Tiger,
    Coweta, Indian Territory.

Applications for Enrollment of Creek Newborn
Act of 1905 Volume IV

Dear Madam:

You are hereby advised that you will be allowed fifteen days from date hereof which to appear before the Commission, at its office in Muskogee, Indian Territory, with your husband, James Tiger, and two witnesses who know the dates of the birth and death of your minor children, Phillip and Joanna Tiger.

This matter should receive your prompt attention.

Respectfully,

Chairman.

(Written on a torn piece of lined paper)

Philip Tiger Born in Feb 12 1092[sic]
Joanna Tiger Born in March 11 1904
Died March 11 1904

(The above letter to Nancy Tiger given again)

BIRTH AFFIDAVIT.

DEPARTMENT OF THE INTERIOR,
COMMISSION TO THE FIVE CIVILIZED TRIBES.

IN RE Application for Enrollment, as a citizen of the Creek Nation, of ~~Indians~~ Joanna Tiger, born on the 11" day of March, 1904

Name of Father:	James Tiger	a citizen of the	Creek	Nation.
Name of Mother:	Nancy Tiger	a citizen of the	Creek	Nation.

Post-Office: Coweta Ind. Ter.

AFFIDAVIT OF MOTHER.

UNITED STATES OF AMERICA,
    Indian Territory.
Western Judicial   District.

I, Nancy Tiger, on oath state that I am about 33 years of age and a citizen by blood, of the Creek Nation; that I am the lawful wife of James Tiger, who is a citizen, by blood of the Creek Nation; that a female child was born to me

Applications for Enrollment of Creek Newborn
Act of 1905 Volume IV

on 11" day of March, 1904, that said child has been named Joanna Tiger, and ~~is now living~~. that said child Joanna Tiger died on the 11" day of March 1905.

                                         her
                                Nancy x Tiger
WITNESSES TO MARK: mark
  { *(Name Illegible)*
    Ned Kelley

Subscribed and sworn to before me this 14" *day of* March, *1905.*

My Com Expires   W.A. Brigham
Oct. 28" 1906.   *Notary Public.*

AFFIDAVIT OF ATTENDING PHYSICIAN OR MID-WIFE.

UNITED STATES OF AMERICA,
  Indian Territory.
Western Judicial   District.

    I, Yanah Lynch, a Neighbor Woman, on oath state that I attended on Mrs. Nancy Tiger, wife of James Tiger on the 11" day of March, 1904; that there was born to her on said date a female child; that said child is now ~~living~~ dead and is said to have been named Joanna Tiger. That she got there after my child had been born.
                                her
                            Yanah x Lynch
WITNESSES TO MARK: mark
  { R. M. Easley
    Ned Kelley

Subscribed and sworn to before me this 14" *day of* March, *1905.*

My Com Expires   W.A. Brigham
Oct. 28" 1906.   *Notary Public.*

NC 254.
DEPARTMENT OF THE INTERIOR,
COMMISSION TO THE FIVE CIVILIZED TRIBES.
MUSKOGEE, I. T. JUNE 23, 1905.

    In the matter of the application for the enrollment of Phillip and Joanna Tiger, as citizens by blood of the Creek Nation.

    James Tiger, being duly sworn, testified as follows:

Applications for Enrollment of Creek Newborn
Act of 1905   Volume IV

Examination by the Commission:
Q What is your name? A James Tiger.
Q How old are you? A About 33.
Q What is your post office address? A Coweta.
Q Are you the father of Phillip and Joanna Tiger? A Yes sir.
Q Do you remember when Phillip was born A I think February 12, 1902.
Q Is Phillip Tiger living? A Yes sir.
Q When was Joanna Tiger born? A March 11, 1904.
Q Is she living? A No sir.
Q When did she die? A Last March 19.
Q Did you write down in a book or on a pice[sic] of paper anywhere the dates of the birth and death of this child? A Yes, sir, I have a record.
Q Did you bring that with you? A I have it here on a piece of paper.
Q Did you copy it from the record at home? A Yes sir.

    Witness presents a piece of paper on which is written "Philip Tiger, Born in Feb. 12 ~~190~~ 1092[sic]. Joanna Tiger Born in March 11 1904 Died March 11 1905."

Q When did you write it down in that book or record at home? A Same day it was born.
Q When did you write the record of her death in the book? A Sam[sic] day she died.
Q How old was Joanna Tiger when she died? A One year old.
Q Just one year old? A Just exactly one year old to the day.
Q Do you remember when you made out these affidavits about the death and birth of Joanna Tiger? A Pretty near two months ago.
Q You just remember that you made them, now how long before you made this affidavit out did Joanna Die? A About two or three months.
Q She died about two or three months before you made this affidavit out? A Yes sir.
Q Are you sure it had been dead as much as a month before you made it out? A I think she had been dead bout two or three months, I don't know, I won't be positive.
Q Before this affidavit was made by Nancy Tiger about Joanna? Do you remember going in there to a Notary Public with Nancy Tiger, your wife, Yarnah Lynch, a negro woman, and Ned Kelly--you went in before the Notary Public and swore to some affidavits, do you remember that? A Yes sir.
Q You say this child died about two or three months before that? A I am not sure of that.
[sic] Are you sure it was as much as two weeks or one month before you made out the affidavit? A I guess just about one month.
Q Do you know New Years? A Yes sir.
Q Did this child die before New Years? A He died about March.
Q You don't know what day? A The 11th..
Q How do you know that? A I had in down in a book.
Q When did you put it in a book? A Same day she died.

------oOo-------

    Nancy Tiger, being duly sworn, testified as follows, through official interpreter Jesse McDermott.

Applications for Enrollment of Creek Newborn
Act of 1905   Volume IV

Examination by the Commission:
Q What is your name? A Nancy Tiger.
Q What is your age? A About 33.
Q What is your post office address? A Coweta.
Q Nancy do you remember when you made out this affidavit about the birth and death of your child, Joanna? A No sir I do not know.
Q You remember going in with James, Yarnar[sic] Lynch and Ned Kelly before a Notary Public, don't you remember that? A Yes sir.
Q Well how long had your child been dead then, Joanna I mean? A About two months.
Q Had been dead about two months before that? A Yes sir.
Q Are you sure that your child Joanna was dead as much as one month before you made that affidavit? A Yes sir, it was a good while after she had died.
Q Who interpretered[sic] this affidavit for you? A Ned Kelly.
Q Can he talk pretty good Creek and English? A Yes sir.
Q He put it down as you say now, the 11th of March, and the affidavit was made out in March, and two months after that child died you say you went before the Notary Public, can you explain that-- A The child was dead when we made out the affidavit.
Q How long had the child been dead? A I don't know, I can't remember.

Thomas Tiger, being duly sworn, testified as follows:

By Commission.
Q What is your name? Thomas Tiger.
Q Are you any kind to James Tiger? A Brother.
Q Do you or did you know a child of his and Nancy Tiger by the name of Joanna Tiger? A Yes sir.
Q When was Joanna born? A Born 11th of March, 1904.
Q Do you know when she died? A Yes sir.
Q How do you know that, were you there? A Yes, sir I was at the burying.
Q Can you read and write? A Yes sir.
Q And figure? A Yes sir.
Q What day was it she died? A Same days she was born,--I mean when she was a year old, 11th day of March, this year.
Q You mean to say that is was a year old to the day? A Yes sir, just exactly one year old.
Q How do you know? A By the dates.
Q How is it that those dates are so fresh in your mind now what helps you to remember them? A Cause there are twelve months in a year and the baby was born 1904, and twelve months after the baby was a year old.
Q How do you remember she was born on the 11th day of March, and how do you get 11? A Cause I remember it.
Q Did you look at a calendar either on the birth day or death day of that child? A I have a record of all my children--
Q You wrote them down yourself? A Yes sir.

Applications for Enrollment of Creek Newborn
Act of 1905   Volume IV

Q Did you write down the date of the birth and death of Joanna Tiger yourself? A Yes sir.
Q Have you got that record with you? A No sir. I Left it at home.
Q Were you with them on that day they went before the Notary Public to make out the affidavits? A I made an affidavit myself that same day.
Q You made an affidavit yourself? A Yes sir.
Q Not in this case, in your own child's case? A Yes sir.
Q So that helps you to remember the day yu went before the Notary Public because you made one yourself? A Yes sir.
Q Is the day you went before the Notary Public to make out an affidavit and saw these people make one out also about that child, is that day as fresh in your mind as the 2 March Elevens you speak about, the birth day and death day of Joanna? Is it? A I don't know.
Q What day in March was it that you went before the Notary Public? A I don't remember I never had that written down.
Q Do you remember the 11th so well because it was written down? A Yes sir.
Q But you can't remember going before the Notary Public? A Yes sir.
Q Well now how log was it before that day in March that you went before the Notary Public? A You mean how long after the child had been dead? Q Yes, how long after? A About two weeks.
Q Are you sure it was as much as two weeks? A I think it was.
Q You think it has been dead at least two weeks when you went to make that affidavit out? A Yes, sir, I think it was two weeks
Q Do you remember what day of the week March 11 was? Was it Monday, Tuesday, Wednesday or what? You say you marked it down in a book and you were there when that child died, and that you remember it well, do you remember what day of the week it was? A I think it was Tuesday, I am not sure. I don't remember just exactly what day it was.

Statement by the first witness: I can recollect that the child was a year old or going on a year old when it died. The child died just the day before it was a year old. That is why I remember it.

-------oOo-------

Nicey Tiger, being duly sworn, testified as follows:
Through Occicial[sic] Interpreter, Jesse McDermott.

Examination by the Commission:
Q What is your name? A Nicey Tiger.
Q What is your age? A 19.
Q Do you know James and Nancy Tiger? A Yes sir.
" James ir[sic] your husband's brother? A Yes sir.
Q Do you know a child of theirs named Joanna Tiger? A Yes sir.
Q Is she dead? A Yes sir.
Q Do you know when she died? A March 11.
Q This year? A Yes sir.

Applications for Enrollment of Creek Newborn
Act of 1905 Volume IV

Q Well do you remember going in the month of March before a Notary Public and making affidavit about your child, Mary Tiger? A Yes sir.
Q How long before that had Joanna Tiger been dead? A About one week.
Q Are you sure it was as much as a week? A Yes sir.
Q Well I will tell you now Nicey to refresh your memory when you went before that Notary Public it is as shown by his jurat,*(illegible)* is was[sic] on March 14. Now a week or seven days before that would make March the 7th. Now March 7th and March 11th are not alike, you certainly have been mistaken? A I was mistaken.
Q How do you remember that the child died March 11, what make you remember that? A I don't know.
Q Were you present when the child died? A No sir, but was there during its sickness.
Q Were you present when Joanna was born? A No sir.

Lona Merrick, being duly sworn, states that the above and foregoing is a true and correct transcript of her stenographic notes as taken in said case on said date.

Lona Merrick

Subscribed and sworn to before me this 23rd day of June, 1905.

Edw C Griesel
Notary Public.

NC 254.
DEPARTMENT OF THE INTERIOR,
COMMISSION TO THE FIVE CIVILIZED TRIBES.
MUSKOGEE, IND. TER. JUNE 23, 1905.

In the matter of the application for the enrollment of Phillip and Joanna Tiger as citizens by blood of the Creek Nation.

James Tiger, being duly sworn, testified as follows:

Examination by the Commission:
Q What is your name? A James Tiger.
Q Did you have a doctor to attend on Joanna at the time of her death? A No sir.
Q Didn't have any? A No sir.
Q Did you have any medicine man of any kind? A Yes sir.
Q Who did you have? A I just gave her the medicine myself.
Q When you buried her did you by a coffin her? A No sir, I made the coffin myself.
Q Did you by any material --burying material for her? A I bought some clothes and tacks.
Q Did you pay for them the day you got the goods or did you get them on credit? A I paid cash for them.
Q Where did you buy them? A At Catoosa.

Applications for Enrollment of Creek Newborn
Act of 1905   Volume IV

Q What was the name of the man you bought them from? A I don't know, I sent Thomas Tiger the money to get them for me. I didn't by them myself. I had to make the coffin.
Q Well who did you send after the material? A Thomas Tiger. I sent word to him to go get the material for me and he did.

-----oOo------

Thomas Tiger, being duly sworn, testified as follows:

Examination by the Commission.
Q Did you by the material for James Tiger? A Yes sir.
Q Whose store did you get them at? A Downs' I think.
Q That is a store in Catossa[sic]? A Yes sir.
Q Did you pay cash or them? A Yes sir.
Q Did you by any goods or supplies of any kind on credit about the time this child died? A No, sir, James Tiger sent me the money to go and get the goods.
Q Does he keep a blank[sic] account or does he keep it in cash with him? A I don't know how he keeps his money, but he sent me the money by Jasper Sarty, and I went and got the goods. He was the man that came and told me about the child being dead, and James wanted me to go to town for the burying material.
Q Did they give you at the store a bill or receipt for the goods you bought? A No sir.
Q Do you know what day of the week it was that the child died? A I think it was on Friday night the child died and I went to town on Saturday.

The calendar for the year 1905 examined and the 11th day of March falls on Saturday.

James Tiger, recalled testified as follows:

Q When you went before the Notary Public to make out that affidavit did you say to him that Joanna died March 11, or did you just tell him how long she had been dead and let him firgure[sic] it out? A I told him she died March 11.
Q Did you bury her the same day she died? A Yes, sir, same day.
Q Do you remember what you did the next day; well if she died on March 11, that was Saturday, did you go to church on Sunday the next day or not? A I didn't go to church Saturday or Sunday.
Q Now how long had she been dead and buried before you ~~made~~ went to the Notary Public? A I don't know how much it was, but after I studied about it, it was two or three days.
Q You said this morning it was two or three months? Why did you say two or three months? A I told him I wasn't sure it was three months.

Witness is notified that the Commission desires the testimony of Yarnar[sic] Lynch, who attended on the mother after the birth of the child.

Applications for Enrollment of Creek Newborn
Act of 1905   Volume IV

Lona Merrick, being duly sworn, states that the above and foregoing is a true and correct transcript of her stenographic notes as taken in said cause on said date.

Lona Merrick

Subscribed and sworn to before me this 23rd day of June, 1905.

Edw C Griesel
Notary Public.

N.C. 254.

DEPARTMENT OF THE INTERIOR,
COMMISSIONER TO THE FIVE CIVILIZED TRIBES,
Near Coweta, Indian Territory, January 22, 1907.

In the matter of the application for the enrollment of Joanna Tiger as a citizen by blood of the Creek Nation.

THOMAS TIGER, being duly sworn, by J. MCDermott, a notary public, testified as follows:

BY THE COMMISSIONER:

Q What is your name? A Thomas Tiger.
Q What is your age? A About 28.
Q What is your postoffice address? A Coweta.
Q Are you a Creek citizen? A Yes sir.
Q Do you know James Tiger? A Yes sir.
Q Do you know his wife, Nancy Tiger? A Yes sir.
Q Do you or did you know a child of theirs named Joanna? A Yes sir.
Q Joanna is now living dead is she not? A Yes sir.
Q Do you know when she died? A Yes sir.
Q You have testified about her death before, have you not? A Yes sir.

In your testimony on June 23, 1905, you stated that you had a record of the date of her death at home.

Q Have you that record? A Yes sir.

The witness presents a Daybook and on the last page of said book appears the following entry, second from the bottom of a list of six names: "Joanna Tiger died Mar 11, 1905"

Applications for Enrollment of Creek Newborn
Act of 1905   Volume IV

Q Are all of these names that appear on this page the names of your children? A No, four are my brother's children and the balance are mine.
Q When did you make this record about the death of Joanna? A Just as soon as I got home from the burying.
Q Were there any others present at the burial besides her immediate relatives? A Yes, Moty Tiger, Alex Thompson and several others were present.

Statement by the witness.

The methodist[sic] denomination at the Spring Town church was holding a district conference the very time that Joanna and it might be that you could get the exact date of her death by referring to the minutes of the church.

Q Where is the church located? A About a mile southeast of here.
Q Who is the janitor of that church? A Francis Asbury.
Q Where does he live? A Just a short distance west of the church.

I, Jesse McDermott, on oath state that the above and foregoing is a full and true transcript of my notes as taken in said cause on said date.

Jesse McDermott

Subscribed and sworn to before me, this 23rd day of January, 1907.

Noel C Ownby
Notary Public.

My Commission
Expires May 13, 1909.

N.C. 254.   F.H.W.
DEPARTMENT OF THE INTERIOR,
COMMISSIONER TO THE FIVE CIVILIZED TRIBES.

In the matter of the application for the enrollment of Joanna Tiger, deceased, as a citizen by blood of the Creek Nation.

D E C I S I O N.

The record in this case shows that on March 16, 1905 an application was filed, in affidavit form, for the enrollment of Joanna Tiger, as a citizen by blood of the Creek Nation. Further proceedings were had on June 23, 1905.

The evidence in this case shows that the name of the father of the applicant appears as James Tiger in the birth affidavit and in the testimony but it is clear from the evidence and the records of this office that Joanna Tiger, deceased, was the minor child

Applications for Enrollment of Creek Newborn
Act of 1905   Volume IV

of Jim and Nancy Tiger, whose names appear on a partial schedule of citizens by blood of the Creek Nation.

It further appears in evidence that said Joanna Tiger was born March 11, 1904, and died March 11, 1905.

The Act of Congress approved March 3, 1905, (33 Stats., 1048), provides in part as follows:

"That the Commission to the Five Civilized Tribes is authorized for sixty days after the date of the approval of this Act to receive and consider applications for enrollments of children born subsequent to May twenty five, nineteen hundred and one, and prior to March fourth, nineteen hundred and five, and living on said latter date, to citizens of the Creek tribe of Indians whose enrollment has been approved by the Secretary of the Interior prior to the date of the approval of this Act; and to enroll and make allotments to such children."

It is, therefore, ordered and adjudged that the said Joanna Tiger, deceased, is entitled to be enrolled as a citizen by blood of the Creek Nation, in accordance with the provisions of law above quoted, and the application for her enrollment as such is accordingly granted.

Tams Bixby   Commissioner.

Muskogee, Indian Territory.
JAN 25 1907

NBC 254.

Muskogee, Indian Territory, March 7, 1907.

Nancy Tiger,
    Care of James Tiger,
        Coweta, Indian Territory.

Dear Madam:

You are hereby advised that on March 2, 1907, the Secretary of the Interior approved the enrollment of your deceased minor child, Joanna Tiger, as a citizen by blood of the Creek Nation, and that the name of said child appears upon the roll of new born citizens by blood of the Creek Nation enrolled Act of Congress approved March 3, 1905, as number 1228.

This child is now entitled to an allotment, and application therefor should be made by a duly appointed administrator at the Creek Land Office, Muskogee, Indian Territory.

Respectfully,

Commissioner.

(NOTE: The form used for Joanna Tiger's enrollment information was a Cherokee Nation Roll form. It is unclear why a Cherokee Nation form was used, but the word

Applications for Enrollment of Creek Newborn
Act of 1905   Volume IV

'Copy' was hand-written at the top of the form. The following is a condensed version of a form used to list Joanna Tiger's vital information.)

Residence: *(blank)*   Copy   **Card No**. 284
Post Office: Cowita[sic] I.T.   **Field No.** *(blank)*

Dawes Roll No. *(blank)*   *(Date hand written)* 3/4/5   **Tribal Enrollment**: *(blank)*
Name: Tiger Joanna   **Age**: 1   **Sex**: F   **Blood**: Full
Name of Father: James Tiger   **Year**: 1122 *(?)*
Name of Mother: Nancy Tiger   **Year**: 1123 *(?)*   **Born: 3-11-04**

(Hand-written in center of form) App received 3-14-05

Cr NC 255

Muskogee, Indian Territory, June 9, 1905.

Nicey Tiger,
      Coweta, Indian Territory.

Dear Madam:

      In the matter of the application for the enrollment of your minor child, Mary Tiger, as a citizen of the Creek Nation, you are advised that the Commission cannot identify you on its rolls of Creek citizens.

      You are requested to furnish the Commission with your maiden name, the names of your parents, the Creek Indian Town to which you claim to belong, your roll number as it appears on your deeds to land in the Creek Nation, and any other information which will help to identify you as a citizen of said Nation.

      Respectfully,

      Chairman.

DEPARTMENT OF THE INTERIOR,
COMMISSIONER TO THE FIVE CIVILIZED TRIBES.

REFER IN REPLY TO THE FOLLOWING:
NC-255

Muskogee, Indian Territory, **August 4, 1905.**

Thomas Tiger,
      Coweta, Indian Territory.

Applications for Enrollment of Creek Newborn
Act of 1905   Volume IV

Dear Sir:

You are hereby advised that on **July 28, 1905**, the Secretary of the Interior approved the enrollment of your minor child, **Mary Tiger**, as a citizen by blood of the **Creek** Nation, and that the name of said child appears upon the roll of new born citizens of the **Creek** Nation as Number **168**.

The child is now entitled to an allotment, and application therefor should be made without delay at the Land Office for the Nation in which the prospective allotment is located.

An entire allotment for said child must be selected at the time of the original application.

Respectively,

Commissioner.

Department of the Interior,
COMMISSION TO THE FIVE CIVILIZED TRIBES.

IN RE APPLICATION FOR ENROLLMENT, as a citizen of the Creek Nation, of Mary Tiger, born on the 1st day of February, 1902

Name of Father: Thomas Tiger   a citizen of the   Creek   Nation.
Name of Mother: Nicey Tiger   a citizen of the   Creek   Nation.

Postoffice,   Coweta Ind. Ter.

AFFIDAVIT OF MOTHER.

UNITED STATES OF AMERICA,
Indian Territory.
Western Judicial   District.

I, Nicey Tiger, on oath state that I am 19 years of age and a citizen by blood, of the Creek Nation; that I am the lawful wife of Thomas Tiger, who is a citizen, by blood of the Creek Nation; that a female child was born to me on 1st day of February, 1902, that said child has been named Mary Tiger, and is now living.

                                                her
                                      Nicey x Tiger
WITNESSES TO MARK: mark
    Jas Tiger
    Jasper Sarty

Applications for Enrollment of Creek Newborn
Act of 1905   Volume IV

Subscribed and sworn to before me this 14" *day of* March, 1905.

My Com Expires   W A Brigham
Oct 25" 1906   **NOTARY PUBLIC.**

AFFIDAVIT OF ATTENDING PHYSICIAN OR MID-WIFE.

UNITED STATES OF AMERICA,
Indian Territory.
Western Judicial   District.

I, Yanah Lynch , a Midwife , on oath state that I attended on Mrs. Nicey Tiger , wife of Thomas Tiger on the 1ˢᵗ day of February , 190*(ink spot)*; that there was born to her on said date a female child; that said child is now living and is said to have been named Mary Tiger

                               her
                        Yanah x Lynch
WITNESSES TO MARK: mark
 Jas Tiger
 Jasper Sarty

Subscribed and sworn to before me this 14" *day of* March, 1905.

My Com Expires   W A Brigham
Oct 25" 1906   **NOTARY PUBLIC.**

BIRTH AFFIDAVIT.

DEPARTMENT OF THE INTERIOR.
COMMISSION TO THE FIVE CIVILIZED TRIBES.

IN RE APPLICATION FOR ENROLLMENT, as a citizen of the Creek Nation, of Melissa Harjo, born on the 1st day of October , 1904

Name of Father: Tulsa Harjo   a citizen of the   Creek   Nation.
Name of Mother: Mollie Harjo   a citizen of the   Creek   Nation.

              Postoffice   Okemah, I.T.

Applications for Enrollment of Creek Newborn
Act of 1905   Volume IV

AFFIDAVIT OF MOTHER.

UNITED STATES OF AMERICA, Indian Territory, }
Western Judicial   DISTRICT.

I, Mollie Harjo , on oath state that I am 28 years of age and a citizen by Blood , of the Creek Nation; that I am the lawful wife of Tulsa Harjo , who is a citizen, by Blood of the Creek Nation; that a Female child was born to me on 1st day of October , 1904 , that said child has been named Melissa Harjo , and was living March 4, 1905.

                                                          her
                                         Mollie x Harjo

Witnesses To Mark: mark
{ S J Haynes
{ John H. Phillips

Subscribed and sworn to before me this 14th day of March , 1905.

                                        John H. Phillips
My Commission Expires Sept. 6th, 1906   Notary Public.

AFFIDAVIT OF ATTENDING PHYSICIAN OR MID-WIFE.

UNITED STATES OF AMERICA, Indian Territory, }
Western Judicial   DISTRICT.

I, Sarhoska , a Mid- wife , on oath state that I attended on Mrs. Mollie Harjo , wife of Tulsa Harjo on the 1st day of October , 1904 ; that there was born to her on said date a Female child; that said child was living March 4, 1905, and is said to have been named Melissa Harjo

                                          her
                                      Sarhoska x

Witnesses To Mark: mark
{ S J Haynes
{ John H. Phillips

Subscribed and sworn to before me this 14th day of March , 1905.

                                        John H. Phillips
My Commission Expires Sept. 6th, 1906   Notary Public.

Applications for Enrollment of Creek Newborn
Act of 1905 Volume IV

BIRTH AFFIDAVIT.

DEPARTMENT OF THE INTERIOR.
COMMISSION TO THE FIVE CIVILIZED TRIBES.

IN RE APPLICATION FOR ENROLLMENT, as a citizen of the Creek Nation, of Lizzie Harjo, born on the 15 day of June, 1903

Name of Father: Tulsa Harjo   a citizen of the   Creek   Nation.
Name of Mother: Mollie Harjo   a citizen of the   Creek   Nation.

Postoffice   Okemah, I.T.

AFFIDAVIT OF MOTHER.

UNITED STATES OF AMERICA, Indian Territory, ⎫
Western Judicial   DISTRICT. ⎭

    I, Mollie Harjo, on oath state that I am 28 years of age and a citizen by Blood, of the Creek Nation; that I am the lawful wife of Tulsa Harjo, who is a citizen, by Blood of the Creek Nation; that a Female child was born to me on 15th day of June, 1903, that said child has been named Lizzie Harjo, and was living March 4, 1905.

                                                            her
                                              Mollie x Harjo
Witnesses To Mark: mark
  { S J Haynes
    John H. Phillips

    Subscribed and sworn to before me this 14th day of March, 1905.

                                         John H. Phillips
My Commission Expires Sept. 6th, 1906   Notary Public.

AFFIDAVIT OF ATTENDING PHYSICIAN OR MID-WIFE.

UNITED STATES OF AMERICA, Indian Territory, ⎫
Western Judicial   DISTRICT. ⎭

    I, Sarhoska, a mid-wife, on oath state that I attended on Mrs. Mollie Harjo, wife of Tulsa Harjo on the 15th day of June, 1905[sic]; that there was born to her on said date a Female child; that said child was living March 4, 1905, and is said to have been named Lizzie Harjo   her
                                         Sarhoska x
                                           mark

Applications for Enrollment of Creek Newborn
Act of 1905   Volume IV

Witnesses To Mark:
    { S J Haynes
      John H. Phillips

    Subscribed and sworn to before me this 14th day of March , 1905.

                                              John H. Phillips
My Commission Expires Sept. 6th, 1906   Notary Public.

N C 256   COPY

                                Okemah, Ind. Ter., 4/10-1905

Commission to the 5 Civilized Tribes,
               Muskogee, I T

Dear Sir

    I send you two affidavits for enrollment some time ago but I did not give you my former name for you might have some trouble to find my name. My filing paper shows that I was enrolled by Mollie (Yahola) Those aft. for Lizzie Harjo and Melissa Harjo. I am

                                    Mollie (Yahola) Harjo.

                            COPY

NC 256

                          Muskogee, Indian Territory, April 17, 1905.

Mollie Harjo,
       Okemah, Indian Territory.

Dear Madam:

    The Commission acknowledged receipt of your letter of April 11, 1905, in which you state that you sent sometime ago, affidavits concerning the dates of the birth of your two children, Lizzie and Melissa Harjo, and stating the name under which you filed was Mollie Yarhola.

    In reply you are advised that the affidavits referred to have been received and filed with the Commission. You are further advised that the Commission desires to know your number on the approved roll as the same appears on your deed or allotment certificate.

Applications for Enrollment of Creek Newborn
Act of 1905 Volume IV

Respectfully,

(Signed) Tams Bixby

Chairman.

Creek Indian ROLL, NO 7738.

K.I.D.

BA- 592 & 593B.

DEPARTMENT OF THE INTERIOR,
COMMISSION TO THE FIVE CIVILIZED TRIBES.
MUSKOGEE, INDIAN TERRITORY, March 16, 1905.

-ooOoo-

In the matter of the application for the enrollment of Louis Bemo and Dora Bemo , as a citizen by blood of the Creek Nation.

CHARLIE BEMO, being duly sworn, testified as follows:

EXAMINATION BY THE COMMISSION:
Q What is your name? A Charlie Bemo.
Q How old are you? A 27.
Q What is your postoffice address? A Fry, I. T.
Q Have you a child names[sic] Louis Bemo? A Yes, sir.
Q When was Louis born? A October 3, 1903.
Q Is he living? A Yes, sir.
Q Have you a child named Dora Bemo? A Yes, sir.
Q When was she born? A April 3, 1902.
Q Are you a citizen of the Creek Nation? A No, sir.
Q Are you a citizen of any Nation? A Seminole.
Q What is the name of the mother of these children? A Maggie Cox.
Q Is Maggie Cox a citizen of the Creek Nation? A Yes, sir.

Maggie Cox is identified on Creek Indian Card, Field Number 2550, and her name is contained in the partial list of citizens by blood of the Creek Nation, approved by the Secretary of the Interior March 28, 1902, Roll Number 7556.

Q If it should be found that your children, Louis Bemo and Dora Bemo, have rights in both the Creek and Seminole Nation, in which Nation do you elect to have them enrolled and receive their allotment of land? A In the Creek Nation.

Applications for Enrollment of Creek Newborn
Act of 1905   Volume IV

  Zera Ellen Parrish, being duly sworn on her oath states that as stenographer to the Commission to the Five Civilized Tribes she reported the above case and that this is a full, true and correct transcript of her stenographic notes in same.

           Zera Ellen Parrish

Subscribed and sworn to before me this 18 day of March, 1905.

           Edw C Griesel
            Notary Public.

BIRTH AFFIDAVIT.

DEPARTMENT OF THE INTERIOR.
COMMISSION TO THE FIVE CIVILIZED TRIBES.

Corrected later
 14th

  IN RE APPLICATION FOR ENROLLMENT, as a citizen of the CREEK Nation, of Dora Bemo, born on the 3 day of April, 1902

Name of Father:	Charlie Bemo	a citizen of the	Seminole Nation.
Name of Mother:	Maggie Bemo	a citizen of the	Creek Nation.

      Postoffice Fry

     AFFIDAVIT OF ~~MOTHER~~. Father

UNITED STATES OF AMERICA, Indian Territory,
  WESTERN   DISTRICT.

  I, Charlie Bemo, on oath state that I am 27 years of age and a citizen by blood, of the Seminole Nation; that I am the lawful ~~wife~~ husband of Maggie Bemo, who is a citizen, by blood of the Creek Nation; that a female child was born to me on 3 day of April, 1902, that said child has been named Dora Bemo, and is now living.

            His
         Charlie x Bemo
Witnesses To Mark: mark
 { Irwin Donovan
   EC Griesel

  Subscribed and sworn to before me this 16 day of March, 1905.

           Edw C Griesel
            Notary Public.

Applications for Enrollment of Creek Newborn
Act of 1905 Volume IV

BIRTH AFFIDAVIT.

DEPARTMENT OF THE INTERIOR.
COMMISSION TO THE FIVE CIVILIZED TRIBES.

IN RE APPLICATION FOR ENROLLMENT, as a citizen of the CREEK Nation, of Louis Bemo, born on the 3 day of October, 1903

Name of Father:	Charlie Bemo	a citizen of the	~~Cr~~ Seminole Nation.
Name of Mother:	Maggie Bemo	a citizen of the	Creek Nation.

Postoffice   Fry

AFFIDAVIT OF ~~MOTHER~~. Father

UNITED STATES OF AMERICA, Indian Territory,
WESTERN   DISTRICT.

I, Charlie Bemo, on oath state that I am 27 years of age and a citizen by blood, of the Seminole Nation; that I am the lawful ~~wife~~ husband of Maggie Cox, who is a citizen, by blood of the Creek Nation; that a male child was born to me on 3 day of October, 1903, that said child has been named Louis Bemo, and is now living.

His
Charlie x Bemo
mark

Witnesses To Mark:
{ Irwin Donovan
  EC Griesel

Subscribed and sworn to before me this 16 day of March, 1905.

Edw C Griesel
Notary Public.

BIRTH AFFIDAVIT.

DEPARTMENT OF THE INTERIOR.
COMMISSION TO THE FIVE CIVILIZED TRIBES.

IN RE APPLICATION FOR ENROLLMENT, as a citizen of the Creek Nation, of Lewis Bemore, born on the 3 day of Oct, 1903

Name of Father:	Charlie Bemore	a citizen of the	Creek Nation.
Name of Mother:	Maggie Bemore	a citizen of the	Creek Nation.

Postoffice   Coweta, Indian Territory.

Applications for Enrollment of Creek Newborn
Act of 1905   Volume IV

AFFIDAVIT OF MOTHER.

UNITED STATES OF AMERICA, Indian Territory,
Western   DISTRICT.

    I, Maggie Bemore , on oath state that I am 24 years of age and a citizen by blood , of the Creek Nation; that I am the lawful wife of Charlie Bemore , who is a citizen, by blood of the Seminole Nation; that a male child was born to me on 3 day of Oct , 1903 , that said child has been named Lewis Bemore , and is now living.

                                          Maggie Bemore

Witnesses To Mark:

    Subscribed and sworn to before me this 1st day of April , 1905.

                                          R. C. Allen

My commission expires March 15, 1908.   Notary Public.

AFFIDAVIT OF ATTENDING PHYSICIAN OR MID-WIFE.

UNITED STATES OF AMERICA, Indian Territory,
Western   DISTRICT.

    I, Annie Cox , a Mid-wife , on oath state that I attended on Mrs. Maggie Bemore , wife of Charlie Bemore on the 3 day of Oct , 1903 ; that there was born to her on said date a male child; that said child is now living and is said to have been named Lewis Bemore

                                          Annie Cox

Witnesses To Mark:

    Subscribed and sworn to before me this 1st day of April , 1905.

                                          R. C. Allen

My commission expires March 15, 1908.   Notary Public.

Applications for Enrollment of Creek Newborn
Act of 1905   Volume IV

BIRTH AFFIDAVIT.

DEPARTMENT OF THE INTERIOR.
COMMISSION TO THE FIVE CIVILIZED TRIBES.

IN RE APPLICATION FOR ENROLLMENT, as a citizen of the CREEK Nation, of Dora Bemore, born on the 14 day of April, 1902

Name of Father:	Charlie Bemore	a citizen of the	Seminole Nation.
Name of Mother:	Maggie Bemore	a citizen of the	Creek Nation.

Postoffice   Coweta, I.T.

AFFIDAVIT OF MOTHER.

UNITED STATES OF AMERICA, Indian Territory,
WESTERN   DISTRICT.

I, Maggie Bemore, on oath state that I am 24 years of age and a citizen by birth, of the Creek Nation[sic] Nation; that I am the lawful wife of Charlie Bemore, who is a citizen, by birth of the Seminole Nation; that a female child was born to me on 14 day of April, 1902, that said child has been named Dora Bemore, and is now living.

Maggie Bemore

Witnesses To Mark:

Subscribed and sworn to before me this 1st day of April, 1905.

R. C. Allen
My commission expires March 15, 1908.   Notary Public.

AFFIDAVIT OF ATTENDING PHYSICIAN OR MID-WIFE.

UNITED STATES OF AMERICA, Indian Territory,
WESTERN   DISTRICT.

I, Sophia Simon, a Mid-wife, on oath state that I attended on Mrs. Maggie Bemore, wife of Charlie Bemore on the 14 day of April, 1902; that there was born to her on said date a female child; that said child is now living and is said to have been named Dora Bemore

her
Sophia x Simon
mark

Witnesses To Mark:
- Joe Fennell
- M. R. Pryor

Applications for Enrollment of Creek Newborn
Act of 1905 Volume IV

Subscribed and sworn to before me this 1st day of April, 1905.

R. C. Allen
Notary Public.

My commission expires March 15, 1908.

No. 257

Muskogee, Indian Territory, November 12, 1906.

Chief Clerk,
    Seminole Enrollment Division,
        General Office.

Dear Sir:

    You are hereby advised that the named of Dora and Lewis Bemore, children of Charlie Bemore, an alleged citizen of the Seminole Nation, and Maggie Bemore, a citizen of the Creek Nation, is contained in the schedule of New Born citizens by blood of the Creek Nation, approved August 22, 1905, by the Secretary of the Interior, opposite Roll Nos. 1269[sic] and 270.

Respectfully,

Commissioner.

NC 257.

Muskogee, Indian Territory, July 14, 1905.

Commissioner to the Five Civilized Tribes,
    Seminole Enrollment Division,
        Muskogee, Indian Territory.

Gentlemen:

    March 16, 1905, application was made to the Commission to the Five Civilized Tribes for the enrollment of Dora Bemore, born April 14, 1902, and Lewis Bemore, born October 3, 1903, as citizens by blood of the Creek Nation. It is stated in said application that the father of said children is Charlie Bemore, a citizen of the Seminole Nation, and that the mother is Maggie Bemore, a citizen of the Creek Nation.

    You are requested to inform the Creek Enrollment Division as to whether application has been made for the enrollment of said Dora and Lewis Bemore, as citizens of the Seminole Nation, and if so, what disposition has been made of the same.

Applications for Enrollment of Creek Newborn
Act of 1905 Volume IV

Respectfully,

Commissioner.

DEPARTMENT OF THE INTERIOR.
COMMISSIONER TO THE FIVE CIVILIZED TRIBES.

Muskogee, Indian Territory July 18, 1905.

Chief Clerk,
    Creek Enrollment Division.

Dear Sir:

    Receipt is hereby acknowledged of your letter of July 14, 1905 (NC-257) stating that application was made to the Commission to the Five Civilized Tribes for the enrollment of Dora Bemore, born April 14, 1902, and Lewis Bemore, born October 3, 1903, children of Charlie Bemore, a citizen of the Seminole Nation, and Maggie Bemore, a citizen of the Creek Nation, as citizens by blood of the Creek Nation and requesting to be informed as to whether application has been made for the enrollment of said children as citizens of the Seminole Nation.

    In reply to your letter you are advised that it does not appear from an examination of the records of this office that any application was made to the Commission to the Five Civilized Tribes for the enrollment of Said Dora Bemore and Lewis Bemore as citizens of the Seminole Nation.

Respectfully,

Tams Bixby   Commissioner.

NC-259

Muskogee, Indian Territory, July 26, 1905.

Maggie Washington,
    Beggs, Indian Territory.

Dear Madam:

    In the matter of the application for the enrollment of your minor children, George and Sadie Washington, as a citizen of the Creek Nation, you are advised that it is impossible, without further information, to identify you on the rolls of citizens of said Nation.

Applications for Enrollment of Creek Newborn
Act of 1905   Volume IV

You are requested to state your maiden name, the names of your parents, the Creek Indian Town to which you belong, and, if possible the roll number as same appears on your deeds to land in the Creek Nation.

This matter should receive your prompt attention.

                Respectfully,

                              Commissioner.

(The letter below typed as given on microfilm.)

                Copy

                        Beggs, Ind. Terr.
                        July 29, 1905.

Commission to the Five Civilized Tribes
    Muskogee,
                Ind. Terr.

Dear Sir: In replying to your letter of the 26 instant, stating that it being impossible for to enrolled my two (2) minor children George & Sadie Washington. the notary in making out those affadavitt give my name Maggie. but my name is Aggie Washington. but my former name is Aggie Harry. which said name will appear on the Tuskegee roll. being the daughter of Henry Harry & Nicy Harry. the name Aggie Washington is derive from my husband, Dixon Washington, whose name will be found on the Kechepartagee town. the mother being Martha Suvier. Our deed have never been delivered yet. now let me here from your office at once weather same has been approved or not and if necessary I will come down, or furnished more information.
    Hoping to here from you soon.
                Signed   Aggie Washington
                                  Beggs, Ind. Terr

NC-259.

                    Muskogee, Indian Territory, August 2, 1905.

Aggie Washington,
    Beggs, Indian Territory.

Dear Madam:

    Receipt is hereby acknowledged of your letter of July 29, 1905 stating that your name is Aggie Washington instead of Maggie Washington as you signed it in your

Applications for Enrollment of Creek Newborn
Act of 1905   Volume IV

affidavits as to the birth of your children, George Washington and Sadie Washington, and also stating that you were enrolled under the name of Aggie Harry.

The information contained in your letter has enabled this office to identify you upon the final roll of citizens by blood of the Creek Nation.

In the matter of the application for the enrollment of your minor children George and Sadie Washington it will be necessary for you to have the inclosed[sic] affidavits executed, taking care to sign your name as the same appears in the body of the affidavits. In case the midwife signs the affidavits by mark such signature must be attested by two disinterested witnesses. Be careful to see that the notary public, before whom the affidavits are sworn to, attaches his name and seal to each affidavit.

You should give this matter your prompt attention.

Respectfully,

Commissioner.

CTD-17.
Env.

BIRTH AFFIDAVIT.

DEPARTMENT OF THE INTERIOR.
COMMISSION TO THE FIVE CIVILIZED TRIBES.

IN RE APPLICATION FOR ENROLLMENT, as a citizen of the Creek Nation, of George Washington, born on the 22 day of March, 1903

Name of Father:	Dixon Washington	a citizen of the	Creek	Nation.
Name of Mother:	Maggie Washington	a citizen of the	Creek	Nation.

Postoffice   Beggs, I. T.

AFFIDAVIT OF MOTHER.

UNITED STATES OF AMERICA, Indian Territory,
Western   DISTRICT.

I, Maggie Washington, on oath state that I am 26 years of age and a citizen by blood, of the Creek Nation; that I am the lawful wife of Dixon Washington, who is a citizen, by blood of the Creek Nation; that a male child was born to me on the 22 day of March, 1903, that said child has been named George Washington, and was living March 4, 1905.

Maggie Washington

Applications for Enrollment of Creek Newborn
Act of 1905   Volume IV

Witnesses To Mark:

Subscribed and sworn to before me this 8 day of April, 1905.

H H Barker
Notary Public.

AFFIDAVIT OF ATTENDING PHYSICIAN OR MID-WIFE.

UNITED STATES OF AMERICA, Indian Territory,
Western   DISTRICT.

I, Micy Harry, a Midwife, on oath state that I attended on Mrs. Maggie Washington, wife of Dixon Washington on the 22 day of March, 1903 ; that there was born to her on said date a male child; that said child was living March 4, 1905, and is said to have been named George Washington

her
Micy x Harry
mark

Witnesses To Mark:
Falba King
H H Barker

Subscribed and sworn to before me this 8 day of April, 1905.

H.H. Barker
Notary Public.

My Com. Ex. 7/14-06.

BIRTH AFFIDAVIT.

DEPARTMENT OF THE INTERIOR.
COMMISSION TO THE FIVE CIVILIZED TRIBES.

IN RE APPLICATION FOR ENROLLMENT, as a citizen of the Creek Nation, of George Washington, born on the 22nd day of March, 1903

Name of Father:	Dixon Washington	a citizen of the	Creek	Nation.
Name of Mother:	Aggie Washington	a citizen of the	Creek	Nation.

Postoffice   Beggs, I. T.

Applications for Enrollment of Creek Newborn
Act of 1905 Volume IV

AFFIDAVIT OF MOTHER.

UNITED STATES OF AMERICA, Indian Territory,
Western DISTRICT.

I, Aggie Washington, on oath state that I am 26 years of age and a citizen by blood, of the Creek Nation; that I am the lawful wife of Dixon Washington, who is a citizen, by blood of the Creek Nation; that a male child was born to me on the 22nd day of March, 1903, that said child has been named George Washington, and was living March 4, 1905.

             Aggie Washington

Witnesses To Mark:

Subscribed and sworn to before me this 10th day of Aug, 1905.

             H H Barker
                Notary Public.

Com. Ex. 7-14-06

AFFIDAVIT OF ATTENDING PHYSICIAN OR MID-WIFE.

UNITED STATES OF AMERICA, Indian Territory,
Western DISTRICT.

I, Micey Harry, a midwife, on oath state that I attended on Mrs. Aggie Washington, wife of Dixon Washington on the 22nd day of March, 1903; that there was born to her on said date a male child; that said child was living March 4, 1905, and is said to have been named George Washington

             her
           Micey x Harry
             mark

Witnesses To Mark:
 Dixon Washington
 H H Barker

Subscribed and sworn to before me this 10th day of Aug, 1905.

             H.H. Barker
                Notary Public.

Com. Ex. 7-14-06

Applications for Enrollment of Creek Newborn
Act of 1905   Volume IV

BIRTH AFFIDAVIT.

DEPARTMENT OF THE INTERIOR.
COMMISSION TO THE FIVE CIVILIZED TRIBES.

IN RE APPLICATION FOR ENROLLMENT, as a citizen of the Creek Nation, of Sadie Washington, born on the 12th day of January, 1905

Name of Father:	Dixon Washington	a citizen of the	Creek	Nation.
Name of Mother:	Aggie Washington	a citizen of the	Creek	Nation.

Postoffice   Beggs, I. T.

AFFIDAVIT OF MOTHER.

UNITED STATES OF AMERICA, Indian Territory,   }
 Western   DISTRICT.

I, Aggie Washington, on oath state that I am 26 years of age and a citizen by blood, of the Creek Nation; that I am the lawful wife of Dixon Washington, who is a citizen, by blood of the Creek Nation; that a female child was born to me on the 12th day of January, 1905, that said child has been named Sadie Washington, and was living March 4, 1905.

Aggie Washington

Witnesses To Mark:
{

Subscribed and sworn to before me this 10th day of Aug, 1905.

H H Barker
Notary Public.

Com. Ex. 7-14-06

AFFIDAVIT OF ATTENDING PHYSICIAN OR MID-WIFE.

UNITED STATES OF AMERICA, Indian Territory,   }
 Western   DISTRICT.

I, Micey Harry, a midwife, on oath state that I attended on Mrs. Aggie Washington, wife of Dixon Washington on the 12th day of January, 1905; that there was born to her on said date a female child; that said child was living March 4, 1905, and is said to have been named Sadie Washington

her
Micey x Harry
mark

Applications for Enrollment of Creek Newborn
Act of 1905   Volume IV

Witnesses To Mark:
 { Dixon Washington
   H H Barker

Subscribed and sworn to before me this 10th day of Aug, 1905.

                         H.H. Barker
                         Notary Public.

Com. Ex. 7-14-06

BIRTH AFFIDAVIT.

DEPARTMENT OF THE INTERIOR.
COMMISSION TO THE FIVE CIVILIZED TRIBES.

IN RE APPLICATION FOR ENROLLMENT, as a citizen of the Creek Nation, of Sadie Washington, born on the 12 day of Jan, 1905

| Name of Father: | Dixon Washington | a citizen of the | Creek | Nation. |
| Name of Mother: | Maggie Washington | a citizen of the | Creek | Nation. |

                 Postoffice   Beggs, I. T.

AFFIDAVIT OF MOTHER.

UNITED STATES OF AMERICA, Indian Territory, }
       Western   DISTRICT.

I, Maggie Washington, on oath state that I am 26 years of age and a citizen by blood, of the Creek Nation; that I am the lawful wife of Dixon Washington, who is a citizen, by blood of the Creek Nation; that a female child was born to me on the 12t day of Jan. , 1905, that said child has been named Sadie Washington, and was living March 4, 1905.

                         Maggie Washington

Witnesses To Mark:
{

Subscribed and sworn to before me this 8 day of April, 1905.

                         H H Barker
                         Notary Public.

Applications for Enrollment of Creek Newborn
Act of 1905 Volume IV

AFFIDAVIT OF ATTENDING PHYSICIAN OR MID-WIFE.

UNITED STATES OF AMERICA, Indian Territory, }
Western DISTRICT.

I, Martha Adams , a midwife , on oath state that I attended on Mrs. Maggie Washington , wife of Dixon Washington on the 12 day of January , 1905 ; that there was born to her on said date a female child; that said child was living March 4, 1905, and is said to have been named Sadie Washington

                 her
               Maartha x Adams
                 mark

Witnesses To Mark:
  { Falba King
    H H Barker

Subscribed and sworn to before me this 8 day of April, 1905.

               H.H. Barker
                 Notary Public.

My Com. Ex. 7/14-06

BIRTH AFFIDAVIT.

DEPARTMENT OF THE INTERIOR.
COMMISSION TO THE FIVE CIVILIZED TRIBES.

IN RE APPLICATION FOR ENROLLMENT, as a citizen of the Creek Nation, of Dorothy Vera McBirney, born on the 28th day of November , 1902

Name of Father: James H McBirney   a citizen of the   U.S.   Nation.
Name of Mother: Vera McBirney nee Clinton   a citizen of the   Creek   Nation.

               Postoffice   Tulsa Ind. Ter.

AFFIDAVIT OF MOTHER.

UNITED STATES OF AMERICA, Indian Territory, }
Western DISTRICT.

I, Vera McBirney nee Clinton , on oath state that I am 25 years of age and a citizen by blood , of the Creek Nation; that I am the lawful wife of James H. McBirney , who is a citizen, by *(blank)* of the United States ~~Nation~~; that a female child was born to me on 28th day of November , 1905, that said child has been named Dorothy Vera McBirney , and is now living.

Applications for Enrollment of Creek Newborn
Act of 1905   Volume IV

Vera McBirney nee Clinton

Witnesses To Mark:
{ Robert A. McBirney
{ Lea McBirney

Subscribed and sworn to before me this 15 day of March , 1905.

Robert E. Lynch
Notary Public.

Com Ex. 7/3/1906

AFFIDAVIT OF ATTENDING PHYSICIAN OR MID-WIFE.

UNITED STATES OF AMERICA, Indian Territory, }
    Western   DISTRICT.

    I, Fred S. Clinton , a Physician , on oath state that I attended on Mrs. Vera McBirney , wife of James H. McBirney on the 28th day of November , 1902 ; that there was born to her on said date a   female   child; that said child is now living and is said to have been named Dorothy V. McBirney

Fred S. Clinton

Witnesses To Mark:
{ M B *(Illegible)*
{ P. E. Coyne

Subscribed and sworn to before me this 15 day of March, 1905.

Robert E. Lynch
Notary Public.

Com Ex. 7/3/1906

BIRTH AFFIDAVIT.

DEPARTMENT OF THE INTERIOR.
COMMISSION TO THE FIVE CIVILIZED TRIBES.

    IN RE APPLICATION FOR ENROLLMENT, as a citizen of the CREEK Nation, of James Franklin Miller , born on the 27" day of Jany , 1905

Name of Father:	Benjamin Miller	a citizen of the	U.S.	Nation.
Name of Mother:	Margaret A Miller	a citizen of the	Creek	Nation.

Postoffice   Sapulpa, I.T.

Applications for Enrollment of Creek Newborn
Act of 1905   Volume IV

AFFIDAVIT OF MOTHER.

UNITED STATES OF AMERICA, Indian Territory, }
WESTERN DISTRICT. }

I, Margaret A. Miller , on oath state that I am 17 years of age and a citizen by blood , of the Creek Nation; that I am the lawful wife of Benjamin Miller , who is a citizen, by ----- of the United States Nation; that a male child was born to me on 27 day of January , 1905 , that said child has been named James Franklin Miller , and is now living.

Margaret A. Miller

Witnesses To Mark:
{

Subscribed and sworn to before me this 20 day of March , 1905.

Edward Merrick
Notary Public.

BIRTH AFFIDAVIT.

DEPARTMENT OF THE INTERIOR.
COMMISSION TO THE FIVE CIVILIZED TRIBES.

IN RE APPLICATION FOR ENROLLMENT, as a citizen of the CREEK Nation, of George Thomas Miller, born on the 15th day of August , 1903

Name of Father:	Benjamin F. Miller	a citizen of the	U.S.	Nation.
Name of Mother:	Margaret A Miller	a citizen of the	Creek	Nation.

Postoffice   Sapulpa, I.T.

AFFIDAVIT OF MOTHER.

UNITED STATES OF AMERICA, Indian Territory, }
WESTERN DISTRICT. }

I, Margaret A. Miller , on oath state that I am 17 years of age and a citizen by blood , of the Creek Nation; that I am the lawful wife of Benjamin F. Miller , who is a non citizen, by blood of the Creek Nation; that a male child was born to me on 15 day of August A.D. , 1903 , that said child has been named George Thomas Miller , and is now living.

Margaret A. Miller

Witnesses To Mark:
{

Applications for Enrollment of Creek Newborn
Act of 1905   Volume IV

Subscribed and sworn to before me this 12th day of April A.D. , 1905.

F.L. Mars

My Commission expires July 11, 1906.   Notary Public.

AFFIDAVIT OF ATTENDING PHYSICIAN OR MID-WIFE.

UNITED STATES OF AMERICA, Indian Territory,
WESTERN   DISTRICT.

I, Mrs. Grace Cue , a mid-wife , on oath state that I attended on Mrs. Margaret A. Miller , wife of Benjamin F. Miller on the 15th day of August A.D. , 1903 ; that there was born to her on said date a   male   child; that said child is now living and is said to have been named George Thomas Miller

Mrs. Grace Cue

Witnesses To Mark:

Subscribed and sworn to before me this 12th day of April A.D. , 1905.

F.L. Mars

My Commission expires July 11, 1906.   Notary Public.

BIRTH AFFIDAVIT.
DEPARTMENT OF THE INTERIOR.
COMMISSION TO THE FIVE CIVILIZED TRIBES.

IN RE APPLICATION FOR ENROLLMENT, as a citizen of the CREEK Nation, of George Thomas Miller, born on the 15 day of Aug , 1903

Name of Father:	Benjamin Miller	a citizen of the	U.S.	~~Nation.~~
Name of Mother:	Margaret A Miller	a citizen of the	Creek	Nation.

Postoffice   Sapulpa, I.T.

AFFIDAVIT OF MOTHER.

UNITED STATES OF AMERICA, Indian Territory,
WESTERN   DISTRICT.

I, Margaret A. Miller , on oath state that I am 17 years of age and a citizen by blood , of the Creek Nation; that I am the lawful wife of Benjamin F. Miller , who is a citizen, ~~by~~ ----- of the United States Nation; that a male child was born to me on

Applications for Enrollment of Creek Newborn
Act of 1905   Volume IV

15" day of August , 1903 , that said child has been named George Thomas Miller , and is now living.

Margaret A. Miller

Witnesses To Mark:
{

Subscribed and sworn to before me this 20 day of March , 1905.

Edward Merrick
Notary Public.

BIRTH AFFIDAVIT.

DEPARTMENT OF THE INTERIOR.
COMMISSION TO THE FIVE CIVILIZED TRIBES.

IN RE APPLICATION FOR ENROLLMENT, as a citizen of the CREEK Nation, of James Franklin Miller, born on the 27th day of January , 1905

Name of Father:	Benjamin F. Miller	a citizen of the Creek	Nation.
Name of Mother:	Margaret A Miller	a citizen of the Creek	Nation.

Postoffice   Sapulpa, I.T.

AFFIDAVIT OF MOTHER.

UNITED STATES OF AMERICA, Indian Territory,
WESTERN   DISTRICT.

I, Margaret A. Miller , on oath state that I am 17 years of age and a citizen by blood , of the Creek Nation; that I am the lawful wife of Benjamin F. Miller , who is a non citizen, by blood of the Creek Nation; that a male child was born to me on 27 day of January , 1905 , that said child has been named James Franklin Miller , and is now living.

Margaret A. Miller

Witnesses To Mark:
{

Subscribed and sworn to before me this 12th day of April A.D. , 1905.

F.L. Mars
Notary Public.

My Commission expires July 11, 1906.

Applications for Enrollment of Creek Newborn
Act of 1905   Volume IV

AFFIDAVIT OF ATTENDING PHYSICIAN OR MID-WIFE.

UNITED STATES OF AMERICA, Indian Territory,
    WESTERN   DISTRICT.

I, Mrs. Maggie M. Miller, a mid-wife, on oath state that I attended on Mrs. Margaret A. Miller, wife of Benjamin F. Miller on the 27 day of January, 1905; that there was born to her on said date a male child; that said child is now living and is said to have been named James Franklin Miller

                      Mrs. Maggie M Miller

Witnesses To Mark:

    Subscribed and sworn to before me this 12th day of April, 1905.

                      F.L. Mars

My Commission expires July 11, 1906.   Notary Public.

BIRTH AFFIDAVIT.

DEPARTMENT OF THE INTERIOR.
COMMISSION TO THE FIVE CIVILIZED TRIBES.

IN RE APPLICATION FOR ENROLLMENT, as a citizen of the CREEK Nation, of Roly Francis, born on the 7 day of June, 1902

Name of Father:	Wm Francis	a citizen of the	Creek	Nation.
Name of Mother:	Minkey Francis	a citizen of the	Creek	Nation.

              Postoffice   Eufaula

AFFIDAVIT OF MOTHER.

UNITED STATES OF AMERICA, Indian Territory,
    WESTERN   DISTRICT.

I, Wm. Francis, on oath state that I am 32 years of age and a citizen by blood, of the Creek Nation; that I am the lawful ~~wife~~ husband of Minkey Francis, who is a citizen, by blood of the Creek Nation; that a male child was born to me on 7 day of June, 1902, that said child has been named Roly Francis, and is now living.

                      William Francis

Applications for Enrollment of Creek Newborn
Act of 1905   Volume IV

Witnesses To Mark:

Subscribed and sworn to before me this 11th day of Mar, 1905.

My Commission
Ex July 25 1907

J McDermott
Notary Public.

Department of the Interior,
COMMISSION TO THE FIVE CIVILIZED TRIBES.

IN RE APPLICATION FOR ENROLLMENT, as a citizen of the Creek Nation, of Roly Francis, born on the 7 day of June, 1902

Name of Father: William Francis   a citizen of the   Creek   Nation.
Hickory Ground
Name of Mother: Minky Francis   a citizen of the   Creek   Nation.
Tuskegee Town

Post-Office: Eufaula, Ind. Ter.

AFFIDAVIT OF MOTHER.

UNITED STATES OF AMERICA,
   Indian Territory.
  Western   District.

Child is present

I, Minky Francis, on oath state that I am about 26 years of age and a citizen by blood, of the Creek Nation; that I am the lawful wife of William Francis, who is a citizen, by blood of the Creek Nation; that a male child was born to me on 7 day of June, 1902, that said child has been named Roly Francis, and ~~is now~~ was living on March 4, 1905.

                      her
               Minky x Francis
WITNESSES TO MARK: mark
  Alex Posey
  DC Skaggs

Subscribed and sworn to before me this 3 *day of* April, *1905.*

                    Drennan C Skaggs
                        NOTARY PUBLIC.

Applications for Enrollment of Creek Newborn
Act of 1905 Volume IV

AFFIDAVIT OF ATTENDING PHYSICIAN OR MID-WIFE.

UNITED STATES OF AMERICA,
   Indian Territory.
Western   District.

I, Nellie Francis , a midwife , on oath state that I attended on Mrs. Minky Francis , wife of William Francis on the 7 day of June , 1902 ; that there was born to her on said date a male child; that said child is now was living on March 4, 1905, and is said to have been named Roly Francis

                                             her
                                     Nellie x Francis

WITNESSES TO MARK: mark
   Alex Posey
   DC Skaggs

Subscribed and sworn to before me this 3 *day of* April, *1905.*

                                       Drennan C Skaggs
                                           NOTARY PUBLIC.

BIRTH AFFIDAVIT.

DEPARTMENT OF THE INTERIOR.
COMMISSION TO THE FIVE CIVILIZED TRIBES.

    IN RE APPLICATION FOR ENROLLMENT, as a citizen of the CREEK Nation, of Sam Francis , born on the 1 day of May , 1904

Name of Father:	Wm Francis	a citizen of the Creek	Nation.
Name of Mother:	Minkey Francis	a citizen of the Creek	Nation.

                              Postoffice   Eufaula

AFFIDAVIT OF MOTHER.

UNITED STATES OF AMERICA, Indian Territory,
    WESTERN   DISTRICT.

    I, Wm. Francis , on oath state that I am 32 years of age and a citizen by blood , of the Creek Nation; that I am the lawful wife husband of Minkey Francis , who is a citizen, by blood of the Creek Nation; that a male child was born to me on 1 day of May , 1904 , that said child has been named Sam Francis , and is now living.

                                             William Francis

Applications for Enrollment of Creek Newborn
Act of 1905   Volume IV

Witnesses To Mark:

Subscribed and sworn to before me this 11th day of Mar, 1905.

My Com
Ex July 25 1907

J McDermott
Notary Public.

Department of the Interior,
COMMISSION TO THE FIVE CIVILIZED TRIBES.

IN RE APPLICATION FOR ENROLLMENT, as a citizen of the Creek Nation, of Samuel Francis, born on the 1 day of May, 1904

Name of Father: William Francis   a citizen of the   Creek   Nation. Hickory Ground Town
Name of Mother: Minky Francis   a citizen of the   Creek   Nation. Tuskegee Town

Post-Office: Eufaula, Ind. Ter.

AFFIDAVIT OF MOTHER.

UNITED STATES OF AMERICA,
   Indian Territory.
   Western   District.

Child is present

I, Minky Francis, on oath state that I am about 26 years of age and a citizen by blood, of the Creek Nation; that I am the lawful wife of William Francis, who is a citizen, by blood of the Creek Nation; that a male child was born to me on 1 day of May, 1904, that said child has been named Samuel Francis, and ~~is now~~ was living on March 4, 1905.

                    her
              Minky x Francis
                  mark

WITNESSES TO MARK:
   Alex Posey
   DC Skaggs

Subscribed and sworn to before me this 3 day of April, 1905.

                  Drennan C Skaggs
                      NOTARY PUBLIC.

Applications for Enrollment of Creek Newborn
Act of 1905 Volume IV

AFFIDAVIT OF ATTENDING PHYSICIAN OR MID-WIFE.

UNITED STATES OF AMERICA,
    Indian Territory.
Western   District.

I, Nellie Francis , a midwife , on oath state that I attended on Mrs. Minky Francis , wife of William Francis on the 1 day of May , 1904 ; that there was born to her on said date a male child; that said child is now was living on March 4, 1905, and is said to have been named Samuel Francis

                       her
                       Nellie x Francis
WITNESSES TO MARK: mark
    Alex Posey
    DC Skaggs

Subscribed and sworn to before me this 3 *day of* April, *1905.*

                       Drennan C Skaggs
                       NOTARY PUBLIC.

                       NC-263
                       31
Muskogee, Indian Territory, May 30, 1905.

William Francis,
    Eufaula, Indian Territory.

Dear Sir:

In the matter of the application for the enrollment of your minor children, Roly and Sam Francis, as a citizen of the Creek Nation, you are advised that the Commission requires the affidavits of the mother and midwife in the cases.

There are herewith enclosed two blank forms of birth affidavits. In executing same, care should be taken to see that all blanks are properly filled, all names written in full, and in the event that either of the persons signing the affidavit is unable to write, signature by mark must be attested by two witnesses.

                    Respectfully,

                             Chairman.

2 B A

Applications for Enrollment of Creek Newborn
Act of 1905 Volume IV

BIRTH AFFIDAVIT.

DEPARTMENT OF THE INTERIOR.
COMMISSION TO THE FIVE CIVILIZED TRIBES.

IN RE APPLICATION FOR ENROLLMENT, as a citizen of the Creek Nation, of William Enrigues, born on the 27th day of December, 1903

Name of Father:	Jesus Enrigues	a citizen of the Mexican	Nation.
Name of Mother:	Lizzie Enrigues	a citizen of the Creek	Nation.

Postoffice   Henry, Oklahoma Territory

AFFIDAVIT OF MOTHER.

UNITED STATES OF AMERICA, Indian Territory, ⎫
    Western   DISTRICT. ⎭

    I, Lizzie Enrigues (nee Gooden), on oath state that I am 23 years of age and a citizen by blood, of the Creek Nation; that I am the lawful wife of Jesus Enrigues, who is a citizen, by blood of the Mexican Nation; that a male child was born to me on 27th day of December, 1903, that said child has been named William Enrigues, and was living March 4, 1905.

                                                      her
                                              Lizzie x Enrigues
Witnesses To Mark: mark
    ⎧ *(Illegible)* C Perryman
    ⎩ Chas. E. Stewart

    Subscribed and sworn to before me this 20th day of March, 1905.

                                        (Name Illegible)
                                             Notary Public.
    My commission expires July 10th 1906

AFFIDAVIT OF ATTENDING PHYSICIAN OR MID-WIFE.

UNITED STATES OF AMERICA, Indian Territory, ⎫
    Western   DISTRICT. ⎭

    I, Sordie Gooden, a midwife, on oath state that I attended on Mrs. Lizzie Enrigues, wife of Jesus Enrigues on the 27th day of December, 1903; that there was born to her on said date a male child; that said child was living March 4, 1905, and is said to have been named William Enrigues

                                                      her
                                            Sordie x Gooden
                                                 mark

Applications for Enrollment of Creek Newborn
Act of 1905   Volume IV

Witnesses To Mark:
{ *(Illegible)* C Perryman
  Chas. E. Stewart

    Subscribed and sworn to before me this 20th day of March, 1905.

(Name Illegible)
Notary Public.

My commission expires July 10th 1906

BIRTH AFFIDAVIT.

DEPARTMENT OF THE INTERIOR.
COMMISSION TO THE FIVE CIVILIZED TRIBES.

    IN RE APPLICATION FOR ENROLLMENT, as a citizen of the CREEK Nation, of Ellen Deer, born on the 16th day of Sept., 1901

| Name of Father: | Silas Deer | a citizen of the | Creek | Nation. |
| Name of Mother: | Nancy Deer | a citizen of the | Creek | Nation. |

    Postoffice   Haskell, I.T.

AFFIDAVIT OF ATTENDING PHYSICIAN OR MID-WIFE.

UNITED STATES OF AMERICA, Indian Territory,
    Western   DISTRICT.

    I, Betty Grayson, a midwife, on oath state that I attended on Mrs. Nancy Deer, wife of Silas Deer on the 16th day of Sept, 1901; that there was born to her on said date a female child; that said child is now living and is said to have been named Ellen Deer

                                        her
                                Betty x Grayson
Witnesses To Mark: mark
{ B. A. McBride
  (Illegible) M. Carver

    Subscribed and sworn to before me this 10th day of April, 1905.

                                      E. B. Harris
                                      Notary Public.

Applications for Enrollment of Creek Newborn
Act of 1905   Volume IV

Disinterested Person
AFFIDAVIT OF <s>ATTENDING PHYSICIAN OR MID-WIFE</s>.

UNITED STATES OF AMERICA, Indian Territory, ⎫
    Western   DISTRICT. ⎭

know
I, R. P. De Graffenried , an acquaintance , on oath state that I <s>attended on</s> Mrs. Nancy McBride , wife of B.A. McBride & on <s>the</s> or about 16" day of September , 1901 ; that there was born to her on said date a female child; that said child was living March 4, 1905, to the best of my knowledge and is said to have been named Ellen Deer

R P deGraffenried

Witnesses To Mark:
{ Subscribed and sworn to before me this 11" day of August, 1905.

Henry G. Hains
Notary Public.

BIRTH AFFIDAVIT.

DEPARTMENT OF THE INTERIOR.

COMMISSION TO THE FIVE CIVILIZED TRIBES.

IN RE APPLICATION FOR ENROLLMENT, as a citizen of the CREEK Nation, of Ellen Deer, born on the 16th day of Sept. , 1901

Name of Father: Silas Deer   a citizen of the   Creek   Nation.
Name of Mother: Nancy Deer   a citizen of the   Creek   Nation.

Postoffice   Haskell, I.T.

AFFIDAVIT OF MOTHER.

UNITED STATES OF AMERICA, Indian Territory, ⎫
                             DISTRICT. ⎭

I, Davis Asbury on oath state that I was personaly[sic] acquainted with both Nancy and Silas Deer parents of Ellen Deer and to best of my memory she was born in the fall of 1901 and that said Ellen Deer is a citizen and is now living

his
Davis x Asbury
mark

Witnesses To Mark:
{ B.S. Tatum
  B A McBride

Applications for Enrollment of Creek Newborn
Act of 1905 Volume IV

Subscribed and sworn to before me this 4th day of August, 1905.

                                        Ralph Dresback
                                        Notary Public.

AFFIDAVIT OF ATTENDING PHYSICIAN OR MID-WIFE.

UNITED STATES OF AMERICA, Indian Territory,
    Western   **DISTRICT.**

I, Betty Grayson, a midwife, on oath state that I attended on Mrs. Nancy Deer, wife of Silas Deer on the 16 day of September, 1901; that there was born to her on said date a Female child; that said child was living March 4, 1905, and is said to have been named Ellen Deer

                                      her
                            Betty x Grayson
Witnesses To Mark: mark
  { B.S. Tatum
    B A McBride

Subscribed and sworn to before me this 4th day of August, 1905.

                                      Ralph Dresback
                                      Notary Public.

BIRTH AFFIDAVIT.
DEPARTMENT OF THE INTERIOR.
COMMISSION TO THE FIVE CIVILIZED TRIBES.

IN RE APPLICATION FOR ENROLLMENT, as a citizen of the CREEK Nation, of Ellen Deer, born on the 16 day of Sept., 1901

Name of Father:	Silas Deer	a citizen of the	Creek	Nation.
Name of Mother:	Nancy "	a citizen of the	Creek	Nation.

                              Postoffice   Haskell

---

child present

                          AFFIDAVIT OF ~~MOTHER~~.
                                  Step father

UNITED STATES OF AMERICA, Indian Territory,
    WESTERN   **DISTRICT.**

I, B.A. McBride, on oath state that I am 40 years of age and a citizen by -----, of the U.S. Nation; that I am the lawful ~~wife-step-father~~ husband of Nancy Deer (dc'd), who is a citizen, by *(blank)* of the *(blank)* Nation; that a female child was born to

Applications for Enrollment of Creek Newborn
Act of 1905   Volume IV

~~me~~ her on 16 day of Sept. , 1901 , that said child has been named Ellen Deer , and is now living.

B A McBride

Witnesses To Mark:
{

Subscribed and sworn to before me this 20 day of March, 1905.

Edw C Griesel
Notary Public.

NC-265.

Muskogee, Indian Territory, July 26, 1905.

B. A. McBride,
    Haskell, Indian Territory.

Dear Sir:

    On March 20, 1905 you appeared before the Commission to the Five Civilized Tribes and made application for the enrollment[sic] of Ellen Deer, daughter of Silas Deer, deceased, and Nancy Deer, deceased, as a citizen by blood of the Creek Nation.

    You are advised that before the rights of said child as a citizen by blood of the Creek Nation can be finally determined it will be necessary for you to file with this office the affidavits of two disinterested witnesses as to the birth of said child disinterested parties who are acquainted with said Ellen Deer, know when she was born, the names of her parents and whether or not she was living March 4, 1905 March 4, 1905.

    You should give this matter your immediate attention.

Respectfully,

Commissioner.

DEPARTMENT OF THE INTERIOR,
COMMISSIONER TO THE FIVE CIVILIZED TRIBES.

REFER IN REPLY TO THE FOLLOWING:
C-356

Muskogee, Indian Territory, October 3, 1905.

Silas Deer,
    Haskell, Indian Territory.

Dear Sir:

Applications for Enrollment of Creek Newborn
Act of 1905   Volume IV

You are hereby advised that on **September 27, 1905**, the Secretary of the Interior approved the enrollment of your minor child, **Ellen Deer**, as a citizen by blood of the **Creek** Nation, and that the name of said child appears upon the roll of new born citizens of the **Creek** Nation as Number **356**.

The child is now entitled to an allotment, and application therefor should be made without delay at the Land Office for the Nation in which the prospective allotment is located.

An entire allotment for said child must be selected at the time of the original application.

Respectively,

Tams Bixby

Commissioner.

N.C. 266

DEPARTMENT OF THE INTERIOR,
COMMISSIONER TO THE FIVE CIVILIZED TRIBES.
Muskogee, Indian Territory, August 8, 1905.

In the matter of the application for the enrollment of Thomas Brown as a citizen by blood of the Creek Nation.

Co-den-ny being duly sworn testified as follows:

By Commissioner:

Q What is your name? [sic] Co-den-ny that's my Indian name the way I am enrolled. My English name is Fortyfour Brown.
Q What is your age? A 34
Q What is your post office address? A Mounds.
Q Are you a full blood Indian? A Yes, sir.
Q Have you a child named Thomas Brown? A Yes, sir.
Q Is he living? A Yes, sir.
Q What is the name of the mother of that child? A You-con-co-con-thla-nay
Q Has she an English name? [sic] Her English name is Annie Brown
Q Is her English name Annie or Hannah? A Hannah

I, Anna Garrigues, on oath state that the above and foregoing is a true and correct copy of my stenographic notes taken in said cause on said date.

Applications for Enrollment of Creek Newborn
Act of 1905 Volume IV

Anna Garrigues

Subscribed and sworn to before
me this 8th day of August, 1905.

Edw C Griesel
Notary Public.

BIRTH AFFIDAVIT.

DEPARTMENT OF THE INTERIOR.
COMMISSION TO THE FIVE CIVILIZED TRIBES.

IN RE APPLICATION FOR ENROLLMENT, as a citizen of the CREEK Nation, of Thomas Brown, - - - - - - - - - - -, born on the 27th, day of November, , 1904

Name of Father: Forty-four Brown, - - - - - - a citizen of the Creek, - - - - Nation.
Name of Mother: Annie Brown, - - - - - - - - - a citizen of the Creek, - - - - Nation.

Postoffice   Mounds, I.T. - - - - - -

AFFIDAVIT OF MOTHER.

UNITED STATES OF AMERICA, Indian Territory,
WESTERN   DISTRICT.

I, Annie Brown, - - - - - - - - - - - - -, on oath state that I am Twenty two years of age and a citizen by Blood - - - - -, of the Creek - - - - - - - - - - Nation; that I am the lawful wife of Forty-four Brown - - - - - - - - - - - - - - , who is a citizen, by Blood, - - - - - of the Creek, - - - - - - - - Nation; that a Male - - - child was born to me on 27th, - - - day of November, , 1901 , that said child has been named Thomas Brown, - - - - - - - - - - -, and is now living.

her
Annie x Brown
mark

Witnesses To Mark:
{ T.A. Hubbard
{ D Bigpond

Subscribed and sworn to before me this 20th,   day of March, - - - - - - , 1905.

R Bantou
My Commission expires Sept. 4, 1906   Notary Public.

Applications for Enrollment of Creek Newborn
Act of 1905 Volume IV

AFFIDAVIT OF ATTENDING PHYSICIAN OR MID-WIFE.

UNITED STATES OF AMERICA, Indian Territory, ⎫
    Western   DISTRICT. ⎭

    I, Jensie Barnett, - - - - - --- - - , a acting midwife , on oath state that I attended on Mrs. Annie Brown - - - - - - - - , wife of Forty-four Brown, - - - - - on the 27th, day of November, , 1904 ; that there was born to her on said date a male child; that said child is now living and is said to have been named Thomas Brown, - - - - - - - -

                                          her
                                   Jensie x Barnett
Witnesses To Mark: mark
  ⎧ T.A. Hubbard
  ⎩ D Bigpond

    Subscribed and sworn to before me this 20th, day of March, - - - - - - - 1905.

                                R. Bantou
      My Commission expires Sept. 4, 1906   Notary Public.

BIRTH AFFIDAVIT.

DEPARTMENT OF THE INTERIOR.
COMMISSION TO THE FIVE CIVILIZED TRIBES.

    IN RE APPLICATION FOR ENROLLMENT, as a citizen of the Creek Nation, of Thomas Brown , born on the 27 day of Nov , 1904

Name of Father: Co-den-ny   a citizen of the   Creek   Nation.
Name of Mother: You-con-co-con-thla-nay   a citizen of the   Creek   Nation.

                        Postoffice   Mounds

                AFFIDAVIT OF MOTHER.   Child Present

UNITED STATES OF AMERICA, Indian Territory, ⎫
    Western   DISTRICT. ⎭

    I, You-con-co-con-thla-nay , on oath state that I am 20 years of age and a citizen by blood , of the Creek Nation; that I am the lawful wife of Co-den-ny , who is a citizen, by blood of the Creek Nation; that a male child was born to me on 27 day of Nov , 1904 , that said child has been named Thomas Brown , and was living March 4, 1905.   Her
                                 You-con-co-con-thla-nay x
                                                       mark

Applications for Enrollment of Creek Newborn
Act of 1905   Volume IV

Witnesses To Mark:
{ David Shelby
{ Jesse McDermott

    Subscribed and sworn to before me this 27 day of April , 1905.

                                         Edw C Griesel
                                                 Notary Public.

AFFIDAVIT OF ATTENDING ~~PHYSICIAN OR MID-WIFE~~.
                         Father

UNITED STATES OF AMERICA, Indian Territory, }
    Western   DISTRICT.

    I, Co-den-ny , ~~a~~ ----- , on oath state that I attended on Mrs. You-con-co-con-thla-nay , my wife ~~of~~ *(blank)* on the 27 day of Nov , 1904 ; that there was born to her on said date a male child; that said child was living March 4, 1905, and is said to have been named Thomas Brown   His
                                 Co-den-ny x
Witnesses To Mark: mark
{ David Shelby
{ Jesse McDermott

    Subscribed and sworn to before me this 27 day of April , 1905.

                                     Edw C Griesel
                                        Notary Public.

                                     Cr NC-266

             Muskogee, Indian Territory, June 9, 1905.

Annie Brown (or You-con-co-con-thla-nay)
    Mound, Indian Territory.

Dear Madam:

    In the matter of the application for the enrollment of your minor child, Thomas Brown, as a citizen of the Creek Nation, there are on file with the Commission affidavits executed by you and the father of said child which you have signed as "Annie Brown" and "You-con-co-con-thla-nay." You are listed for enrollment in the Creek Nation as You-con-co-con-thla-nay. A note on the card in said case states that your English name is Hannah Brown.

Applications for Enrollment of Creek Newborn
Act of 1905   Volume IV

You are requested to advise the Commission as to the different names under which you are known.

The father of said child has been identified as Co-den-ny. There is also an affidavit on file with the Commission to which his name is signed as "Forty-four Brown." You are requested to advise the Commission as to whether Forty-fur Brown is the English name of said Co-den-ny.   Respectfully,

                      Chairman.

NC-266

            Muskogee, Indian Territory, July 26, 1905.

Forty-four Brown (or Co-den-ny)
   Mounds, Indian Territory.

Dear Sir:

  In the matter of the application for the enrollment of your minor child Thomas Brown, as a citizen by blood of the Creek Nation, there are on file affidavits executed by you and the mother of said child in which the name of the mother of said child appears as Annie Brown and You-con-co-con-thla-nay. Your wife is listed for enrollment in the Creek Nation as You-con-co-con-thla-nay. A note on the card in said case states that her English name is Hannah Brown.

  You are requested to advise this office as to whether or not your wife is also known by the English name of Annie Brown and as to whether Annie Brown and You-con-co-con-thla, nay are one and the same person.

  You are identified upon the final roll of Creek citizens by blood as Co-den-ny.

  You are also requested to inform this office as to whether you are known by the name of Forty-four Brown.
            Respectfully,

                    Commissioner.

NC-267.

            Muskogee, Indian Territory, July 26, 1905.

Ada Carr,
   Checotah, Indian Territory.

Dear Madam:

Applications for Enrollment of Creek Newborn
Act of 1905 Volume IV

    In the matter of the application for the enrollment of your daughter Verna Vinita Carr as a citizen by blood of the Creek Nation you are advised that, before the rights of said child as such citizen can be finally determined, it will be necessary for you to file with this office wither the original or a certified copy of the marriage license and certificate between you and Thomas Carr the citizen father of said child.

                  Respectfully,

                                  Commissioner.

NC-267.

                        Muskogee, Indian Territory, August 14, 1905.

Ada Carr,
      c/o Thomas Carr,
            Checotah, Indian Territory.

Dear Madam:

    In the matter of the application for the enrollment of your minor daughter Vera Vinita Carr, as a citizen by blood of the Creek Nation, you are advised that it will be necessary for you to furnish this office with the affidavit of Thomas Carr, the father of said child, relative to her birth and for that purpose there is inclosed[sic] herewith a blank for proof of birth which has been properly filled out.

                  Respectfully,

                              Acting Commissioner.

CTD-43.
Env.

BIRTH AFFIDAVIT.

DEPARTMENT OF THE INTERIOR.
COMMISSION TO THE FIVE CIVILIZED TRIBES.

    IN RE APPLICATION FOR ENROLLMENT, as a citizen of the Creek Nation, of Indian Ty, Verna, Vinita, Carr , born on the 31st day of May , 1903

Name of Father:	Thomas, Carr	a citizen of the Creek	Nation.
Name of Mother:	Ada, Carr	a citizen of the Creek	Nation.

                    Postoffice   Checotah. , Ind. Tery.

Applications for Enrollment of Creek Newborn
Act of 1905 Volume IV

AFFIDAVIT OF MOTHER.

UNITED STATES OF AMERICA, Indian Territory,
Western, DISTRICT.

I, Ada, Carr , on oath state that I am 19 years of age and a citizen by Marriage, , of the Creek Nation; that I am the lawful wife of Thomas, Carr , who is a citizen, by Blood of the Creek Nation; that a Female child was born to me on 31st, day of May, , 1903. , that said child has been named Verna, Vinita, Carr. , and was living March 4, 1905.

Ada Carr

Witnesses To Mark:

Subscribed and sworn to before me this 18th day of March, , 1905.

MY COMMISSION EXPIRES JULY 6, 1906.   N. G. Turk
Notary Public.

AFFIDAVIT OF ATTENDING PHYSICIAN OR MID-WIFE.

UNITED STATES OF AMERICA, Indian Territory,
Western DISTRICT.

I, Eliza, Collins. , a Midwife, , on oath state that I attended on Mrs. Ada, Carr. , wife of Thomas Carr on the 31st day of May , 1903 ; that there was born to her on said date a Female child; that said child was living March 4, 1905, and is said to have been named Verna, Vinita, Carr

Eliza Collins

Witnesses To Mark:

Subscribed and sworn to before me this 18th day of March, , 1905.

MY COMMISSION EXPIRES JULY 6, 1906.   N. G. Turk
Notary Public.

BIRTH AFFIDAVIT.

DEPARTMENT OF THE INTERIOR.
COMMISSION TO THE FIVE CIVILIZED TRIBES.

IN RE APPLICATION FOR ENROLLMENT, as a citizen of the Creek Nation, of Verna Vinita Carr , born on the 31st day of May , 1903

Applications for Enrollment of Creek Newborn
Act of 1905 Volume IV

Name of Father: Thomas Carr   a citizen of the   Creek   Nation.
Name of Mother: Ada Carr   a citizen of the United States Nation.

                        Postoffice   Checotah, Ind. Ter.

AFFIDAVIT OF ~~MOTHER~~. Father

UNITED STATES OF AMERICA, Indian Territory,
    Western -----   **DISTRICT.**

    I, Thomas Carr, on oath state that I am 25 years of age and a citizen by blood, of the Creek Nation; that I am the lawful ~~wife of~~ husband of Ada Carr, who is a citizen, by *(blank)* of the United States ~~Nation~~; that a female child was born to ~~me~~ us on 31st day of May, 1903, that said child has been named Verna Vinita Carr, and was living March 4, 1905 and that I am the father of said child.

                                                    Thomas Carr

Witnesses To Mark:

    Subscribed and sworn to before me this 28 day of March, 1905.

                                                J D Faulkner
            My commission expires Feby. 12th 1907.   Notary Public.

CERTIFICATE OF RECORD.

United States of America,
    Indian Territory,   } *ss.*
    Northern District.

    I, **ROBERT P. HARRISON**, Clerk of the United States Court in the Western District, Indian Territory, do hereby certify that the instrument hereto attached was filed for record in my office the 5 day of Dec.   1902 at   M., and duly recorded in Book N. , Marriage Record, Page 425

    WITNESS my hand and seal of said Court at Muscogee, in said Territory, this 5   day of   Dec.   A. D. 1902
                                  R.P. Harrison   *Clerk.*
By   J Harlan   *Deputy.*

Applications for Enrollment of Creek Newborn
Act of 1905 Volume IV

𝔐ARRIAGE 𝔏ICENSE.
••••••••

𝔘nited 𝔖tates of 𝔄merica,
  Indian Territory,   } ss.   *No.* **455**
  Northern District.

To Any Person Authorized by Law to Solemnize Marriage---Greeting:

𝔜ou are 𝔥ereby 𝔈ommanded *to Solemnize the Rite and Publish the Banns of Matrimony between Mr.*   Thomas Carr   *of*   Checotah *, in the Indian Territory, aged*   20   *years and M*iss Ada Bell Williams   *of*   Checotah   *in the Indian Territory aged*   17   *years according to law, and do you officially sign and return this License to the parties therein named.*

WITNESS my hand and official seal at Muscogee Indian Territory this   21st *day of*   November   *A.D. 190* 2

                                                    R.P. Harrison
                                                    Clerk of the U.S. Court

By   *(Name Illegible)*   *Deputy*

CERTIFICATE OF MARRIAGE.
••••••

𝔘nited 𝔖tates of 𝔄merica,
  Indian Territory,   } ss.
  Northern District.

I,   W. M. Marlin   *, a Minister of the Gospel, DO HEREBY CERTIFY that on the*   26   *day of*   November   *A. D. 1902, I did duly and according to law as commanded in the foregoing License, solemnize the Rite and Publish the Banns of Matrimony between the parties therein named.*

WITNESS my hand this   26   *day of*   November   *A. D. 1902*

My credentials are recorded in the office of the Clerk of the United States Court, Indian Territory, Western District, Book   B   *, Page*   152   .
                                                    W. M. Marlin
                                                    A Minister of the Gospel

Note—This License and Certificate of Marriage must be returned to the Office of the Clerk of the United States Court in the Northern District, Indian Territory, from whence it was issued, within sixty days from the date thereof, or the party to whom the license was issued will be liable in the amount of the One Hundred Dollars ($100.00)

Applications for Enrollment of Creek Newborn
Act of 1905   Volume IV

NC-268.

Muskogee, Indian Territory, July 26, 1905.

Josie A. Morton,
    Okemah, Indian Territory.

Dear Madam:

    In the matter of the application for the enrollment of your minor son Ellis N. Morton as a citizen by blood of the Creek Nation it will be necessary, before the rights of said child as such citizen can be finally determined, for you to file with this office wither the original or a certified copy of the marriage license and certificate between you and Mossie Morton the citizen father of said child.

                  Respectfully,

                                      Commissioner.

MARRIAGE LICENSE

United States of America, ⎞
  Indian Territory,   (SS.   No. 931.
  Northern District. ⎠

TO ANY PERSON AUTHORIZED BY LAW TO SOLEMNIZE MARRIAGE---GREETING:

    You are hereby commanded to solemnize the Rite and publish the Banns of Matrimony between Mr. Mossie M. Morton of Okmulgee, in the Indian Territory, aged 28 years, and Miss Josie A. Dean of Okmulgee, in the Indian Territory, aged 18 years, according to law, and do you officially sign and return this License to the parties therein named.
    WITNESS my hand and official seal at Muscogee[sic], Indian Territory, this 14" day of September, A. D. 1900.

          (SEAL)   Chas A Davidson
                                             Clerk of the U.S. Court.

By L A Winston
    Deputy.

CERTIFICATE OF MARRIAGE.

United States of America, ⎞
  Indian Territory,   (SS.
  Northern District. ⎠

Applications for Enrollment of Creek Newborn
Act of 1905 Volume IV

    I, A. M. Lusk, a Minister of the Gospel, DO HEREBY CERTIFY, that on the 16 day of Sept., A.D. 1900, I did duly and according to law as commanded in the foregoing License, solemnize the Rite and publish the Banns of Matrimony between the parties therein named.
    WITNESS my hand that 16 day of Sept., A. D. 1900.
    My credentials are recorded in the office of the Clerk of the United States Court, Indian Territory, Third Judicial Division, Book A, Page 138.

                signed.   A. M. Lusk
                                    A Minister of the Gospel.

ENDORSEMENTS:

                    CERTIFICATE OF RECORD.

United State of America. I
      Indian Territory,   (SS.
      Northern District. I

    I, Charles A. Davidson, Clerk of the United States Court in the Northern District, Indian Territory, do hereby certify that the instrument hereto attached was filed for record in my office the 6 day of Oct 1900, at _____M., and duly recorded in Book J., Marriage Record, Page 119.
    WITNESS my hand and seal of said Court at Muscogee[sic], in said Territory this 5 day of Dec. A.D. 1900.

        Seal   Chas A. Davidson
                                                Clerk.

Northern Dist. Ind. Ter. Filed Oct. 6, 1900. Chas. A. Davidson, Clerk, U.S. Courts.

    I, D. C. Skaggs, on oath state that the above and foregoing is a full and complete copy of the original now on file in the office of the Commissioner to the Five Civilized Tribes at Muskogee, Indian Territory.

                                    D.C. Skaggs

Subscribed and sworn to before me this 3 day of August, 1905.

                                Edw C Griesel
                                    Notary Public.
            My Commission expires Nov. 29-1908.

Applications for Enrollment of Creek Newborn
Act of 1905 Volume IV

BIRTH AFFIDAVIT.

DEPARTMENT OF THE INTERIOR.
COMMISSION TO THE FIVE CIVILIZED TRIBES.

IN RE APPLICATION FOR ENROLLMENT, as a citizen of the Creek Nation, of Ellis M. Morton, born on the 1st day of September, 1904

Name of Father: Mossie Morton   a citizen of the   Creek   Nation.
Name of Mother: Josie A. Morton   a citizen of the United States Nation.

Postoffice   Okemah, I.T.

AFFIDAVIT OF MOTHER.

UNITED STATES OF AMERICA, Indian Territory,
Western   DISTRICT.

I, Josie A. Morton, on oath state that I am 22 years of age and a citizen by -----, of the United States ~~Nation~~; that I am the lawful wife of Mossie Morton, who is a citizen, by blood of the Creek Nation; that a male child was born to me on the 1st day of September, 1904, that said child has been named Ellis M. Morton, and is now living.

Josie A. Morton

Witnesses To Mark:
{

Subscribed and sworn to before me this 8" day of March, 1905.

Seal   Drennan C Skaggs
            Notary Public.

AFFIDAVIT OF ATTENDING PHYSICIAN OR MID-WIFE.

UNITED STATES OF AMERICA, Indian Territory,
Western   DISTRICT.

I, Robert Allan, a Physician, on oath state that I attended on Mrs. Josie A Morton, wife of Mossie Morton on the 1st day of September, 1904; that there was born to her on said date a male child; that said child is now living and is said to have been named Ellis M. Morton

Robert Allan

Witnesses To Mark:
{

Subscribed and sworn to before me this 8" day of March, 1905.

Applications for Enrollment of Creek Newborn
Act of 1905   Volume IV

Seal   Drennan C Skaggs
              Notary Public.

DEPARTMENT OF THE INTERIOR,
COMMISSION TO THE FIVE CIVILIZED TRIBES.
April 17, 1905, Bristow, I.T.

In the matter of the application for the enrollment of La-sa-wee Littlehead, as a citizen by blood of the Creek Nation.

Whiteman Littlehead being duly sworn, by E.C. Griesel, a notary public, testified as follows: Through fficial interpreter, Tom W. Flynn.

By Commission:
Q What is your name? A Whiteman Littlehead.
Q How old are you? A About 25.
Q What is your post office? A Bristow.
Q You are a citizen of the Creek Nation? A Yes sir.
Q You are the father of La-sa-wee Littlehead? A Yes sir.
Q Who is the mother of this child? A Yar-la-wee Littlehead.
Q She is also a citizen of the Creek Nation? A Yes sir.
Q When was this child born? A March the 4th, 1905.
Q On what day of the week was this? A On Saturday.
Q What time of the day was this child born? A One o'clock at noon. After dinner.
Q After dinner? A Yes.
Q Who was present at the birth of this child? A Yas-ta-ko-thla-nan.
Q What relation is she to the mother of this child? A An aunt, sister to her father.
Q[sic]

------oOo-------

Yar-la-wee being duly sworn by E.C. Griesel, a Notary Public. Public, testified as follows: Through official interpreter Whiteman Littlehead.

By Commission.
Q What is your name? A Yar-la-wee Littlehead.
Q How old are you? A About 20.
Q What is your post office? A Bristow.
Q Are you the mother of this child? La-sa-wee Littlehead? A Yes, sir.
Q When was this child born? A I do not know.
Q How old is that child now? A About two months.
Q How do you know this? A You are asking too many question, I have told you all I know.

Case is fully explained to her through the interpreter, and then she answer[sic] March 4th, 1905.

Applications for Enrollment of Creek Newborn
Act of 1905   Volume IV

E.C. Griesel, being duly sworn, on oath, states that the above and foregoing is a true and correct transcript of his stenographic[sic] notes as taken in said cause on said date.

Edw C Griesel

Subscribed and sworn to before me this 5 day of May, 1905.

Zera E Parrish
Notary Public.

BIRTH AFFIDAVIT.

DEPARTMENT OF THE INTERIOR.
COMMISSION TO THE FIVE CIVILIZED TRIBES.

IN RE APPLICATION FOR ENROLLMENT, as a citizen of the Creek Nation, of Charles Percy Berryhill, born on the 1st day of August, 1902

Name of Father:	Andrew J. Berryhill	a citizen of the	Creek	Nation.
Name of Mother:	Lula Berryhill	a citizen of the	U.S.	Nation.

Postoffice   Bixby, Ind. Ter.

AFFIDAVIT OF ~~MOTHER~~. Father

UNITED STATES OF AMERICA, Indian Territory,
Western DISTRICT.

I, Andrew J. Berryhill, on oath state that I am 49 years of age and a citizen by Blood, of the Creek Nation; that I am the lawful ~~wife~~ husband of Lula Berryhill, who is a citizen, by birth of the U.S. Nation; that a male child was born to me on 1st day of August, , 1902, that said child has been named Charles Percy Berryhill, and was living March 4, 1905.

Andrew J Berryhill

Witnesses To Mark:
{

Subscribed and sworn to before me this 18 day of March, 1905.

Allen Henry
Notary Public.

My commission expires Oct. 19, 1907.

Applications for Enrollment of Creek Newborn
Act of 1905   Volume IV

AFFIDAVIT OF ATTENDING PHYSICIAN OR MID-WIFE.

UNITED STATES OF AMERICA, Indian Territory,
Western DISTRICT.

I, Cora Woods, a mid-wife, on oath state that I attended on Mrs. Lula Berryhill, wife of Andrew J. Berryhill on the 1st day of August, 1902 ; that there was born to her on said date a male child; that said child was living March 4, 1905, and is said to have been named Charles Percy Berryhill

Cora Woods

Witnesses To Mark:

Subscribed and sworn to before me this 18 day of March, 1905.

Allen Henry
Notary Public.
My commission expires Oct. 19, 1907.

BIRTH AFFIDAVIT.

DEPARTMENT OF THE INTERIOR.
COMMISSION TO THE FIVE CIVILIZED TRIBES.

IN RE APPLICATION FOR ENROLLMENT, as a citizen of the Creek Nation, of Charles Percy Berryhill, born on the 1st day of August, 1902

| Name of Father: | Andrew J. Berryhill | a citizen of the | Creek | Nation. |
| Name of Mother: | Lula Berryhill | a citizen of the | U.S. | Nation. |

Postoffice   Bixby, Ind. Ter.

AFFIDAVIT OF MOTHER.

UNITED STATES OF AMERICA, Indian Territory,
Western DISTRICT.

I, Lula Berryhill, on oath state that I am Thirty Four years of age and a citizen by birth, of the United States Nation; that I am the lawful wife of Andrew J. Berryhill, who is a citizen, by blood of the Creek Nation; that a male child was born to me on 1st day of August, 1902, that said child has been named Charles Percy Berryhill, and was living March 4, 1905.

Lula Berryhill

Witnesses To Mark:

Applications for Enrollment of Creek Newborn
Act of 1905   Volume IV

Subscribed and sworn to before me this 20th day of March, 1905.

                     Chas M. Sherrill
                     Notary Public.

BIRTH AFFIDAVIT.

DEPARTMENT OF THE INTERIOR.
COMMISSION TO THE FIVE CIVILIZED TRIBES.

IN RE APPLICATION FOR ENROLLMENT, as a citizen of the CREEK Nation, of Charles Percy Berryhill, born on the 1 day of Aug, 1902

Name of Father: Andrew J. Berryhill   a citizen of the   Creek   Nation.
Name of Mother: Lula   "   a citizen of the   U.S.   Nation.

                 Postoffice   Bixby

AFFIDAVIT OF MOTHER.

UNITED STATES OF AMERICA, Indian Territory,
    WESTERN   DISTRICT.

I, Andrew J. Berryhill, on oath state that I am 49 years of age and a citizen by blood, of the Creek Nation; that I am the lawful ~~wife~~ hus of Lula Berryhill, who is a citizen, by ----- of the U.S. Nation; that a male child was born to me on 1 day of Aug, 1902, that said child has been named Charles Percy Berryhill, and is now living.

                 Andrew J Berryhill

Witnesses To Mark:

Subscribed and sworn to before me this 20 day of March, 1905.

                 Edw C Griesel
                 Notary Public.

                     NC 271.

             Muskogee, Indian Territory, June 6, 1905.

Ethel J. Ricketts,
     Sapulpa, Indian Territory.

Applications for Enrollment of Creek Newborn
Act of 1905   Volume IV

Dear Madam:

In the matter of the application for the enrollment of your minor child, Goldie Ardell Ricketts, as a citizen of the Creek Nation, you are advised that there is on file with the commission an affidavit of the midwife in attendance at the birth of said child, which is not signed by the Notary Public.

There is herewith enclosed a blank form of birth affidavit, and in executing same care should be exercised to see that all blanks are properly filled, all names written in full and in the event that the person signing the affidavit is unable to write, signature by mark must be attested by two witnesses. Each affidavit must be executed before a Notary Public and the notarial seal and signature of the officer must be attached to each separate affidavit.

The birth of said child is given as January 2, 1903, and January 2, 1904. For the purpose of correcting this discrepancy in the dates you will be allowed fifteen days from date within which to appear before the Commission at Muskogee, Indian Territory.

Respectfully,

1 BA   Commissioner in Charge.

BIRTH AFFIDAVIT.

DEPARTMENT OF THE INTERIOR.
COMMISSION TO THE FIVE CIVILIZED TRIBES.

                                                                                                       Goldie
IN RE APPLICATION FOR ENROLLMENT, as a citizen of the CREEK Nation, of ~~Dora~~ Ardell Rickets, born on the 2 day of Jan, 1903

| Name of Father: | Robt. J. Rickets | a citizen of the | Creek | Nation. |
| Name of Mother: | Ethel J.   " | a citizen of the | U. S. | Nation. |

Postoffice   Sapulpa

Child Present - Gr

AFFIDAVIT OF MOTHER.

UNITED STATES OF AMERICA, Indian Territory, ⎫
    WESTERN   DISTRICT. ⎭

I, Ethel J. Rickets , on oath state that I am 21 years of age and a citizen by -----, of the U.S. Nation; that I am the lawful wife of Robt. J. Rickets , who is a citizen, by blood of the Creek Nation; that a female child was born to me on 2 day of Jan, 1903 , that said child has been named ~~Dora~~ Goldie Ardell Rickets , and is now living.

Ethel J. Ricketts

Applications for Enrollment of Creek Newborn
Act of 1905 Volume IV

Witnesses To Mark:
{

　　Subscribed and sworn to before me this 20 day of March, 1905.

　　　　　　　　　　　　　　　Edw C Griesel
　　　　　　　　　　　　　　　　　　Notary Public.

---

father
AFFIDAVIT OF ~~ATTENDING PHYSICIAN OR MID-WIFE~~.

UNITED STATES OF AMERICA, Indian Territory, }
　　WESTERN　　　DISTRICT. }

　　　　　　　　　　　　　　　　　　　　　　　　　　　husband
　　I, Robt. J. Rickets, a m―――――, ~~on~~ oath state that I ~~attended on Mrs.~~ ――, ~~wife~~ of Ethel J. Rickets & on the 2 day of Jan., 1903 ; that there was born to her on said date a female child; that said child is now living and is said to have been named Dora[sic] Ardell Rickets

　　　　　　　　　　　　　　Robert J. Ricketts

Witnesses To Mark:
{

　　Subscribed and sworn to before me this 20 day of March, 1905.

　　　　　　　　　　　　　　　Edw C Griesel
　　　　　　　　　　　　　　　　　　Notary Public.

BIRTH AFFIDAVIT.

DEPARTMENT OF THE INTERIOR.
COMMISSION TO THE FIVE CIVILIZED TRIBES.

IN RE APPLICATION FOR ENROLLMENT, as a citizen of the Creek Nation, of Goldie A Ricketts, born on the 2nd day of Jan, 1904

Name of Father:	Robert. J Ricketts	a citizen of the	Creek	Nation.
Name of Mother:	Ethel J. Ricketts	a citizen of the	noncitizen	Nation.

　　　　　　　　　Postoffice　　Sapulpa, Ind. Ter.

Applications for Enrollment of Creek Newborn
Act of 1905 Volume IV

AFFIDAVIT OF MOTHER.

UNITED STATES OF AMERICA, Indian Territory,
Western   DISTRICT.

I, Ethel J. Ricketts , on oath state that I am 21 years of age and a citizen by noncitizen, of the Creek Nation; that I am the lawful wife of Robert J. Ricketts , who is a citizen, by blood of the Creek Nation; that a female child was born to me on 2nd day of January, 1904 , that said child has been named Goldie A. Ricketts , and is now living.

Ethel J. Ricketts

Witnesses To Mark:
{

Subscribed and sworn to before me this 17th day of April , 1905.

James J. Mars
Notary Public.

AFFIDAVIT OF ATTENDING PHYSICIAN OR MID-WIFE.

UNITED STATES OF AMERICA, Indian Territory,
Western   DISTRICT.

I, Maggie M Miller , a midwife , on oath state that I attended on Mrs. Ethel J Ricketts , wife of Robert J. Ricketts on the 2nd day of January , 1904; that there was born to her on said date a female child; that said child is now living and is said to have been named Goldie A Ricketts

Maggie M. Miller

Witnesses To Mark:
{

Subscribed and sworn to before me this 17th day of April, 1905.

(No name given)
Notary Public.

My commission expires May 7, 1908..

BIRTH AFFIDAVIT.

DEPARTMENT OF THE INTERIOR.
COMMISSION TO THE FIVE CIVILIZED TRIBES.

IN RE APPLICATION FOR ENROLLMENT, as a citizen of the CREEK Nation, of Clarence Francis Rickets, born on the 28 day of June, 1902

Applications for Enrollment of Creek Newborn
Act of 1905   Volume IV

Name of Father: Robt. J. Rickets   a citizen of the   Creek   Nation.
Name of Mother: Ethel J.   "   a citizen of the   U. S.   Nation.

Postoffice   Sapulpa

Child Present - Gr

AFFIDAVIT OF MOTHER.

UNITED STATES OF AMERICA, Indian Territory,
WESTERN   DISTRICT.

Ethel

I, ~~Robert~~ J. Rickets , on oath state that I am 21 years of age and a citizen by -----, of the U.S. Nation; that I am the lawful wife of Robt. J. Rickets , who is a citizen, by blood of the Creek Nation; that a male child was born to me on 28 day of June, 1902 , that said child has been named Charles Francis Rickets , and is now living.

Ethel J. Ricketts

Witnesses To Mark:

Subscribed and sworn to before me this 20 day of   March , 1905.

Edw C Griesel
Notary Public.

BIRTH AFFIDAVIT.

DEPARTMENT OF THE INTERIOR.
COMMISSION TO THE FIVE CIVILIZED TRIBES.

IN RE APPLICATION FOR ENROLLMENT, as a citizen of the CREEK Nation, of Clarence Francis Rickets, born on the 28 day of June, 1902

Name of Father: Robt. J. Rickets   a citizen of the   Creek   Nation.
Name of Mother: Ethel J.   "   a citizen of the   U. S.   Nation.

Postoffice   Sapulpa

Child Present Gr

AFFIDAVIT OF MOTHER.

UNITED STATES OF AMERICA, Indian Territory,
WESTERN   DISTRICT.

I, Robert J. Rickets , on oath state that I am 23 years of age and a citizen by blood , of the Creek Nation; that I am the lawful ~~wife~~ hus of Ethel J. Rickets , who is a

Applications for Enrollment of Creek Newborn
Act of 1905 Volume IV

citizen, by ----- of the U.S. Nation; that a male child was born to me on 28 day of June, 1902, that said child has been named Clarence Francis Rickets, and is now living.

Robert J. Ricketts

Witnesses To Mark:
{

Subscribed and sworn to before me this 20 day of March, 1905.

Edw C Griesel
Notary Public.

BIRTH AFFIDAVIT.

DEPARTMENT OF THE INTERIOR.
COMMISSION TO THE FIVE CIVILIZED TRIBES.

IN RE APPLICATION FOR ENROLLMENT, as a citizen of the Creek Nation, of Goldie Ardell Ricketts, born on the 2nd day of Jan, 1904

Name of Father:	Robert. J Ricketts	a citizen of the	Creek Nation.
Name of Mother:	Ethel J. Ricketts	a citizen of the	noncitizen Nation.

Postoffice   Sapulpa, Ind. Ter.

AFFIDAVIT OF MOTHER.

UNITED STATES OF AMERICA, Indian Territory, }
Western   DISTRICT.

I, Ethel J. Ricketts, on oath state that I am 21 years of age and a citizen by noncitizen, of the Creek Nation; that I am the lawful wife of Robert J. Ricketts, who is a citizen, by blood of the Creek Nation; that a female child was born to me on 2nd day of January, 1904, that said child has been named Goldie A. Ricketts, and is now living.

Ethel J. Ricketts

Witnesses To Mark:
{

Subscribed and sworn to before me this 17th day of April, 1905.

James J. Mars
Notary Public.

Applications for Enrollment of Creek Newborn
Act of 1905   Volume IV

AFFIDAVIT OF ATTENDING PHYSICIAN OR MID-WIFE.

UNITED STATES OF AMERICA, Indian Territory, }
  Western   DISTRICT.

I, Maggie M Miller, a midwife, on oath state that I attended on Mrs. Ethel J Ricketts, wife of Robert J. Ricketts on the 2nd day of January, 1904; that there was born to her on said date a female child; that said child is now living and is said to have been named Goldie A Ricketts

Maggie M. Miller

Witnesses To Mark:
{

Subscribed and sworn to before me this 17th day of April, 1905.

My commission expires May 7, 1908..

(No name given)
Notary Public.

BIRTH AFFIDAVIT.

DEPARTMENT OF THE INTERIOR.
COMMISSION TO THE FIVE CIVILIZED TRIBES.

IN RE APPLICATION FOR ENROLLMENT, as a citizen of the Creek Nation, of Clarence F. Ricketts, born on the 28th day of June, 1902

Name of Father: Robert. J Ricketts   a citizen of the   Creek   Nation.
Name of Mother: Ethel J. Ricketts   a citizen of the   Creek   Nation.

Postoffice   Sapulpa, Ind. Ter.

AFFIDAVIT OF MOTHER.

UNITED STATES OF AMERICA, Indian Territory, }
  Western   DISTRICT.

I, Ethel J. Ricketts, on oath state that I am 21 years of age and a citizen by noncitizen, of the Creek Nation; that I am the lawful wife of Robert J. Ricketts, who is a citizen, by blood of the Creek Nation; that a male child was born to me on 28th day of June, 1902, that said child has been named Clarence F. Ricketts, and is now living.

Ethel J. Ricketts

Witnesses To Mark:
{

Subscribed and sworn to before me this 17th day of April, 1905.

Applications for Enrollment of Creek Newborn
Act of 1905   Volume IV

James J. Mars
Notary Public.

AFFIDAVIT OF ATTENDING PHYSICIAN OR MID-WIFE.

UNITED STATES OF AMERICA, Indian Territory, }
    Western   DISTRICT.

I, Maggie M Miller , a midwife , on oath state that I attended on Mrs. Ethel J Ricketts , wife of Robert J. Ricketts on the 28th day of June , 1902; that there was born to her on said date a male child; that said child is now living and is said to have been named Clarence F. Ricketts

Maggie M. Miller

Witnesses To Mark:

{ Subscribed and sworn to before me this 17th day of April, 1905.

James J. Mars
My commission expires May 7, 1908..   Notary Public.

BIRTH AFFIDAVIT.

DEPARTMENT OF THE INTERIOR.
COMMISSION TO THE FIVE CIVILIZED TRIBES.

IN RE APPLICATION FOR ENROLLMENT, as a citizen of the Creek Nation, of Goldie Ardell Ricketts, born on the 2nd day of Jan, 1904

Name of Father:	Robert. J Ricketts	a citizen of the	Creek Nation.
Name of Mother:	Ethel J. Ricketts	a citizen of the	noncitizen Nation.

Postoffice   Sapulpa, Ind. Ter.

AFFIDAVIT OF MOTHER.

UNITED STATES OF AMERICA, Indian Territory, }
    Western   DISTRICT.

I, Ethel J. Ricketts , on oath state that I am 21 years of age and a citizen by *(blank)* , of the United States Nation; that I am the lawful wife of Robert J. Ricketts , who is a citizen, by blood of the Creek Nation; that a female child was born to me on 2nd day of January, 1904 , that said child has been named Goldie Ardell Ricketts , and was living March 4, 1905.

Ethel J. Ricketts

Applications for Enrollment of Creek Newborn
Act of 1905 Volume IV

Witnesses To Mark:
{

    Subscribed and sworn to before me this 8th day of June, 1905.

                                    James J. Mars
My commission expires May 7, 1908..   Notary Public.

AFFIDAVIT OF ATTENDING PHYSICIAN OR MID-WIFE.

UNITED STATES OF AMERICA, Indian Territory,
    Western   DISTRICT.

    I, Maggie Miller, a midwife, on oath state that I attended on Mrs. Ethel J Ricketts, wife of Robert J. Ricketts on the 2nd day of January, 1904; that there was born to her on said date a female child; that said child was living March 4, 1905, and is said to have been named Goldie Ardell Ricketts

                                    Maggie M. Miller

Witnesses To Mark:
{

    Subscribed and sworn to before me this 8th day of June, 1905.

                                    James J. Mars
My commission expires May 7, 1908.   Notary Public.

Department of the Interior,
COMMISSION TO THE FIVE CIVILIZED TRIBES.

    IN RE APPLICATION FOR ENROLLMENT, as a citizen of the Creek Nation, of Susie, born on the twenty eight day of June, 1903

Name of Father:	Albert Moore	a citizen of the	Creek	Nation.
Name of Mother:	Leah Moore	a citizen of the	Creek	Nation.

                          Post-Office: Stidham I.T.

Applications for Enrollment of Creek Newborn
Act of 1905   Volume IV

AFFIDAVIT OF MOTHER.

UNITED STATES OF AMERICA,
    Indian Territory.
Western   District.

    I, Leah Moore, on oath state that I am twenty years of age and a citizen by Blood, of the Creek Nation; that I am the lawful wife of Albert Moore, who is a citizen, by Blood of the Creek Nation; that a female child was born to me on twenty eight day of June, 1903, that said child has been named Susie, and is now living

                                              her
                                    Leah Moore x
WITNESSES TO MARK: mark
    Preston *(Illegible)*
    (Name Illegible)

Subscribed and sworn to before me this 18 *day of* March, 1905.

                                      Preston *(Illegible)*
                                          NOTARY PUBLIC.

AFFIDAVIT OF ATTENDING PHYSICIAN OR MID-WIFE.

UNITED STATES OF AMERICA,
    Indian Territory.
Western   District.

    I, W.C. Gilliam, a Physician, on oath state that I attended on Mrs. Leah Moore, wife of Albert Moore on the 18 day of June, 1903; that there was born to her on said date a female child; that said child is now living and is said to have been named Susie

                                    W.C. Gilliam
WITNESSES TO MARK:

Subscribed and sworn to before me this 18 *day of* March, 1905.

                                    Preston *(Illegible)*
My comishian[sic]   Notary Public.
expirs[sic] May 18th 1908

Applications for Enrollment of Creek Newborn
Act of 1905   Volume IV

NC-272.

Muskogee, Indian Territory, July 26, 1905.

Leah Moore,
    c/o Albert Moore,
        Stidham, Indian Territory.

Dear Madam:

    In the matter of the application for the enrollment of your daughter Susie Moore as a citizen by blood of the Creek Nation it appears from your affidavit as to the birth of said child that she was born June 28, 1903 and from the affidavit of W. C. Gilliam, the attending physician at her birth, that she was born June 18, 1903.

    For the purpose of correcting this discrepancy there is inclosed[sic] herewith a blank for proof of birth partially filled out which you are requested to have wholly filled out, executed and return to this office with as little delay as possible. Be careful to see that the notary public before whom the affidavits are sworn to attaches his name and seal to each affidavit. In case any signature is by mark it must be attested by two disinterested witnesses.

                     Respectfully,

CTD-5   Commissioner.
Env.

BIRTH AFFIDAVIT.

DEPARTMENT OF THE INTERIOR.
COMMISSION TO THE FIVE CIVILIZED TRIBES.

    IN RE APPLICATION FOR ENROLLMENT, as a citizen of the Creek Nation, of Susie Moore, born on the *(blank)* day of June, 1903

Name of Father: Albert Moore   a citizen of the   Creek   Nation.
   Coweter[sic] Town
Name of Mother: Leah Moore   a citizen of the   Creek   Nation.
   Coweter[sic]
                                   Postoffice   Stidham, Ind. Ter.

Applications for Enrollment of Creek Newborn
Act of 1905   Volume IV

AFFIDAVIT OF MOTHER.

UNITED STATES OF AMERICA, Indian Territory, ⎫
   Western   DISTRICT.   ⎬   (child present)
                                      ⎭

I, Leah Moore , on oath state that I am 20 years of age and a citizen by blood , of the Creek Nation; that I am the lawful wife of Albert Moore , who is a citizen, by blood of the Creek Nation; that a female child was born to me on 18 day of June, 1903 , that said child has been named Susie Moore , and was living March 4, 1905.

                                                her
                                           Leah x Moore
Witnesses To Mark: mark
  { William P Redding
    Lewis Pittman

Subscribed and sworn to before me this 31 day of July , 1905.

                                       Preston *(Illegible)*
                                       Notary Public.

AFFIDAVIT OF ATTENDING PHYSICIAN OR MID-WIFE.

UNITED STATES OF AMERICA, Indian Territory, ⎫
   Western   DISTRICT.   ⎬
                                      ⎭

I, W. C. Gilliam , a physician , on oath state that I attended on Mrs. Leah Moore , wife of Albert Moore on the 18 day of June , 1903 ; that there was born to her on said date a female child; that said child was living March 4, 1905, and is said to have been named Susie Moore

                                         Dr. W. C. Gilliam
Witnesses To Mark:
  {

Subscribed and sworn to before me this 31 day of July, 1905.

My commission   Preston *(Illegible)*
expires May 19th 1908   Notary Public.

Applications for Enrollment of Creek Newborn
Act of 1905   Volume IV

BIRTH AFFIDAVIT.

DEPARTMENT OF THE INTERIOR.
COMMISSION TO THE FIVE CIVILIZED TRIBES.

IN RE APPLICATION FOR ENROLLMENT, as a citizen of the Creek Nation, of Lois Alleen Weaver, born on the 20 day of Sept , 1901

Name of Father: Bert W Weaver   a citizen of the   Creek   Nation.
Name of Mother: Rena Weaver   a citizen of the   Creek   Nation.

Postoffice   Sapulpa, I.T.

AFFIDAVIT OF MOTHER.

UNITED STATES OF AMERICA, Indian Territory,
   Western   DISTRICT.

I, Rena Weaver , on oath state that I am 24 years of age and a citizen by blood , of the Creek Nation; that I am the lawful wife of Bert W Weaver , who is a citizen, by *(blank)* of the Creek Nation; that a Female child was born to me on 20th day of Sept , 1901 , that said child has been named Lois Alleen Weaver , and was living March 4, 1905.

Rena Weaver

Witnesses To Mark:

Subscribed and sworn to before me this 20th day of March , 1905.

My commission expires 10/20-1906   Joseph Brewer
                                                                        Notary Public.

AFFIDAVIT OF ATTENDING PHYSICIAN OR MID-WIFE.

UNITED STATES OF AMERICA, Indian Territory,
   Western   DISTRICT.

I, L J Weaver , a midwife , on oath state that I attended on Mrs. Rena Weaver , wife of Bert W Weaver on the 20th day of Sept , 1901 ; that there was born to her on said date a Female child; that said child was living March 4, 1905, and is said to have been named Lois Alleen Weaver

L J Weaver

Witnesses To Mark:

Subscribed and sworn to before me this 28 day of March, 1905.

Applications for Enrollment of Creek Newborn
Act of 1905 Volume IV

My commission expires 10/20-1906   Joseph Brewer
                                                 Notary Public.

BIRTH AFFIDAVIT.

DEPARTMENT OF THE INTERIOR.
COMMISSION TO THE FIVE CIVILIZED TRIBES.

IN RE APPLICATION FOR ENROLLMENT, as a citizen of the Creek Nation, of Bert Leo Weaver, born on the 12 day of Nov, 1903

Name of Father:	Bert W Weaver	not a citizen of the Creek	Nation.
Name of Mother:	Rena Weaver	a citizen of the Creek	Nation.

Postoffice   Sapulpa, I.T.

AFFIDAVIT OF MOTHER.

UNITED STATES OF AMERICA, Indian Territory,
     Western   DISTRICT.

     I, Rena Weaver, on oath state that I am 24 years of age and a citizen by blood, of the Creek Nation; that I am the lawful wife of Bert W Weaver, who is not a citizen, by ----- of the Creek Nation; that a Female[sic] child was born to me on 12th day of Nov, 1903, that said child has been named Bert Leo Weaver, and was living March 4, 1905.

                                               Rena Weaver

Witnesses To Mark:

     Subscribed and sworn to before me this 20th day of March, 1905.

My commission expires 10/20-1906   Joseph Brewer
                                                 Notary Public.

AFFIDAVIT OF ATTENDING PHYSICIAN OR MID-WIFE.

UNITED STATES OF AMERICA, Indian Territory,
     Western   DISTRICT.

     I, Mrs. L. J. Weaver, a mid-wife, on oath state that I attended on Mrs. Rena Weaver, wife of Bert W Weaver on the 12th day of Nov, 1903 ; that there was born to her on said date a Female[sic] child; that said child was living March 4, 1905, and is said to have been named Bert Leo Weaver

                                               L P Weaver

Applications for Enrollment of Creek Newborn
Act of 1905   Volume IV

Witnesses To Mark:
{

Subscribed and sworn to before me this 20th day of March , 1905.

My commission expires 10/20-1906   Joseph Brewer
                                                                    Notary Public.

Department of the Interior,
COMMISSION TO THE FIVE CIVILIZED TRIBES.

IN RE Application for Enrollment, as a citizen of the Creek Nation, of Samson Grayson , born on the 1th[sic] day of November, 1904

Name of Father:	Robert Grayson	a citizen of the	Creek	Nation.
Name of Father:	Luiza Grayson	a citizen of the	Creek	Nation.

Post Office: Brushhill I T

AFFIDAVIT OF MOTHER.

UNITED STATES OF AMERICA,
  INDIAN TERRITORY,
  Western   District.

I, Luiza Grayson , on oath state that I am 39 years of age and a citizen by Blood, of the Creek Nation; that I am the lawful wife of Robert Grayson , who is a citizen, by Blood of the Creek Nation; that a male child was born to me on first day of November , 1904 , that said child has been named Samson Grayson , and is now living.   her
    { K H Shepherd   Luiza x Grayson
Witness { Warren *(Illegible)*   mark

Subscribed and sworn to before me this 20th day of March, 1904.

                                M. Y. Killingsworth
                                        Notary Public.
            My com expire Apr 10th 1907

Applications for Enrollment of Creek Newborn
Act of 1905 Volume IV

AFFIDAVIT OF ATTENDING PHYSICIAN OR MID-WIFE.

UNITED STATES OF AMERICA,
   INDIAN TERRITORY,
    Western   District.

    I, Sallie Gouge , a mid wife , on oath state that I attended on Mrs. Louiza Grayson , wife of Robert Grayson on the 1th[sic] day of Nov , 1904 ; that there was born to her on said date a male child; that said child is now living and is said to have been named Samson Grayson

                                    her
Witness { K H Shepherd   Sallie x Gouge
         { Warren *(Illegible)*   mark

    Subscribed and sworn to before me this 20th day of March, 1904.

                                    M. Y. Killingsworth
                                           Notary Public.
    My commission expire Apr 10th 1907

NC-276.

                                  Muskogee, Indian Territory, July 26, 1905.

Mary Haynie,
    Coweta, Indian Territory.

Dear Madam:

    In the matter of the application for the enrollment of your son Felix Haynie, born July 8, 1902, you are advised that it will be necessary, before the rights of said child as a citizen by blood of the Creek Nation can be finally determined, for you to file with this office the affidavits of two disinterested witnesses as to the birth of said child. Said witnesses should set forth in their affidavits the name of said child, when he was born, the names of his parents and whether or not he was living March 4, 1905 March 4, 1905.

                                  Respectfully,

                                                  Commissioner.

Applications for Enrollment of Creek Newborn
Act of 1905   Volume IV

United States of America
Western Judicial District   } SS.
Indian Territory

I Mar ch Haynie on oath state that I was at the place of Mrs Mary Bruner alias Mary Haynie wife as above of Felix Haynie now deceased on the 8" day of July 1902; that there was born to her on said date a male child, that said child was living March 4, 1905, and is said to have been name Felix Haynie.

Mar ch Hay-nie

Subscribed and sworn to before me this 10" day of August 1905

My term expires   W.A. Brigham
    Oct. 28" 1906.   Notary Public.

BIRTH AFFIDAVIT.

DEPARTMENT OF THE INTERIOR.
COMMISSION TO THE FIVE CIVILIZED TRIBES.

IN RE APPLICATION FOR ENROLLMENT, as a citizen of the Creek Nation, of Felix Haynie , born on the 8" day of July , 1902

Name of Father: Felix Haynie   a citizen of the   Creek   Nation.
                              alias
Name of Mother: Mary Bruner   Mary Haynie   a citizen of the   Creek   Nation.

                          Postoffice   Coweta, Indian Territory. Ind. Ter.

AFFIDAVIT OF MOTHER.

UNITED STATES OF AMERICA, Indian Territory,
Western Judicial   DISTRICT.

I, Mary Bruner alias Mary Haynie , on oath state that I am 29 years of age and a citizen by blood , of the Creek Nation; that I ~~am~~ was the lawful common law and by Indian custom wife of Felix Haynie now deceased , who ~~is~~ was a citizen, by blood of the Creek Nation; that a male child was born to me on 8" day of July , 1902 , that said child has been named Felix Haynie , and was living March 4, 1905. I had no mid wife or physician at my confinement.

                        Mary Haynie

Applications for Enrollment of Creek Newborn
Act of 1905 Volume IV

Witnesses To Mark:
{

Subscribed and sworn to before me this 10" day of August, 1905.

My term expires   W.A. Brigham
    Oct. 28" 1906.   Notary Public.

AFFIDAVIT OF ATTENDING PHYSICIAN OR MID-WIFE.

UNITED STATES OF AMERICA, Indian Territory, }
  Western Judicial   DISTRICT. }

was at the home of
I, Cornelius Boudinot, a *(blank)*, on oath state that I ~~attended on~~ Mrs. Mary Bruner alias Mary Haynie, wife as above of Felix Haynie now deceased on the 8" day of July, 1902; that there was born to her on said date a male child; that said child was living March 4, 1905, and is said to have been named Felix Haynie

                            Cornelius Boudinot

Witnesses To Mark:
{

Subscribed and sworn to before me this 28 day of March, 1905.

My term expires   W.A. Brigham
    Oct. 28" 1906.   Notary Public.

BIRTH AFFIDAVIT.
DEPARTMENT OF THE INTERIOR.
COMMISSION TO THE FIVE CIVILIZED TRIBES.

IN RE APPLICATION FOR ENROLLMENT, as a citizen of the Creek Nation, of Felix Haynie, born on the 8 day of July, 1902

Name of Father:	Felix Haynie	a citizen of the	Creek	Nation.
Name of Mother:	Mary "	a citizen of the	Creek	Nation.

                        Postoffice   Coweta, Indian Territory. I.T.

Applications for Enrollment of Creek Newborn
Act of 1905 Volume IV

Child Present MAR 28 1905 Gr

AFFIDAVIT OF MOTHER.

UNITED STATES OF AMERICA, Indian Territory,
    (blank)   **DISTRICT.**

    I, Mary Haynie , on oath state that I am 29 years of age and a citizen by blood , of the Creek Nation; that I am the lawful wife of Felix Haynie , who is a citizen, by blood of the Creek Nation; that a male child was born to me on 8" day of July , 1902 , that said child has been named Felix Haynie , and is now living.

                                  Mary Haynie

Witnesses To Mark:

    Subscribed and sworn to before me this 28" day of March , 1905.

                                Edw C Griesel
                                      Notary Public.

No midwife nor physician present and Father dead.

AFFIDAVIT OF ATTENDING PHYSICIAN OR MID-WIFE.

UNITED STATES OF AMERICA, Indian Territory,
    (blank)   **DISTRICT.**

    I, , a , on oath state that I attended on Mrs. , wife of on the day of , 190 ; that there was born to her on said date a male child; that said child is now living and is said to have been named

Witnesses To Mark:

    Subscribed and sworn to before me this 28 day of March, 1905.

                                      Notary Public.

Applications for Enrollment of Creek Newborn
Act of 1905 Volume IV

BIRTH AFFIDAVIT.

DEPARTMENT OF THE INTERIOR.
COMMISSION TO THE FIVE CIVILIZED TRIBES.

IN RE APPLICATION FOR ENROLLMENT, as a citizen of the CREEK Nation, of Edward Ray McDonald, born on the 17 day of Aug., 1904

Name of Father:	Martin J. McDonald	a citizen of the	U. S.	Nation.
Name of Mother:	Mattie B. "	a citizen of the	Creek	Nation.

Postoffice   Coweta

(child present)

AFFIDAVIT OF MOTHER.

UNITED STATES OF AMERICA, Indian Territory, }
WESTERN DISTRICT. }

I, Mattie B. McDonald, on oath state that I am 21 years of age and a citizen by blood, of the Creek Nation; that I am the lawful wife of Martin J. McDonald, who is a citizen, by ----- of the U. S. Nation; that a male child was born to me on 17 day of August, 1904, that said child has been named Edward Ray McDonald, and is now living.

Mattie B. McDonald

Witnesses To Mark:
{

Subscribed and sworn to before me this 21" day of March, 1905.

Edw C Griesel
Notary Public.

BIRTH AFFIDAVIT.

DEPARTMENT OF THE INTERIOR.
COMMISSION TO THE FIVE CIVILIZED TRIBES.

IN RE APPLICATION FOR ENROLLMENT, as a citizen of the Creek Nation, of Edward Ray McDonald, born on the 17th day of August, 1904

Name of Father:	Martin J. McDonald	a citizen of the United States	Nation.
Name of Mother:	Mattie B. McDonald	a citizen of the Creek	Nation.

Postoffice   Coweta Indian Territory

Applications for Enrollment of Creek Newborn
Act of 1905 Volume IV

AFFIDAVIT OF ATTENDING PHYSICIAN OR MID-WIFE.

UNITED STATES OF AMERICA, Indian Territory,
Western DISTRICT.

I, George A. Pursley M.D. , a Physician , on oath state that I attended on Mrs. Mattie B. Dryden McDonald, wife of Martin J. McDonald on the 17th day of August , 1904 ; that there was born to her on said date a male child; that said child was living March 4, 1905, and is said to have been named Edward Ray McDonald

George A. Pursly[sic] M.D.

Witnesses To Mark:

Subscribed and sworn to before me this 2^d day of May, 1905.

My Commission expires
July 2, 1906.

Joshua Ross
Notary Public.

BIRTH AFFIDAVIT.

DEPARTMENT OF THE INTERIOR.
COMMISSION TO THE FIVE CIVILIZED TRIBES.

IN RE APPLICATION FOR ENROLLMENT, as a citizen of the Creek Nation, of Harry Wiseman, born on the 29 day of May , 1903

Name of Father: Charley Wiseman   a citizen of the United States Nation.
Name of Mother: Hepsie Wiseman   a citizen of the   Creek   Nation.
Okfuske[sic] Town
                  Postoffice   Calvin, I.T.

AFFIDAVIT OF MOTHER.

UNITED STATES OF AMERICA, Indian Territory,
Western DISTRICT.

I, Hepsie Wiseman , on oath state that I am 28 years of age and a citizen by blood , of the Creek Nation; that I am the lawful wife of Charley Wiseman , who is a citizen, ~~by~~ *(blank)* of the United States Nation; that a male child was born to me on 29 day of May , 1903 , that said child has been named Harry Wiseman , and was living March 4, 1905.

Hepsie Wiseman

Applications for Enrollment of Creek Newborn
Act of 1905 Volume IV

Witnesses To Mark:
{

Subscribed and sworn to before me this 29 day of March, 1905.

                              Drennan C Skaggs
                              Notary Public.

AFFIDAVIT OF ATTENDING PHYSICIAN OR MID-WIFE.

UNITED STATES OF AMERICA, Indian Territory,
Western DISTRICT.

I, Lizzie Plummer, a mid-wife, on oath state that I attended on Mrs. Hepsie Wiseman, wife of Charlie Wiseman on or about the 29 day of May, 1903 ; that there was born to her on said date a male child; that said child was living March 4, 1905, and is said to have been named Harry Wiseman

                              Lizzie Plummer

Witnesses To Mark:
{

Subscribed and sworn to before me this 29 day of March, 1905.

                              Drennan C Skaggs
                              Notary Public.

BIRTH AFFIDAVIT.

DEPARTMENT OF THE INTERIOR.
COMMISSION TO THE FIVE CIVILIZED TRIBES.

IN RE APPLICATION FOR ENROLLMENT, as a citizen of the CREEK Nation, of Harry Wiseman, born on the 29 day of May, 1903

Name of Father:	Charley Wiseman	a citizen of the	U S	Nation.
Name of Mother:	Hepsey "	a citizen of the	Creek	Nation.

                        Postoffice   Calvin

Applications for Enrollment of Creek Newborn
Act of 1905 Volume IV

(child present)

AFFIDAVIT OF MOTHER.

UNITED STATES OF AMERICA, Indian Territory, }
WESTERN DISTRICT. }

I, Hepsey Wiseman , on oath state that I am 28 years of age and a citizen by blood , of the Creek Nation; that I am the lawful wife of Charley Wiseman , who is a citizen, by *(blank)* of the U. S. Nation; that a male child was born to me on 29" day of May , 1903 , that said child has been named Harry Wiseman , and is now living.

                                        Hepsie Wiseman

Witnesses To Mark:

Subscribed and sworn to before me this 23 day of March , 1905.

                                        Edw C Griesel
                                              Notary Public.

NC-279.

                                    Muskogee, Indian Territory, July 26, 1905.

Ben T. Harmon,
    Coweta, Indian Territory.

Dear Sir:

    In the matter of the application for the enrollment of your daughter Lonie Harmon as a citizen by blood of the Creek Nation, it will be necessary, before the rights of said child as such citizen can be finally determined, for you to file with this office either the original or a certified copy of the marriage license and certificate showing the marriage between you and Mary J. Harmon the noncitizen mother of said child.

                          Respectfully,

                                        Commissioner.

Applications for Enrollment of Creek Newborn
Act of 1905   Volume IV

Department of the Interior,
COMMISSION TO THE FIVE CIVILIZED TRIBES.

In the matter of the death of   Lonie Harman   a citizen of the Creek Nation, who formerly resided at or near   Coweta , Ind. Ter., and died on the   2nd day of July , 1905.

AFFIDAVIT OF RELATIVE.

UNITED STATES OF AMERICA,
 INDIAN TERRITORY,
 Western Judicial   District.

I, Ben T. Harman , on oath state that I am 36 years of age and a citizen by blood , of the Creek   Nation; that my postoffice address is   Coweta   , Ind. Ter.; that I am   Father   of   Lonie Harman   who was a citizen, by blood , of the Creek Nation and that said   Lonie Harman   died on the   2nd day of July   , 1905.

B. T. Harman

Witnesses To Mark:

Subscribed and sworn to before me this 13" day of January , 1906.

My term expires   W.A. Brigham
 Oct. 28" 1906.   *Notary Public.*

AFFIDAVIT OF ACQUAINTANCE.

UNITED STATES OF AMERICA,
 INDIAN TERRITORY,
 (blank)   District.

non
I, A. E. Carder M.D. , on oath state that I am 40 years of age, and a ^ citizen by *(blank)*   of the Creek   Nation; that my postoffice address is   Coweta   , Ind. Ter.; that I was personally acquainted with   Lonie Harman   who was a citizen, by blood, of the Creek   Nation; and that said   Lonie Harman   died on the   2"   day of July   , 1905.   and that I am the physician who attended deceased at her last sickness.

A. E. Carder M.D.

Witnesses To Mark:

Applications for Enrollment of Creek Newborn
Act of 1905   Volume IV

Subscribed and sworn to before me this 15" day of January, 1906.

My term expires
Oct. 28" 1906.

W.A. Brigham
Notary Public.

MARRIAGE LICENSE

United States of America, I
   Indian Territory, (SS.
   Northern District. I

No. 82.

TO ANY PERSON AUTHORIZED BY LAW TO SOLEMNIZE MARRIAGE---GREETING:

   You are hereby commanded to solemnize the Rite and publish the Banns of Matrimony between Mr. B. T. Harman of Choska, in the Indian Territory, aged 28 years, and Miss Mary Wood of Choska, in the Indian Territory, aged 18 years, according to law, and do you officially sign and return this License to the parties therein named.
   Witness my hand and official seal at Wagoner, Indian Territory, this 21st day of Dec., A. D. 1897.

        Seal

James A. Winston
   Clerk of the U.S. Court.

By R. C. Hunter, Deputy.

CERTIFICATE OF MARRIAGE.

United States of America, I
   Indian Territory, (SS.
   Northern District. I

   I, D. R. Rowell, a Minister of the Gospel, do hereby certify, that on the 26 day of December, A.D. 1897, I did duly and according to law as commanded in the foregoing License, solemnize the Rite and publish the Banns of Matrimony between the parties therein named.
   Witness my hand this 26 day of December A. D. 1897.
   My credentials are recorded in the office of the Clerk of the United States Court, Indian Territory, Northern District, Book A, Page 189.

      Signed   D. R. Rowell
                     A Minister of the Gospel.

Applications for Enrollment of Creek Newborn
Act of 1905   Volume IV

CERTIFICATE OF RECORD.

United State of America. I
    Indian Territory,   (SS.
    Northern District. I

I, James A. Winston, Clerk of the United States Court in the Northern District, Indian Territory, do hereby certify that the instrument hereto attached was filed for record in my office the 4 day of Feby 1898, at _____ M., and duly recorded in Book F, Marriage Record, Page 331.

Witness my hand and seal of said Court at Vinita, in said Territory this 7 day of Feby A.D. 1898.

    No seal   Signed by stamp   Jas A. Winston
                                                             Clerk.

Endorsed on back:
    Filed Dec. 28 1897   Jas. A. Winston, Clerk.

I, D. C. Skaggs, on oath state that the above and foregoing is a full and complete copy of the original now on file in the office of the Commissioner to the Five Civilized Tribes at Muskogee, Indian Territory.

                                  D.C. Skaggs

                                              Jan.
Subscribed and sworn to before me this 9 day of ~~August~~, 1906.

                                    H.G. Hains
                                            Notary Public.

BIRTH AFFIDAVIT.
DEPARTMENT OF THE INTERIOR.
COMMISSION TO THE FIVE CIVILIZED TRIBES.

IN RE APPLICATION FOR ENROLLMENT, as a citizen of the Creek Nation, of Lonie Harman, born on the 8" day of November, 1904

Name of Father:	Ben T. Harman	a citizen of the	Creek	Nation.
Name of Mother:	Mary J. Harman	a ^non citizen of the	-----	Nation.

                              Postoffice   Coweta

Applications for Enrollment of Creek Newborn
Act of 1905   Volume IV

AFFIDAVIT OF MOTHER.

UNITED STATES OF AMERICA, Indian Territory,
Western Judicial   DISTRICT.

I, Mary J. Harman , on oath state that I am 24 years of age and a citizen by non citizen , of the Creek   Nation; that I am the lawful wife of Ben T. Harman , who is a citizen, by   blood of the Creek   Nation; that a female   child was born to me on   8" day of November , 1904 , that said child has been named   Lonie Harman , and was living March 4, 1905.

Mary J Harman

Witnesses To Mark:

Subscribed and sworn to before me this 20" day of March , 1905.

My term expires W.A. Brigham
Oct. 28" 1906. Notary Public.

AFFIDAVIT OF ATTENDING PHYSICIAN OR MID-WIFE.

UNITED STATES OF AMERICA, Indian Territory,
Western Judicial   DISTRICT.

I, May Murphy , a Midwife , on oath state that I attended on Mrs. Mary J. Harman , wife of Ben T. Harman on the 8" day of November , 1904 ; that there was born to her on said date a   female   child; that said child was living March 4, 1905, and is said to have been named Lonie Harman

May Murphy

Witnesses To Mark:

Subscribed and sworn to before me this 20" day of March , 1905.

My term expires W.A. Brigham
Oct. 28" 1906. Notary Public.

N. C. 280

DEPARTMENT OF THE INTERIOR,
COMMISSIONER TO THE FIVE CIVILIZED TRIBES.
Muskogee, Indian Territory, July 12, 1905.

In the matter of the application for the enrollment of Lizzie Wash, deceased, as a citizen of the Creek Nation.

Applications for Enrollment of Creek Newborn
Act of 1905 Volume IV

Peter Wash, being duly sworn, testified as follows through Jesse McDermott official interpreter.

Q What is your name? A Peter Wash.
Q Have you any other name? A No, sir
Q What is the name of your father? A Quagus Fixico
Q Is he living? A No, sir
Q What was the name of your mother? A I don't know.
Q To what Creek Indian town do you belong? A Hutchchuppa
Q To what Creek Indian town did your father belong? A Kialigee
Q How old are you? A About thirty two.
Q Wat is your post office? A Oktaha.
Q What is the name of your wife? A Lizzie.
Q Did you ever have a wife named Rhoda? A Yes, but she has been dead a long time
Q Did you have any children by her? A Yes
Q What are their names? A George, Austin and Wesley.
Q Are they all living? A Yes
Q Where do they live? A Two here in the Creek Nation and the other lives in Cherokee
Q Which one in Cherokee? A Wesley
Q What is his post office? A I take his mail out myself. He lives with his aunt.

Witness states: My nick name is Leader and I have been told it was on the roll as such. Witness files certificate No. 1457 of his marriage with Miss Casitka which is made a part of the record in this case

Q Who is this Miss Casitka? mentioned in this case. ? A It is the Indian name for this lady here (pointing to Mrs. Wash_ I didn't know her English name and when I procured my marriage license I gave the clerk her Indian name.
Q Did you have a child by her named Lizzie Wash? A Yes, sir
Q When was that child born? A December 7, 1904.
Q Is that child living? A No
Q When did she die? A On 29th day last April
Q Do you know how long she lived? A About four months.

Witness is identified on Creek Indian card 106 as Peter Washington and his name is contained in a partial list of Creek citizens approved by the Secretary of the Interior March 13, 1902 opposite roll number 390

Q Are you married to this woman now? A Yes.

Lizzie Wash being duly sworn testified as follows through Jesse McDermott official interpreter.

Q What is your name? A Lizzie Wash
Q How old are you? A About thirty
Q What is your post office address? A Oktaha

Applications for Enrollment of Creek Newborn
Act of 1905 Volume IV

Q We have an affidavit executed by you on March 20, 1905 relative to the birth of your child, Lizzie Wash, was that child living at that time you came in here? A Yes.
Q When did your child Lizzie die? A On the 29th of the fourth month.
Q You are a citizen of the Cherokee Nation are you? A Yes
Q What name are you enrolled under in the Cherokee Nation? A Lizzie Hildebrand.
Q Has application ever been made for the enrolment of yes child, Lizzie, in the Cherokee Nation? A No, sir.
Q Where was the child buried? A Near where I live in the Creek Nation
Q How old was this child when you came in here to make application for it[sic] A Nearly four months old
Q You brought it in with you, did you? A Yes,
Q Did you have a midwife when this child was born? A Two ladies by the name of Hepsie and Lindsey were present when the child was born but they did not assist me.
Q Are they related to you? A Not to me but to my husband.

The witness is advised that in the absence of affidavit of midwife, if there was no midwife, that this office requires the affidavits of two disinterested witnesses as to the birth of said child dis-interested witnesses to the birth of this child.

    I, Anna Garrigues, on oath state that the above and foregoing is a true and correct copy of my stenographic notes taken in said case on said date.

Anna Garrigues

Subscribed and sworn to before me this 12th day of July 1905.

J. McDermott
Notary Public.

N.C. 280.   F.H.W.

DEPARTMENT OF THE INTERIOR,
COMMISSIONER TO THE FIVE CIVILIZED TRIBES.

    In the matter of the application for the enrollment of Lizzie Washington, deceased, as a citizen by blood of the Creek Nation.

DECISION.

    The record in this case shows that on March 21, 1905, application was filed, in affidavit form, for the enrollment as a citizen by blood of the Creek Nation, of Lizzie Wash, minor child of Peter and Lizzie Washington.
    It appearing from the records of this office that the father of the applicant is identified under the surname of Washington, reference is herein made to the said applicant as Lizzie Washington. A supplemental affidavit executed July 12, 1905, is attaché to and made a part of the record herein. Further proceedings were had Jul 12, 1905.

Applications for Enrollment of Creek Newborn
Act of 1905 Volume IV

The evidence and the records in possession of this office show that said Lizzie Washington, deceased, was the child of Lizzie Washington, a citizen of the Cherokee Nation, and Peter Washington, whose name appears on a partial schedule of citizens by blood of the Creek Nation approved by the Secretary of the Interior March 13, 1902, opposite roll No. 390.

The records of this office fail to show that any application has been made for the enrollment of the said Lizzie Washington, deceased, in the Cherokee Nation.

The evidence further shows that said Lizzie Washington was born December 4, 1904, and died April 29, 1905.

The act of Congress approved March 3, 1905, (33 Stats., 1048), provides:

"That the Commission to the Five Civilized Tribes is authorized for sixty days after the date of the approval of this act to receive and consider applications for enrollment, of children, born subsequent to May twenty-fifth, nineteen hundred and one, and prior to March fourth, nineteen hundred and five, and living on said latter date, to citizens of the Creek tribe of Indians whose enrollment has been approved by the Secretary of the Interior prior to the approval of this act; and to enroll and make allotments to such children."

It is, therefore, ordered and adjudged that the said Lizzie Washington, deceased, is entitled to be enrolled as a citizen by blood of the Creek Nation in accordance with the provisions of law above quoted, and the application for her enrollment as such is accordingly granted.

Tams Bixby Commissioner.
Muskogee, Indian Territory.

(COPY)

MARRIAGE LICENSE

UNITED STATES OF AMERICA,)		
)		
Indian Territory,)	SS.	No. 1457
)		
Western District.)		

TO ANY PERSON AUTHORIZED BY LAW TO SOLEMNIZE MARRIAGE---GREETING:

YOU ARE HEREBY COMMANDED to solemnize the Rite and Publish the Banns of Matrimony between Mr. Peter Washington of Oktaha, in the Indian Territory, aged 32 years, and Miss Casitka, of Oktaha, in the Indian Territory, aged 30 years, according to law, and do you officially sign and return this License to the parties therein named.

WITNESS my hand and official seal at Muskogee, Indian Territory, this 15 day of April, A. D. 1904.

Applications for Enrollment of Creek Newborn
Act of 1905 Volume IV

(SEAL)   R. P. Harrison
            Clerk of the U.S. Court.
By Chas. F. Runyan Deputy.

CERTIFICATE OF MARRIAGE.

- - - - - - - - -

UNITED STATES OF AMERICA,)
)
   Indian Territory,   ) SS.
)
   Western District.   )
                     Clerk U. S. Court

    I, R. P. Harrison, ~~a Minister of the Gospel~~, DO HEREBY CERTIFY, that on the 15 day of April, A.D. 1904, I did duly and according to law as commanded in the foregoing License, solemnize the Rite and Publish the Banns of Matrimony between the parties therein named.

    WITNESS my hand that 15 day of April, A. D. 1904.

                  R. P. Harrison
                  ~~A Minister of the Gospel~~
                  Clerk U. S. Court
_____ By Chas. F. Runyan, Dep. _____

    Note-- This License and Certificate of Marriage must be returned to the office of the Clerk of the United States Court in the Western District, Indian Territory, from whence it was issued, within sixty days from the date thereof, of the party to whom the license was issued will be liable in the amount of the One Hundred Dollars ($100.00).

CERTIFICATE OF RECORD.

UNITED STATES OF AMERICA,)   (SEAL)
)
   Indian Territory,   ) SS.
)
   Western District.   )

    I, ROBERT P. HARRISON, Clerk of the United States Court in the Western District, Indian Territory, do hereby certify that the instrument hereto attached was filed for record in my office the 15 day of April 1904, at _____M., and duly recorded in Book Q, Marriage Record, Page 173.

    WITNESS my hand and seal of said Court at Muskogee, in said Territory this 15 day of April, A.D. 1904.

Applications for Enrollment of Creek Newborn
Act of 1905 Volume IV

R. P. Harrison
Clerk.

By John Harlan Deputy.

Department of the Interior
Commissioner to the Five Civilized Tribes
F I L E D, 7-12-05

Tams Bixby.

BIRTH AFFIDAVIT.

DEPARTMENT OF THE INTERIOR.
COMMISSION TO THE FIVE CIVILIZED TRIBES.

IN RE APPLICATION FOR ENROLLMENT, as a citizen of the CREEK Nation, of Lizzie Wash, born on the 7 day of Dec., 1904

Name of Father:	Peter Wash	a citizen of the	Creek Nation.
Name of Mother:	Lizzie "	a citizen of the	Cherokee Nation.

Postoffice   Oktahah

(Child present)

AFFIDAVIT OF MOTHER.

UNITED STATES OF AMERICA, Indian Territory, ⎫
    WESTERN   DISTRICT. ⎭

I, Lizzie Wash, on oath state that I am 30 years of age and a citizen by blood, of the Cherokee Nation; that I am the lawful wife of Peter Wash, who is a citizen, by blood of the Creek Nation; that a female child was born to me on 7 day of Dec., 1904, that said child has been named Lizzie Wash, and is now living.

                                  Lizzie   her
                                  ~~Peter~~ x Wash
Witnesses To Mark: mark
    { H.G. Hains
       Jesse McDermott

Subscribed and sworn to before me this 20 day of March, 1905.

                                  J McDermott
                                      Notary Public.

Applications for Enrollment of Creek Newborn
Act of 1905 Volume IV

AFFIDAVIT OF ~~ATTENDING PHYSICIAN OR MID-WIFE~~.
father

UNITED STATES OF AMERICA, Indian Territory, }
  Western   DISTRICT.

husband
I, Peter Wash , a m , ~~on oath state that I attended on Mrs.   , wife~~ of Lizzie Wash on the 7 day of Dec , 1904 ; that there was born to her on said date a   female child; that said child is now living and is said to have been named Lizzie Wash

                          Peter   his
                          ~~Lizzie~~ x Wash

Witnesses To Mark: mark
{ H.G. Hains
  Jesse McDermott

Subscribed and sworn to before me this 20 day of March, 1905.

                          J. McDermott
                          Notary Public.

BIRTH AFFIDAVIT.

DEPARTMENT OF THE INTERIOR.
COMMISSION TO THE FIVE CIVILIZED TRIBES.

IN RE APPLICATION FOR ENROLLMENT, as a citizen of the Creek Nation, of Lizzie Wash, born on the 7 day of Dec. , 1904

Name of Father:	Peter Wash	a citizen of the	Creek	Nation.
Name of Mother:	Lizzie Wash	a citizen of the	Cherokee	Nation.

                      Postoffice   Oktaha

AFFIDAVIT OF ~~MOTHER~~. Father

UNITED STATES OF AMERICA, Indian Territory, }
  Western   DISTRICT.

I, Peter Wash , on oath state that I am 32 years of age and a citizen by blood , of the Creek Nation; that I ~~am~~ was the lawful ~~wife~~ husband of Lizzie Wash , who is a citizen, by blood of the Cherokee Nation; that a female child was born to me on 7 day of December , 1904 , that said child has been named Lizzie Wash , and was living March 4, 1905. & died April 29, 1905.

                          his
                     Peter x Wash

Witnesses To Mark: mark
{ H.G. Hains
  Anna Garrigues

Applications for Enrollment of Creek Newborn
Act of 1905   Volume IV

Subscribed and sworn to before me this 12" day of July, 1905.

                                     Henry G. Hains
                                     Notary Public.

Cr NC-280

Muskogee, Indian Territory, June 13, 1905.

Lizzie Wash,
      Oktaha, Indian Territory.

Dear Madam:

      In the matter of the application for the enrollment of your minor child, Lizzie Wash, as a citizen of the Creek Nation, you are advised that the Commission requires the affidavit of the midwife or physician in attendance at its birth.

      For this purpose, there is herewith enclosed a blank form of birth affidavit, and in executing same care should be exercised to see that all blanks are properly filled, all names written in full and in the event that the person signing the affidavit is unable to write, signature by mark must be attested by two witnesses.

                              Respectfully,

                                                  Chairman.

1 B A

NC. 280.

Muskogee, Indian Territory, July 14, 1905.

Commissioner to the Five Civilized Tribes,
      Cherokee Enrollment Division,
            Muskogee, Indian Territory.

Gentleman:

      March 21, 1905, application was made to the Commission to the Five Civilized Tribes for the enrollment of Lizzie Wash, born December 7, 1904, as a citizen by blood of the Creek Nation. It is stated in said application that the father of said child is Peter Wash, a citizen of the Creek Nation, and that the mother is Lizzie Wash, a citizen of the Cherokee Nation.

Applications for Enrollment of Creek Newborn
Act of 1905   Volume IV

You are requested to inform the Creek Enrollment Division as to whether application was made for the enrollment of said Lizzie Wash, as a citizen of the Cherokee nation, and if so, what disposition has been made of the same.

Respectfully,

Commissioner.

REFER IN REPLY TO THE FOLLOWING:

**DEPARTMENT OF THE INTERIOR,
COMMISSIONER TO THE FIVE CIVILIZED TRIBES.**

Muskogee, Indian Territory, July 18, 1905.

Chief Clerk,
    Creek Enrollment Division,
        Muskogee, Indian Territory.

Dear Sir:

Replying to your letter of July 14, 1905, (NC. 280) asking to be advised whether or not any application has ever been made for the enrollment, as a citizen of the Cherokee Nation, of Lizzie Wash, a child of Peter Wash, a citizen of the Creek Nation, and Lizzie Wash, a citizen of the Cherokee Nation, you are advised that from an examination of the records of the Cherokee Enrollment Division id does not appear that any application has ever been made for the enrollment of said child as a citizen of that nation.

Respectfully,

GHL   Tams Bixby   Commissioner.

N.C.280.

Muskogee, Indian Territory, July 5, 1906,

Lizzie Wash (or Washington),
    Care Peter Washington,
        Oktaha, Indian Territory.

Dear Madam:

In the matter of the application for the enrollment of your minor child, Lizzie Wash, you are advised that this office requires in lieu of the affidavit of the midwife, the affidavit of two disinterested witnesses relative to her birth.

Applications for Enrollment of Creek Newborn
Act of 1905   Volume IV

You are advised that the name of the father of said child appears on the roll of Creek Indians by blood as Peter Washington and it necessarily follows that the name of the child should be Lizzie Washington. To correct this discrepancy in names, you are requested to appear at this office at an early date to give testimony under oath.

Respectfully,

Commissioner.

Nc[sic] 280

Muskogee, Indian Territory, November 12, 1906

Chief Clerk,
    Cherokee Enrollment Division,
        General Office.

Dear Sir:

March 21, 1905 application was made, in affidavit form for the enrollment as a citizen of the Creek nation of Lizzie Wash, born December 7, 1904 to Peter Wash, a citizen by blood of the Creek Nation and Lizzie Wash, enrolled as a citizen of the Cherokee Nation under the name of Lizzie Hilderbrand.

You are requested to advise this Division if application has been made for the enrollment of said child as a citizen of the Cherokee nation under the provision of the Act of Congress approved April 26, 1906, and if so, please state the status of same.

Respectfully,

Commissioner.

NBC 280.

Muskogee, Indian Territory, March 7, 1907.

Peter Washington,
    Oktaha, Indian Territory.

Dear Sir:

You are hereby advised that on March 2, 1907 the Secretary of the Interior approved the enrollment of your deceased minor child Lizzie Washington as a citizen by blood of the Creek Nation, and that the name of said child appears upon the roll of new born citizens by blood of the Creek Nation enrolled Act of Congress approved March 3, 1905, as number 1229.

Applications for Enrollment of Creek Newborn
Act of 1905 Volume IV

This child is now entitled to allotment, and application therefor should be made without delay by the duly appointed administrator at the Creek Land Office, Muskogee, Indian Territory.

Respectfully,

Commissioner.

Cr NC-281

Muskogee, Indian Territory, June 13, 1905.

Lizzie Weaver,
    Stidham, Indian Territory.

Dear Madam:

In the matter of the application for the enrollment of your minor child, May Weaver, as a citizen of the Creek Nation, you are advised that there are on file with the Commission affidavits executed by you in which the date of her birth is given as September 14 and September 15, 1901.

You are requested to advise the Commission as to the correct date of the birth of said child.

Respectfully,

Chairman.

NC.281.

Muskogee, Indian Territory, July 14, 190[sic]

Commissioner to the Five Civilized Tribes,
    Cherokee Enrollment Division,
        Muskogee, Indian Territory.

Gentlemen:

March 21, 1905, application was made to the Commission to the Five Civilized Tribes for the enrollment of May Weaver, born September 14, 1901, Billie Weaver, born July 14, 1902, and Amos Weaver, born October 21, 1904, as citizens by blood of the Creek Nation. It is states in said application that the father of said children is Edward Weaver, a citizen of the Creek nation, and that the mother is Lizzie Weaver, a citizen of the Cherokee Nation.

Applications for Enrollment of Creek Newborn
Act of 1905 Volume IV

You are requested to inform the Creek Enrollment Division as to whether application has been made for the enrollment of said May, Billie and Amos Weaver, as citizens of the Cherokee Nation, and if so, what disposition has been made of the same.

Respectfully,

Commissioner.

REFER IN REPLY TO THE FOLLOWING:

**DEPARTMENT OF THE INTERIOR,
COMMISSIONER TO THE FIVE CIVILIZED TRIBES.**

Muskogee, Indian Territory, July 19, 1905.

Chief Clerk,
    Creek Enrollment Division,
        Muskogee, Indian Territory.

Dear Sir:

Replying to your letter of July 14, 1905, (NC. 281) asking to be advised whether or not any application has ever been made for the enrollment, as citizens of the Cherokee Nation, of May Weaver, Billie Weaver, and Amos Weaver, children of Edward Weaver, a citizen of the Creek Nation, and Lizzie Weaver, a citizen of the Cherokee Nation, you are advised that from an examination of the records of the Cherokee Enrollment Division it does not appear that any application has ever been made for the enrollment of said children as citizens of that nation.

Respectfully,

GHL   Tams Bixby   Commissioner.

NC 281

Muskogee, Indian Territory, November 12, 1906.

Chief Clerk,
    Cherokee Enrollment Division,
        General Office.

Dear Sir:

You are hereby advised that the names of May, Billie and Amos Weaver, children of Edward Weaver, a citizen by blood of the Creek Nation, and Lizzie Weaver, an alleged citizen by blood of the Cherokee Nation, are contained in the schedule of New Born

Applications for Enrollment of Creek Newborn
Act of 1905   Volume IV

citizens by blood of the Creek Nation, approved by the Secretary of the Interior August 22, 1905, opposite Roll Nos. 285, 286 and 287.

Respectfully,

Commissioner.

BIRTH AFFIDAVIT.

DEPARTMENT OF THE INTERIOR.
COMMISSION TO THE FIVE CIVILIZED TRIBES.

IN RE APPLICATION FOR ENROLLMENT, as a citizen of the Creek Nation, of Amos Weaver, born on the 21st day of October, 1904

Name of Father: Edward Weaver   a citizen of the   Creek   Nation.
Name of Mother: Lizzie Weaver   a citizen of the United States Nation.

Postoffice   Steadham[sic], I.T.

AFFIDAVIT OF MOTHER.

UNITED STATES OF AMERICA, Indian Territory,
Western Jud.   DISTRICT.

I, Lizzie Weaver, on oath state that I am 23 years of age and a citizen by *(blank)*, of the United States Nation; that I am the lawful wife of Edward Weaver, who is a citizen, by Blood of the Creek Nation; that a Male child was born to me on 21st day of October, 1904, that said child has been named Amos Weaver, and was living March 4, 1905.

her
Lizzie x Weaver
mark

Witnesses To Mark:
{ *(Name Illegible)*
  ALJ Merriwether

Subscribed and sworn to before me this 29 day of April, 1905.

My term expire Oct. 1908   Geo B Robinson
                                                          Notary Public.

Applications for Enrollment of Creek Newborn
Act of 1905 Volume IV

AFFIDAVIT OF ATTENDING PHYSICIAN OR MID-WIFE.

UNITED STATES OF AMERICA, Indian Territory,
Western Judicial   DISTRICT.

I, Sarah Greenleaf , a Midwife , on oath state that I attended on Mrs. Lizzie Weaver , wife of Edward Weaver on the 21st day of October , 1904; that there was born to her on said date a Male   child; that said child was living March 4, 1905, and is said to have been named Amos Weaver

           her
        Sarah x Greenleaf
          mark

Witnesses To Mark:
 { ALJ Meriwether
  (Name Illegible)

Subscribed and sworn to before me this 29 day of April , 1905.

My term expire Oct. 11, 1908   Geo B Robinson
                 Notary Public.

BIRTH AFFIDAVIT.

DEPARTMENT OF THE INTERIOR.
COMMISSION TO THE FIVE CIVILIZED TRIBES.

IN RE APPLICATION FOR ENROLLMENT, as a citizen of the CREEK Nation, of Amos Weaver, born on the 20 day of Dec. , 1904

Name of Father: Edward Weaver   a citizen of the   Creek   Nation.
Name of Mother: Lizzie   "   a citizen of the Cher (?)   Nation.

            Postoffice   Stidham, I.T.

         AFFIDAVIT OF ~~MOTHER~~. Father

UNITED STATES OF AMERICA, Indian Territory,
  WESTERN   DISTRICT.

I, Edward Weaver , on oath state that I am 25 years of age and a citizen by blood , of the Creek Nation; that I am the lawful ~~wife~~ hus of Lizzie Weaver, who is a citizen, by ----- of the Cherokee (?) Nation; that a male child was born to me on 20 day of Dec. , 1904 , that said child has been named Amos Weaver , and is now living.

                 Edward Weaver

Witnesses To Mark:
 {

Applications for Enrollment of Creek Newborn
Act of 1905 Volume IV

Subscribed and sworn to before me this 21 day of March, 1905.

Edw C Griesel
Notary Public.

BIRTH AFFIDAVIT.

DEPARTMENT OF THE INTERIOR.
COMMISSION TO THE FIVE CIVILIZED TRIBES.

IN RE APPLICATION FOR ENROLLMENT, as a citizen of the CREEK Nation, of May Weaver, born on the 14 day of Sept. , 1901

Name of Father:	Edward Weaver	a citizen of the	Creek	Nation.
Name of Mother:	Lizzie "	a citizen of the	Cher (?)	Nation.

Postoffice   Stidham, I.T.

AFFIDAVIT OF ~~MOTHER~~. Father

UNITED STATES OF AMERICA, Indian Territory, }
    WESTERN   DISTRICT. }

I, Edward Weaver , on oath state that I am 25 years of age and a citizen by blood , of the Creek Nation; that I am the lawful ~~wife~~ husband of Lizzie Weaver, who is a citizen, by ----- of the (?)Cherokee Nation; that a female child was born to me on 14 day of Sept. , 1901 , that said child has been named May Weaver , and is now living.

Edward Weaver

Witnesses To Mark:
{

Subscribed and sworn to before me this 21 day of March, 1905.

Edw C Griesel
Notary Public.

Applications for Enrollment of Creek Newborn
Act of 1905 Volume IV

BIRTH AFFIDAVIT.

DEPARTMENT OF THE INTERIOR.
COMMISSION TO THE FIVE CIVILIZED TRIBES.

IN RE APPLICATION FOR ENROLLMENT, as a citizen of the CREEK Nation, of Billie Weaver, born on the 14 day of July , 1903

Name of Father:	Edward Weaver	a citizen of the	Creek	Nation.
Name of Mother:	Lizzie "	a citizen of the	Cher (?)	Nation.

Postoffice   Stidham, I.T.

AFFIDAVIT OF ~~MOTHER~~. Father

UNITED STATES OF AMERICA, Indian Territory,
WESTERN   DISTRICT.

I, Edward Weaver , on oath state that I am 25 years of age and a citizen by blood , of the Creek Nation; that I am the lawful ~~wife~~ husb of Lizzie Weaver, who is a citizen, by ----- of the Cherokee(?) Nation; that a male child was born to me on 14" day of July , 1903 , that said child has been named Billie Weaver , and is now living.

Edward Weaver

Witnesses To Mark:
{

Subscribed and sworn to before me this 21 day of March, 1905.

Edw C Griesel
Notary Public.

BIRTH AFFIDAVIT.

DEPARTMENT OF THE INTERIOR.
COMMISSION TO THE FIVE CIVILIZED TRIBES.

IN RE APPLICATION FOR ENROLLMENT, as a citizen of the Creek Nation, of Billie Weaver, born on the 14th day of July , 1903

Name of Father:	Edward Weaver	a citizen of the	Creek	Nation.
Name of Mother:	Lizzie Weaver	a citizen of the United States Nation.		

Postoffice   Steadham[sic], I.T.

Applications for Enrollment of Creek Newborn
Act of 1905   Volume IV

AFFIDAVIT OF MOTHER.

UNITED STATES OF AMERICA, Indian Territory, }
Western Jud.   DISTRICT.

I, Lizzie Weaver , on oath state that I am 23 years of age and a citizen by *(blank)* , of the United States Nation; that I am the lawful wife of Edward Weaver , who is a citizen, by Blood of the Creek Nation; that a Male child was born to me on 14th day of July , 1903, that said child has been named Billy Weaver , and was living March 4, 1905.

                                  her
Witnesses To Mark: Lizzie x Weaver
{ ALJ Merriwether   mark
{ *(Name Illegible)*

Subscribed and sworn to before me this 29 day of April , 1905.

My term expire Oct. 11, 1908   Geo B Robinson
                                        Notary Public.

AFFIDAVIT OF ATTENDING PHYSICIAN OR MID-WIFE.

UNITED STATES OF AMERICA, Indian Territory, }
Western Judicial   DISTRICT.

I, Sarah Greenleaf , a Midwife , on oath state that I attended on Mrs. Lizzie Weaver , wife of Edward Weaver on the 14th day of July , 1903; that there was born to her on said date a Male child; that said child was living March 4, 1905, and is said to have been named Billy Weaver

                                  her
                              Sarah x Greenleaf
Witnesses To Mark: mark
{ *(Name Illegible)*
{ ALJ Meriwether

Subscribed and sworn to before me this 29 day of April , 1905.

My term ex Oct. 11, 1908   Geo B Robinson
                                     Notary Public.

Applications for Enrollment of Creek Newborn
Act of 1905   Volume IV

BIRTH AFFIDAVIT.

DEPARTMENT OF THE INTERIOR.
COMMISSION TO THE FIVE CIVILIZED TRIBES.

IN RE APPLICATION FOR ENROLLMENT, as a citizen of the Creek Nation, of May Weaver, born on the 15th day of September, 1901

Name of Father: Edward Weaver   a citizen of the   Creek   Nation.
Name of Mother: Lizzie Weaver   a citizen of the United States Nation.

Postoffice   Steadham[sic], I.T.

AFFIDAVIT OF MOTHER.

UNITED STATES OF AMERICA, Indian Territory,
Western Judicial   DISTRICT.

I, Lizzie Weaver, on oath state that I am 23 years of age and a citizen by *(blank)*, of the United States Nation; that I am the lawful wife of Edward Weaver, who is a citizen, by Blood of the Creek Nation; that a Female child was born to me on 15th day of September, 1901, that said child has been named May Weaver, and was living March 4, 1905.

            her
           Lizzie x Weaver
Witnesses To Mark: mark
 ALJ Merriwether
 (Name Illegible)

Subscribed and sworn to before me this 29 day of April, 1905.

My term expires Oct. 11, 1908   Geo B Robinson
              Notary Public.

AFFIDAVIT OF ATTENDING PHYSICIAN OR MID-WIFE.

UNITED STATES OF AMERICA, Indian Territory,
Western Judicial   DISTRICT.

I, Sarah Greenleaf, a Midwife, on oath state that I attended on Mrs. Lizzie Weaver, wife of Edward Weaver on the 15th day of September, 1901; that there was born to her on said date a Female child; that said child was living March 4, 1905, and is said to have been named May Weaver

              her
            Sarah x Greenleaf
              mark

Applications for Enrollment of Creek Newborn
Act of 1905 Volume IV

Witnesses To Mark:
{ ALJ Meriwether
{ *(Name Illegible)*

Subscribed and sworn to before me this 29 day of April, 1905.

My term ex Oct. 11, 1908   Geo B Robinson
                                                 Notary Public.

BIRTH AFFIDAVIT.

DEPARTMENT OF THE INTERIOR.
COMMISSION TO THE FIVE CIVILIZED TRIBES.

IN RE APPLICATION FOR ENROLLMENT, as a citizen of the CREEK Nation, of Sarah Squire, born on the 29 day of Dec., 1902

Name of Father: John Squire   a citizen of the   Creek   Nation.
Name of Mother: Annie "   a citizen of the   "   Nation.

                   Postoffice   Bixby

(child present)

AFFIDAVIT OF MOTHER.

UNITED STATES OF AMERICA, Indian Territory,
     WESTERN   DISTRICT.

I, ~~Sara~~ Annie Squire, on oath state that I am 28 years of age and a citizen by blood, of the Creek Nation; that I am the lawful wife of John Squire, who is a citizen, by blood of the Creek Nation; that a female child was born to me on 29 day of Dec., 1902, that said child has been named Sarah Squire, and is now living.

                                       Annie Squire

Witnesses To Mark:
{

Subscribed and sworn to before me this 21 day of March, 1905.

                                       Edw C Griesel
                                             Notary Public.

Applications for Enrollment of Creek Newborn
Act of 1905   Volume IV

AFFIDAVIT OF ATTENDING ~~PHYSICIAN~~ OR MID-WIFE.

UNITED STATES OF AMERICA, Indian Territory, ⎫
    Western   DISTRICT.   ⎭

    I, Rozella Buck , a midwife , on oath state that I attended on Mrs. Annie Squire, wife of John Squire on the 29 day of Dec. , 1902 ; that there was born to her on said date a female child; that said child is now living and is said to have been named Sarah Squire

                                                                Her
                                                          Rosella x Buck
Witnesses To Mark: mark
⎧ J. McDermott
⎩ EC Griesel
Subscribed and sworn to before me this 21 day of March, 1905.

                                                          Edw C Griesel
                                                              Notary Public.

BIRTH AFFIDAVIT.
DEPARTMENT OF THE INTERIOR.
COMMISSION TO THE FIVE CIVILIZED TRIBES.

    IN RE APPLICATION FOR ENROLLMENT, as a citizen of the Creek Nation, of Ernest Ralph Rothhammer, born on the 6th day of August , 1901

| Name of Father: | Joseph Rothhammer | a citizen of the | U. S. | Nation. |
| Name of Mother: | Louisa J. Rothhammer | a citizen of the | Creek | Nation. |

                                Postoffice   Stone bluff Ind Ter

(child appears 3-21-05.)
AFFIDAVIT OF MOTHER.

UNITED STATES OF AMERICA, Indian Territory, ⎫
    Western   DISTRICT.   ⎭

    I, Louisa J. Rothhammer , on oath state that I am 41 years of age and a citizen by Blood , of the Creek Nation; that I am the lawful wife of Joseph Rothhammer , who is a citizen, by US[sic] of the *(blank)* Nation; that a male child was born to me on 6th day of August , 1901 , that said child has been named Ernest Ralph Rothhammer, and is now living.

                                             Louisa J Rothhammer
Witnesses To Mark:
⎧
⎩

Applications for Enrollment of Creek Newborn
Act of 1905 Volume IV

Subscribed and sworn to before me this 20th day of March, 1905.

Ralph Deerback
Notary Public.

AFFIDAVIT OF ATTENDING PHYSICIAN OR MID-WIFE.

UNITED STATES OF AMERICA, Indian Territory, }
   Western   DISTRICT.

I, Lucinda A Smith, a midwife, on oath state that I attended on Mrs. Louisa J. Rothhammer, wife of Joseph Rothhammer on the 6th day of August, 1901; that there was born to her on said date a   male   child; that said child is now living and is said to have been named Ernest Ralph Rothhammer

Lucinda S Smith

Witnesses To Mark:
{

Subscribed and sworn to before me this 20th day of March, 1905.

Ralph Dreback
Notary Public.

DEPARTMENT OF THE INTERIOR,
COMMISSIONER TO THE FIVE CIVILIZED TRIBES.

REFER IN REPLY TO THE FOLLOWING:

NC-284

Muskogee, Indian Territory, **August 4, 1905.**

B. R. DuBois,
   Muskogee, Indian Territory.

Dear Sir:

    You are hereby advised that on **July 28, 1905**, the Secretary of the Interior approved the enrollment of your minor child, **Elizabeth Gladys Dubois**, as a citizen by blood of the **Creek** Nation, and that the name of said child appears upon the roll of new born citizens of the **Creek** Nation as Number **170**.

    The child is now entitled to an allotment, and application therefor should be made without delay at the Land Office for the Nation in which the prospective allotment is located.

Applications for Enrollment of Creek Newborn
Act of 1905   Volume IV

An entire allotment for said child must be selected at the time of the original application.

Respectively,

Commissioner.

BIRTH AFFIDAVIT.

DEPARTMENT OF THE INTERIOR.
COMMISSION TO THE FIVE CIVILIZED TRIBES.

IN RE APPLICATION FOR ENROLLMENT, as a citizen of the Creek Nation, of Elizabeth Gladys Du Bois, born on the 10th day of October, 1902

Name of Father:	B. R. Du Bois	a citizen of the	Creek	Nation.
Name of Mother:	Elizabeth C. Du Bois	a citizen of the	U. S.	Nation.

Postoffice   Muskogee I. T.

AFFIDAVIT OF MOTHER.

State of Alabama
~~UNITED STATES OF AMERICA, Indian Territory,~~
Tallapoosa County   DISTRICT.

I, Elizabeth C. Du Bois , on oath state that I am 38 years of age and a citizen by birth, of the United States ~~Nation~~; that I am the lawful wife of B. R. Du Bois , who is a citizen, by blood of the Creek Nation; that a female child was born to me on 10th day of October, 1902, that said child has been named Elizabeth Gladys Du Bois , and was living March 4, 1905. That my residence is Muskogee, Indian Territory Indian Territory.

Elizabeth C. Du Bois

Witnesses To Mark:
  G. W. Davis
  W. L. Ga?ntt

Subscribed and sworn to before me this 20 day of March, 1905.

J.H. Ashunt
Notary Public. 9-4-08
J.P.

Applications for Enrollment of Creek Newborn
Act of 1905 Volume IV

AFFIDAVIT OF ATTENDING PHYSICIAN OR MID-WIFE.

UNITED STATES OF AMERICA, Indian Territory, }
Western DISTRICT.

I, J.O. Callahan , a physician , on oath state that I attended on Mrs. Elizabeth C Du Bois , wife of B. R. Du Bois on the 10th day of October , 1902 ; that there was born to her on said date a female child; that said child was living March 4, 1905, and is said to have been named Elizabeth Gladys Du Bois

J.O. Callahan

Witnesses To Mark:
{

Subscribed and sworn to before me this 23rd day of March, 1905.

My Commission Expires Jul. 8, 1906   W.H. Wainwright
                                        Notary Public.

BIRTH AFFIDAVIT.

DEPARTMENT OF THE INTERIOR.
COMMISSION TO THE FIVE CIVILIZED TRIBES.

IN RE APPLICATION FOR ENROLLMENT, as a citizen of the Creek Nation, of Elizabeth Gladys Du Bois, born on the 10th day of October , 1902

Name of Father: B. R. Du Bois   a citizen of the   Creek   Nation.
Name of Mother: Elizabeth C. Du Bois   a citizen of the   U. S.   Nation.

Postoffice   Muskogee I. T.

Father

AFFIDAVIT OF MOTHER.

State of Alabama
UNITED STATES OF AMERICA, Indian Territory, }
Tallapoosa County DISTRICT.

I, B. R. Du Bois , on oath state that I am 35 years of age and a citizen by blood , of the Creek Nation; that I am the lawful wife husband of Elizabeth C. Du Bois , who is a citizen, by ----- of the U. S. Nation; that a female child was born to me her on 10th day of October , 1902 , that said child has been named Elizabeth Gladys Du Bois , and was living March 4, 1905.

B. R. Du Bois

Witnesses To Mark:
{

Applications for Enrollment of Creek Newborn
Act of 1905 Volume IV

Subscribed and sworn to before me this 20 day of May, 1905.

J.H. Ashunt NP & *(Illegible)*
Notary Public. & J.P.

BIRTH AFFIDAVIT.

DEPARTMENT OF THE INTERIOR.
COMMISSION TO THE FIVE CIVILIZED TRIBES.

(Child present)

IN RE APPLICATION FOR ENROLLMENT, as a citizen of the CREEK Nation, of Lucinda Noon, born on the 15 day of June, 1904

Name of Father:	Wiley Noon	a citizen of the	Creek	Nation.
Name of Mother:	Louisa "	a citizen of the	Creek	Nation.

Postoffice   Butler I.T.

AFFIDAVIT OF MOTHER.

UNITED STATES OF AMERICA, Indian Territory,
WESTERN   DISTRICT.

I, Louisa Noon, on oath state that I am 25 years of age and a citizen by blood, of the Creek Nation; that I am the lawful wife of Wiley Noon, who is a citizen, by blood of the Creek Nation; that a female child was born to me on 15" day of June, 1904, that said child has been named Lucinda Noon, and is now living.

Her
Louisa x Noon
mark

Witnesses To Mark:
{ J McDermott
{ EC Griesel

Subscribed and sworn to before me this 23" day of Mar, 1905.

Edw C Griesel
Notary Public.

Applications for Enrollment of Creek Newborn
Act of 1905 Volume IV

Father   No Mid wife
AFFIDAVIT OF <s>ATTENDING PHYSICIAN OR MID WIFE</s>.

UNITED STATES OF AMERICA, Indian Territory, ⎫
    WESTERN   DISTRICT. ⎭

I, Wiley Noon , <s>a</s> *(blank)* , on oath state that I attended on <s>Mrs</s>. my , wife <s>of</s> on the 15 day of June , 1904 ; that there was born to her on said date a female child; that said child is now living and is <s>said to have been</s> named Lucinda Noon

His
Wiley x Noon
mark

Witnesses To Mark:
  { J. McDermott
    EC Griesel

Subscribed and sworn to before me this 23" day of Mar, 1905.

Edw C Griesel
Notary Public.

United States of America)
Indian Territory   )ss.
Western Judicial District)

     Mickey being duly sworn on oath deposes and says that she is a resident and citizen of the Creek Nation, Indian Territory, by birth, that i[sic] know Louisa Noon wife of Wiley Noon. And know that a female child was born to Louisa Noon on the 15th day of June, 1904 and that said daughter is now liveing[sic].

I further state that i[sic] have no interst[sic] in this claim and make this statement as a disinterested party. Said child being named Lucinda Noon.

her
Mickey x
mark

Witness To mark
and Signature.

Bennie McCozo
Chas Rider

Subscribed and sworn to before me this 23rd day of August, 1905.

Chas Rider
Notary Public.

My Commission Expires July 11th, 1906.

Applications for Enrollment of Creek Newborn
Act of 1905 Volume IV

United States of America)
Indian Territory   )ss.
Western Judicial District)

     Palmer Mickey being duly sworn on oath deposes and says that he is a resident and citizen of the Creek Nation, Indian Territory, by birth, that i[sic] know Louisa Noon wife of Wiley Noon. And know that a female child was born to Louisa Noon on the 15th day of June, 1904 and that said daughter is now liveing[sic].

I further state that i[sic] have no interst[sic] in this claim and make this statement as a disinterested party. Said child being named Lucinda Noon.

                                                           his
                                       Palmer Mickey x
                                                     mark

Witness To mark
and Signature.

Bennie McCozo
Chas Rider

Subscribed and sworn to before me this 23rd day of August, 1905.

                                                  Chas Rider
                                                           Notary Public.
My Commission Expires July 11th, 1906.

REFER IN REPLY TO THE FOLLOWING:	
NC-285.	**DEPARTMENT OF THE INTERIOR,** **COMMISSIONER TO THE FIVE CIVILIZED TRIBES.**

                                        Muskogee, Indian Territory, July 26, 1905.

Wiley Noon,
        Butler, Indian Territory.

Dear Sir:

     On March 23, 1905 you and your wife Louisa Noon appeared before the Commission to the Five Civilized Tribes and made application for the enrollment of your daughter Lucinda Noon, born June 15, 1904, as a citizen by blood of the Creek Nation, and at that time submitted your affidavits as to the birth of said child, stating also that there was no midwife in attendance at her birth.

Applications for Enrollment of Creek Newborn
Act of 1905 Volume IV

You are advised that in lieu of the affidavit of the attending physician or midwife at the birth of said child it will be necessary for you to furnish this office with the affidavits of two disinterested parties who are acquainted with said child, know the date of her birth, the names of her parents and whether or not she was living on March 4, 1905.

Please give this matter your immediate attention.

Respectfully,

Tams Bixby

Commissioner.

NC.285

Muskogee, Indian Territory, August 2, 1905.

Wiley Noon,
Butner[sic], Indian Territory.

(The above letter typed again.)

Muskogee, Indian Territory, October 26, 1905.

Wiley Noon,
Butner[sic], Indian Territory.

Dear Sir:

Receipt is acknowledged of your letter of October 22, 1905, in which you ask when you can file for your minor child, Lucinda Noon.

In reply you are advised that the matter of the application for the enrollment of said child is pending and when final action is had in same, you will be duly notified.

Respectfully,

Commissioner.

Applications for Enrollment of Creek Newborn
Act of 1905   Volume IV

BA- 925- B.

DEPARTMENT OF THE INTERIOR,
COMMISSION TO THE FIVE CIVILIZED TRIBES.
MUSKOGEE, INDIAN TERRITORY, March 23, 1905.

-ooOoo-

In the matter of the application for the enrollment of your Lillian Scott, as a citizen of the Creek Nation.

James SCOTT, being duly sworn, testified as follows:

EXAMINATION BY COMMISSION:
Q What is your name? A James Scott.
Q How old are you? A About twenty, I believe it is.
Q What is your postoffice address? A Yeager.
Q You have a child born since the 25th of May, 1901, have you not? A Yes, sir.
Q What is its name? A Lillian Scott.
Q When was Lillian born? A October 14, 1904.
Q What is the name of its mother? A Lucy Scott.
Q Is she a citizen of the Creek Nation? A No.
Q Is she a citizen of any Nation in Indian Territory? A Seminole.
Q Was there a mid-wife present at the birth of Lillian? A No.
Q Was there a doctor present at her birth? A No.
Q There was neither a doctor or mid-wife present at her birth? A No.
Q In the event that it should be found that your child, Lillian Scott has rights in both the Seminole and Creek Nation, in which Nation do you elect to have her enrolled and receive her allotment of land? A In the Creek Nation.

Zera Ellen Parrish, being sworn on her oath states that as a stenographer to the Commission to the Five Civilized Tribes she reported the above case and that this is a full, true and correct transcript of her stenographic notes in same.

Zera Ellen Parrish

Subscribed and sworn to
before me this 25th day of
March, 1905.   Edw C Griesel
                                           Notary Public.

Applications for Enrollment of Creek Newborn
Act of 1905 Volume IV

C 286

DEPARTMENT OF THE INTERIOR,
COMMISSION TO THE FIVE CIVILIZED TRIBES.
Holdenville, I. T., March 27, 1905.

In the matter of the application for the enrollment of Lillian Scott as a citizen of the Creek Nation.

LUCY SCOTT, being duly sworn, testified as follows:

Through Alex Posey Official Interpreter:

BY COMMISSION:
Q What is your name? A Lucy Scott.
Q How old are you? A Nineteen.
Q What is your post office address? A Yeager.
Q Are you a citizen of the Creek Nation? A I am a Seminole.
Q Do you make application for the enrollment of your child, Lillian Scott, as a citizen of the Creek Nation? A Yes, sir.
Q Who is the father of this child? A James Scott.
Q Is he a citizen of the Creek Nation? A Yes, sir.
Q If it should be found that your child, Lillian Scott, is entitled to be enrolled in either the Creek or Seminole Nations in which nation do you elect to have her enrolled? A In the Creek Nation.

---oooOOOooo---

I, D. C. Skaggs, on oath state that the above and foregoing is a full and true transcript of my stenographic notes as taken in said cause on said date.

D.C. Skaggs

Subscribed and sworn to before me this 17" day of July, 1905.

J. McDermott
Notary Public.

N.C. 286.

DEPARTMENT OF THE INTERIOR,
COMMISSIONER TO THE FIVE CIVILIZED TRIBES.
Muskogee, Indian Territory, August 8, 1905.

In the matter of the application for the enrollment of Lillian Scott as a citizen by blood of the Creek Nation.

James Scott, being duly sworn, testified as follows:

Applications for Enrollment of Creek Newborn
Act of 1905   Volume IV

By Commissioner.

Q What is your name? A James Scott.
Q What is your age? A About twentyone
Q What is your post office address? A Yeager.
Q Are you a citizen of the Creek Nation? A Yes, sir
Q We have on file here affidavits about your child Lillian in your wifes[sic] affidavit it states that the child was born October 12th, in your affidavit and testimony you say October 14th which is correct? A October 14th.
Q How do you know? A Because I had it on record and looked at the book before I made the affidavit. She didn't look at the book

Witness is advised that in lieu of the affidavit of midwife there being none present, this office requires the affidavits of two disinterested witnesses.

Q Was Lucy Scott a citizen of any nation? A Seminole.
Q Got her land from them? A Yes, sir
Q Is this child living? A Yes, sir.

  Anna Garrigues on oath states that the above and foregoing is a true and correct transcript of her stenographic notes taken in said cause on said date.

                Anna Garrigues

Subscribed and sworn to before me
this 9th day of August 1905.   Henry G. Hains
                  Notary Public.

United States of America
Western Jud Dist. Ind Ter

  Personally appeared before me the undersigned Notary Public, Peter Harjo and Susie Harjo and first being by me duly sworn, each for themselves say, that ~~they~~ we are well acquainted with Lillian Scott, daughter of James Scott and Lucy Scott, that she was born October 14, 1904, and that she was living March 4, 1905 and is still living

	his
Witnesses to mark	Peter Harjo x
	mark
W R Clawson	her
	Susie Harjo x
L L. Clawson	mark

  Subscribed and sworn to before me this 5th day of August 1905.

My Commission Expires June 18th, 1908   W.R. Clawson
                  Notary Public.

Applications for Enrollment of Creek Newborn
Act of 1905 Volume IV

United States of America } SS
Western Jud Dist. Ind. Ter. }

     Personally appeared before me, the undersigned Notary Public, James and Lucy Scott, the parents of Lillian Scott, and upon oath state each for themselves, That we are the parents of Lillian Scott and that she was born Oct. 14, 1904, and was alive March 4, 1905.

	James Scott
Witnesses to mark	her
W R Clawson	Lucy x Scott
L L. Clawson	mark

     Subscribed and sworn to before me this August 5, 1905.

My Commission Expires June 18th, 1908   W.R. Clawson
                                 Notary Public.

BIRTH AFFIDAVIT.

Supplemental to testimony taken
DEPARTMENT OF THE INTERIOR.
COMMISSION TO THE FIVE CIVILIZED TRIBES.

IN RE APPLICATION FOR ENROLLMENT, as a citizen of the Creek Nation, of Lillian Scott, born on the 12 day of October, 1904

| Name of Father: | James Scott | a citizen of the | Creek | Nation. |
| Name of Mother: | Lucy Scott | a citizen of the | Seminole | Nation. |

               Postoffice   Yeager, Ind. Ter.

AFFIDAVIT OF MOTHER.

UNITED STATES OF AMERICA, Indian Territory, }   Child is present
    Western   DISTRICT. }

     I, Lucy Scott, on oath state that I am 19 years of age and a citizen by blood, of the Seminole Nation; that I am the lawful wife of James Scott, who is a citizen, by blood of the Creek Nation; that a female child was born to me on 12 day of October, 1904, that said child has been named Lillian Scott, and was living March 4, 1905. That no one attended on me as midwife or physician in attendance at the birth of said child physician at the birth of the child.   her
                                                Lucy x Scott
                                                 mark

Applications for Enrollment of Creek Newborn
Act of 1905   Volume IV

Witnesses To Mark:
{ D.C. Skaggs
  Alex Posey

Subscribed and sworn to before me this 27 day of March , 1905.

           Drennan C Skaggs
           Notary Public.

         Father
AFFIDAVIT OF ~~ATTENDING PHYSICIAN OR MID-WIFE~~.

UNITED STATES OF AMERICA, Indian Territory, }
 Western   DISTRICT.

                    my wife
  I, James Scott , ~~a~~ *(blank)* , on oath state that I attended on ^ Mrs. Lucy Scott , ~~wife of~~ *(blank)* on the 12 day of October , 1904 ; that there was born to her on said date a *(blank)* child; that said child was living March 4, 1905, and is said to have been named Lillian Scott

                 James Scott

Witnesses To Mark:
{

Subscribed and sworn to before me this 27 day of March , 1905.

           Drennan C Skaggs
           Notary Public.

BIRTH AFFIDAVIT.

DEPARTMENT OF THE INTERIOR.
COMMISSION TO THE FIVE CIVILIZED TRIBES.

  IN RE APPLICATION FOR ENROLLMENT, as a citizen of the CREEK Nation, of Lillian Scott, born on the 14" day of Oct. , 1904

Name of Father:	James Scott	a citizen of the Creek Nation.
Name of Mother:	Lucy "	a citizen of the Seminole Nation.

         Postoffice   Yeager, I.T.

AFFIDAVIT OF ~~MOTHER~~. Father

UNITED STATES OF AMERICA, Indian Territory, }
 WESTERN   DISTRICT.

  I, James Scott , on oath state that I am 21 years of age and a citizen by blood , of the Creek Nation; that I am the lawful ~~wife~~ hus of Lucy Scott , who is a citizen, by

Applications for Enrollment of Creek Newborn
Act of 1905   Volume IV

blood of the Seminole Nation; that a female child was born to me on 14" day of Oct. , 1904 , that said child has been named Lillian Scott , and is now living.

James Scott

Witnesses To Mark:
{

Subscribed and sworn to before me this 23" day of March, 1905.

Edw C Griesel
Notary Public.

REFER IN REPLY TO THE FOLLOWING:
_____

**DEPARTMENT OF THE INTERIOR,
COMMISSIONER TO THE FIVE CIVILIZED TRIBES.**

Muskogee, Indian Territory, July 26, 1905.

Chief Clerk,
    Creek Enrollment Division.

Dear Sir:

    In reply to your verbal inquiry of this date as to whether application was ever made to the Commission to the Five Civilized Tribes for the enrollment of Lillian Scott (NC-286), born October 12, 1904, daughter of James Scott, a Creek citizen, and Lucy Scott, a seminole[sic] citizen, as a citizen of the Seminole Nation, you are advised that it does not appear from an examination of the records of this office that any application has been made for the enrollment of said Lillian Scott as a citizen of the Seminole Nation.

Respectfully,

Tams Bixby   Commissioner.

NC-286.

Muskogee, Indian Territory, July 27, 1905.

James Scott,
    Yeager, Indian Territory.

Dear Sir:

    There are on file with the records of this office an application for the enrollment of, and the affidavits of yourself and wife as to the birth of your daughter Lillian Scott, from one of which affidavits it appears that said child was born August 12, 1904, and

Applications for Enrollment of Creek Newborn
Act of 1905 Volume IV

from another that she was born October 14, 1904. It also appears that there was no physician or midwife in attendance on the mother of said child when she was born.

You are advised that it will be necessary for you to furnish, in lieu of the affidavit of an attending physician or midwife, the affidavits of two disinterested persons who are acquainted with said child, know when she was born, the names of her parents and whether or not she was living March 4, 1905.

You are also requested to furnish this office with the affidavits of yourself and wife stating which of the above dates, if either of them, is the correct date of the birth of said child.

Please give this matter your immediate attention.

    Respectfully,

        Commissioner.

N.C. 286

    Muskogee, Indian Territory, November 12, 1906.

Chief Clerk,
  Seminole Enrollment Division,
    General Office.
Dear Sir:

You are hereby advised that the name of Lillian Scott, born October 14, 1904, to James Scott, a citizen by blood of the Creek Nation, and Lucy Scott, an alleged citizen by blood of the Seminole Nation, is contained in the schedule of New Born citizens by blood of the Creek Nation, approved by the Secretary of the Interior September 27, 1905, opposite Roll No. 360.

    Respectfully,

        Commissioner.

Applications for Enrollment of Creek Newborn
Act of 1905 Volume IV

DEPARTMENT OF THE INTERIOR,
COMMISSIONER TO THE FIVE CIVILIZED TRIBES.

REFER IN REPLY TO THE FOLLOWING:
NC-287

Muskogee, Indian Territory, **August 4, 1905.**

Henry McCoy
    Bixby, Indian Territory.

Dear Sir:

You are hereby advised that on **July 28, 1905**, the Secretary of the Interior approved the enrollment of your minor child, **Ollie McCoy,**, as a citizen by blood of the **Creek** Nation, and that the name of said child appears upon the roll of new born citizens of the **Creek** Nation as Number **171**.

The child is now entitled to an allotment, and application therefor should be made without delay at the Land Office for the Nation in which the prospective allotment is located.

An entire allotment for said child must be selected at the time of the original application.

Respectively,

Commissioner.

BIRTH AFFIDAVIT.

DEPARTMENT OF THE INTERIOR.
COMMISSION TO THE FIVE CIVILIZED TRIBES.

IN RE APPLICATION FOR ENROLLMENT, as a citizen of the Creek Nation, of Ollie McCoy, born on the 15th day of Feby, 1903

Name of Father: Henry McCoy   a citizen of the   Creek   Nation.
Name of Mother: Sallie Clinton McCoy   a citizen of the   Creek   Nation.

Postoffice   Bixby, I.T.

Applications for Enrollment of Creek Newborn
Act of 1905   Volume IV

AFFIDAVIT OF MOTHER.

UNITED STATES OF AMERICA, Indian Territory, }
Western   DISTRICT.

I, Sallie Clinton McCoy, on oath state that I am about 32 years of age and a citizen by blood, of the Creek Nation; that I am the lawful wife of Henry McCoy, who is a citizen, by blood of the Creek Nation; that a female child was born to me on 15th day of Feby, 1903, that said child has been named Ollie McCoy, and is now living.

                                                                             her
Sallie Clinton x McCoy
Witnesses To Mark: mark
{ Henry McCoy Bixby, I.T.
{ Cilla Brown   "   " "

Subscribed and sworn to before me 22 day of March, 1905.

                                                     J. T. *(Illegible)*
                                                     Notary Public.
                                        My Commission Expires July 2nd, 1906.

AFFIDAVIT OF ATTENDING PHYSICIAN OR MID-WIFE.

UNITED STATES OF AMERICA, Indian Territory, }
Western   DISTRICT.

I, Cilla Brown, a midwife, on oath state that I attended on Mrs. Sallie Clinton McCoy, wife of Henry McCoy on the 15th day of Feby, 1903; that there was born to her on said date a female child; that said child is now living and is said to have been named Ollie McCoy

                                                     Cilla Brown
Witnesses To Mark:
{

Subscribed and sworn to before me 22nd day of March, 1905.

                                                   J. T. *(Illegible)*
                                                   Notary Public.
                                        My Commission Expires July 2nd, 1906.

Applications for Enrollment of Creek Newborn
Act of 1905 Volume IV

DEPARTMENT OF THE INTERIOR,
COMMISSIONER TO THE FIVE CIVILIZED TRIBES.

REFER IN REPLY TO THE FOLLOWING:
NC-288

Muskogee, Indian Territory, **August 4, 1905.**

Mary Burton,
    Care of Jesse Burton,
        Muskogee, Indian Territory.

Dear Madam:

You are hereby advised that on **July 28, 1905**, the Secretary of the Interior approved the enrollment of your minor child, **Charles Checotah Burton**, as a citizen by blood of the **Creek** Nation, and that the name of said child appears upon the roll of new born citizens of the **Creek** Nation as Number **172**.

The child is now entitled to an allotment, and application therefor should be made without delay at the Land Office for the Nation in which the prospective allotment is located.

An entire allotment for said child must be selected at the time of the original application.

Respectively,

Commissioner.

DEPARTMENT OF THE INTERIOR,
COMMISSIONER TO THE FIVE CIVILIZED TRIBES.

REFER IN REPLY TO THE FOLLOWING:
NC-288

Muskogee, Indian Territory, **August 4, 1905.**

Mary Burton,
    Care of Jesse Burton,
        Muskogee, Indian Territory.

Dear Madam:

You are hereby advised that on **July 28, 1905**, the Secretary of the Interior approved the enrollment of your minor child, **Rufus Cheestell Burton**, as a citizen by blood of the **Creek** Nation, and that the name of said child appears upon the roll of new born citizens of the **Creek** Nation as Number **173**.

Applications for Enrollment of Creek Newborn
Act of 1905   Volume IV

The child is now entitled to an allotment, and application therefor should be made without delay at the Land Office for the Nation in which the prospective allotment is located.

An entire allotment for said child must be selected at the time of the original application.

Respectively,

Commissioner.

BIRTH AFFIDAVIT.

DEPARTMENT OF THE INTERIOR.
COMMISSION TO THE FIVE CIVILIZED TRIBES.

IN RE APPLICATION FOR ENROLLMENT, as a citizen of the Creek Nation, of Charles Checotah Burton, born on the 8 day of Dec., 1903

Name of Father:	Jesse Burton	a citizen of the	U.S.	Nation.
Name of Mother:	Mary "	a citizen of the	Creek	Nation.

Postoffice   Muskogee

Child Present Gr.

AFFIDAVIT OF MOTHER.

UNITED STATES OF AMERICA, Indian Territory, }
    WESTERN   DISTRICT.

I, Mary Burton, on oath state that I am 21 years of age and a citizen by blood, of the Creek Nation; that I am the lawful wife of Jesse Burton, who is a citizen, by ---- of the U S Nation; that a male child was born to me on 8 day of Dec, 1903, that said child has been named Charles Checotah Burton, and is now living.

Mary Burton

Witnesses To Mark:
{

Subscribed and sworn to before me this 23 day of Mar, 1905.

Edw C Griesel
Notary Public.

Applications for Enrollment of Creek Newborn
Act of 1905 Volume IV

AFFIDAVIT OF ATTENDING PHYSICIAN OR MID-WIFE.

UNITED STATES OF AMERICA, Indian Territory, }
WESTERN DISTRICT.

I, Mary Tiger , a Asst Mid Wife , on oath state that I attended on Mrs. Mary Burton , wife of Jesse Burton on the 8 day of Dec. , 1903 ; that there was born to her on said date a male child; that said child is now living and is said to have been named Charles Checotah Burton

                                                  Her
                                       Mary x Tiger

Witnesses To Mark: mark
{ Orwin Donovan
{ EC Griesel

Subscribed and sworn to before me this 23 day of Mar, 1905.

                                           Edw C Griesel
                                                 Notary Public.

BIRTH AFFIDAVIT.

DEPARTMENT OF THE INTERIOR.
COMMISSION TO THE FIVE CIVILIZED TRIBES.

IN RE APPLICATION FOR ENROLLMENT, as a citizen of the Creek Nation, of Rufus Cheestell Burton, born on the 11day of May , 1902

| Name of Father: | Jesse Burton | a citizen of the | U.S. | Nation. |
| Name of Mother: | Mary " | a citizen of the | Creek | Nation. |

                                  Postoffice   Muskogee

Child Present Gr.

AFFIDAVIT OF MOTHER.

UNITED STATES OF AMERICA, Indian Territory, }
WESTERN DISTRICT.

I, Mary Burton , on oath state that I am 21 years of age and a citizen by blood , of the Creek Nation; that I am the lawful wife of Jesse Burton , who is a citizen, by ----- of the U S Nation; that a male child was born to me on 11 day of May , 1902 , that said child has been named Rufus Cheestell Burton , and is now living.

                                             Mary Burton

Witnesses To Mark:
{

Applications for Enrollment of Creek Newborn
Act of 1905 Volume IV

Subscribed and sworn to before me this 23 day of Mar, 1905.

Edw C Griesel
Notary Public.

AFFIDAVIT OF ATTENDING PHYSICIAN OR MID-WIFE.

UNITED STATES OF AMERICA, Indian Territory,
WESTERN DISTRICT.

I, Mary Tiger, a Asst Mid Wife, on oath state that I attended on Mrs. Mary Burton, wife of Jesse Burton on the 11 day of May, 1902 ; that there was born to her on said date a male child; that said child is now living and is said to have been named Rufus Cheestell Burton

Her
Mary x Tiger
mark

Witnesses To Mark:
- Orwin Donovan
- EC Griesel

Subscribed and sworn to before me this 23 day of Mar, 1905.

Edw C Griesel
Notary Public.

BIRTH AFFIDAVIT.

DEPARTMENT OF THE INTERIOR.
COMMISSION TO THE FIVE CIVILIZED TRIBES.

IN RE APPLICATION FOR ENROLLMENT, as a citizen of the Creek Nation, of Dora Ellen Parks, born on the 12 day of August, 1902

Name of Father: Wm Parks	a citizen of the	U.S. Nation.
Name of Mother: Margaret Atkins Parks	a citizen of the	Creek Nation.

Postoffice Wagoner

(child present)

AFFIDAVIT OF MOTHER.

UNITED STATES OF AMERICA, Indian Territory,
WESTERN DISTRICT.

I, Margaret Atkins Parks, on oath state that I am 32 years of age and a citizen by blood, of the Creek Nation; that I am the lawful wife of Wm Parks, who is a

Applications for Enrollment of Creek Newborn
Act of 1905 Volume IV

citizen, by ----- of the U. S. Nation; that a female child was born to me on 12 day of Aug., 1902, that said child has been named Dora Ellen Parks, and is now living.

Margret[sic] Atkins Parks

Witnesses To Mark:

Subscribed and sworn to before me this 23" day of March, 1905.

Edw C Griesel
Notary Public.

AFFIDAVIT OF ATTENDING PHYSICIAN OR MID-WIFE.

UNITED STATES OF AMERICA, Indian Territory,
WESTERN DISTRICT.

I, Chaney A. Trent, a midwife, on oath state that I attended on Mrs. Margaret Atkins Parks, wife of Wm Parks on the 12 day of August, 1902; that there was born to her on said date a female child; that said child is now living and is said to have been named Dora Ellen Parks

Her
Chaney A. x Trent
mark

Witnesses To Mark:
- H.G. Hains
- E C Griesel

Subscribed and sworn to before me this 23" day of March, 1905.

Edw C Griesel
Notary Public.

DEPARTMENT OF THE INTERIOR,
COMMISSIONER TO THE FIVE CIVILIZED TRIBES.

REFER IN REPLY TO THE FOLLOWING:
NC-290

Muskogee, Indian Territory, August 4, 1905.

Joshua Asbury,
    Weleetka, Indian Territory.

Dear Sir:

You are hereby advised that on **July 28, 1905**, the Secretary of the Interior approved the enrollment of your minor child, **Joseph Asbury**, as a citizen by blood of

Applications for Enrollment of Creek Newborn
Act of 1905   Volume IV

the **Creek** Nation, and that the name of said child appears upon the roll of new born citizens of the **Creek** Nation as Number 174.

The child is now entitled to an allotment, and application therefor should be made without delay at the Land Office for the Nation in which the prospective allotment is located.

An entire allotment for said child must be selected at the time of the original application.

Respectively,

Commissioner.

BIRTH AFFIDAVIT.

DEPARTMENT OF THE INTERIOR.
COMMISSION TO THE FIVE CIVILIZED TRIBES.

IN RE APPLICATION FOR ENROLLMENT, as a citizen of the Creek Nation, of Joseph Asbury, born on the 1st day of November, 1901

Name of Father:	Joshua Asbury	a citizen of the	Creek	Nation.
Name of Mother:	Nancy Grayson	a citizen of the	Creek	Nation.

Postoffice   Weleetka, Ind. Tery.

AFFIDAVIT OF MOTHER.

UNITED STATES OF AMERICA, Indian Territory,
Western Judicial   DISTRICT.

I, Mrs. Joshua Asbury nee Nancy Grayson, on oath state that I am 27 years of age and a citizen by birth, of the Creek Nation; that I ~~am~~ was the lawful wife of Joshua Asbury (now deceased), who ~~is a~~ was a citizen, by birth of the Creek Nation; that a male child was born to me on the 1st day of November, 1901, that said child has been named Joseph Asbury, and was living March 4, 1905.

Mrs. Joshua Asbury nee Nancy Grayson
her x mark

Witnesses To Mark:
 { Chas Coachman
 { Josiah Looney

Subscribed and sworn to before me this 20th day of March, 1905.

(Name Illegible)
Notary Public.

Applications for Enrollment of Creek Newborn
Act of 1905   Volume IV

AFFIDAVIT OF ATTENDING PHYSICIAN OR MID-WIFE.

UNITED STATES OF AMERICA, Indian Territory, ⎫
  Western Judicial   DISTRICT. ⎭

I, Mrs. Miley Asbury , a Mid-Wife , on oath state that I attended on Mrs. Joshua Asbury , wife of Joshua Asbury on the 1st day of November , 1901 ; that there was born to her on said date a   male   child; that said child was living March 4, 1905, and is said to have been named Joseph Asbury

Mrs. Miley Asbury   her x mark

Witnesses To Mark:
  ⎧ Chas. Coachman
  ⎩ Josiah Looney

Subscribed and sworn to before me this 20th day of March , 1905.

(Name Illegible)
Notary Public.

N.C. 291 & 292

DEPARTMENT OF THE INTERIOR,
COMMISSIONER TO THE FIVE CIVILIZED TRIBES.
Muskogee, Indian Territory, August 8, 1905.

In the matter of the application for the enrollment of Eliza Asbury and Samuel Simmons as a citizens by blood of the Creek Nation.

Sarah Asbury being duly sworn testified as follows through Jesse McDermott official interpreter.

By Commissioner.

Q What is your name? A Sarah Asbury.
Q How old are you? A About twentyfive.
Q What is your post office address? A Weleetka
Q What is the names of these two children? A Eliza Asbury and Samuel Simmons.
Q What is the name of the father of Eliza Asbury? A George Asbury.
Q Is he living? A Yes, sir
Q Is he a citizen of the Creek Nation? A Yes, sir
Q What was the name of your father? A Throtho Fixico.
Q What [sic] the name of your mother? A Sewikie.
Q What is the name of the father of Samuel Simmons? A John Simmons

Applications for Enrollment of Creek Newborn
Act of 1905   Volume IV

Q Is he living? A No, dead.
Q Were you married to him? A Yes, sir
Q When did he die? A About two years ago
Q Were you ever know[sic] by the name of Selie? A Yes, sir that is my Indian name.

Anna Garrigues, being duly sworn, states that the above and foregoing is a true and correct copy of her stenographic notes as taken in said cause on said date.

                                        Anna Garrigues

Subscribed and sworn to before me
this 9th day of August 1905.   Henry G. Hains
                                        Notary Public.

BIRTH AFFIDAVIT.

DEPARTMENT OF THE INTERIOR.
COMMISSION TO THE FIVE CIVILIZED TRIBES.

IN RE APPLICATION FOR ENROLLMENT, as a citizen of the Creek Nation, of Eliza Asbury, born on the 24th day of February, 1905

| Name of Father: | George Asbury | a citizen of the | Creek | Nation. |
| Name of Mother: | Sarah Asbury | a citizen of the | Creek | Nation. |

                            Postoffice   Weleetka, Ind. Tery.

AFFIDAVIT OF MOTHER.

UNITED STATES OF AMERICA, Indian Territory,
    Western Judicial   DISTRICT.

I, Sarah Asbury , on oath state that I am about 35 years of age and a citizen by birth , of the Creek Nation; that I am the lawful wife of George Asbury , who is a citizen, by birth of the Creek Nation; that a female child was born to me on 24th day of February , 1905 , that said child has been named Eliza Asbury , and was living March 4, 1905.

                                      Sarah Asbury her x mark

Witnesses To Mark:
    Joseph C. Ricketts
    Josiah Looney

Applications for Enrollment of Creek Newborn
Act of 1905   Volume IV

Subscribed and sworn to before me this 20th day of March , 1905.

(Name Illegible)
Notary Public.

AFFIDAVIT OF ATTENDING PHYSICIAN OR MID-WIFE.

UNITED STATES OF AMERICA, Indian Territory,
Western Judicial   DISTRICT.

I, Harlothoyar King , a mid-wife , on oath state that I attended on Mrs. Sarah Asbury , wife of George Asbury on the 24th day of February , 1905 ; that there was born to her on said date a female child; that said child was living March 4, 1905, and is said to have been named Eliza Asbury

Harlothoyar King her x mark

Witnesses To Mark:
  Joseph C. Ricketts
  Josiah Looney

Subscribed and sworn to before me this 20th day of March , 1905.

(Name Illegible)
Notary Public.

NC-291.

Muskogee, Indian Territory, July 26, 1905.

George Asbury,
  Weleetka, Indian Territory.

Dear Sir:

In the matter of the application for the enrollment of your daughter Eliza Asbury as a citizen by blood of the Creek Nation this office is unable to identify the mother of said child on the final roll of citizens of the Creek Nation.

You are, therefore, requested to immediately inform this office of the name under which your said wife is finally enrolled, the names of her parents and other members of her family. You should also give her final roll number as the same appears upon her allotment certificate or deed, if she has received the same.

Please give this matter your prompt attention.

Applications for Enrollment of Creek Newborn
Act of 1905   Volume IV

Respectfully,

Commissioner.

N.C. 291 & 292

DEPARTMENT OF THE INTERIOR,
COMMISSIONER TO THE FIVE CIVILIZED TRIBES.
Muskogee, Indian Territory, August 8, 1905.

In the matter of the application for the enrollment of Eliza Asbury and Samuel Simmons as a citizens by blood of the Creek Nation.

Sarah Asbury being duly sworn testified as follows through Jesse McDermott official interpreter.

By Commissioner.

Q What is your name? A Sarah Asbury.
Q How old are you? A About twentyfive.
Q What is your post office address? A Weleetka
Q What is the names of these two children? A Eliza Asbury and Samuel Simmons.
Q What is the name of the father of Eliza Asbury? A George Asbury.
Q Is he living? A Yes, sir
Q Is he a citizen of the Creek Nation? A Yes, sir
Q What was the name of your father? A Throtho Fixico.
Q What [sic] the name of your mother? A Sewikie.
Q What is the name of the father of Samuel Simmons? A John Simmons
Q Is he living? A No, dead.
Q Were you married to him? A Yes, sir
Q When did he die? A About two years ago
Q Were you ever know[sic] by the name of Selie? A Yes, sir that is my Indian name.

Anna Garrigues, being duly sworn, states that the above and foregoing is a true and correct copy of her stenographic notes as taken in said cause on said date.

Anna Garrigues

Subscribed and sworn to before me
this 9th day of August 1905.   Henry G. Hains
Notary Public.

Applications for Enrollment of Creek Newborn
Act of 1905 Volume IV

Affidavit of Witnesses.

United States of America,
Western District of the Indian Territory.

We, Dick Barnett and Josiah Looney, on our oaths state that we are personally acquainted with Samuel Simmons, the applicant, herein, and with Sarah Simmons, the mother, and were acquainted with the father John Simmons during his lifetime. We know that John Simmons and Sarah Simmons lived together as husband and wife for a number of years until the death of John Simmons in the Fall of the year 1902. We further swear that during the time that John Simmons and Sarah Simmons lived together as husband and wife, and on or about the 10 day of March, 1902, a child was born to them and is said to have been named Samuel Simmons, and that said child was living with its mother Sarah Simmons on the 4" day of March, 1905.

Dick Barnett

Josiah Looney

Subscribed and sworn to before me this 10 day of August, 1905.

John B. Patterson
Notary Public.

My commission expires the 29 day of Feb., 1908.

BIRTH AFFIDAVIT.

DEPARTMENT OF THE INTERIOR.
COMMISSION TO THE FIVE CIVILIZED TRIBES.

IN RE APPLICATION FOR ENROLLMENT, as a citizen of the Creek Nation, of Samuel Simmons, born on the 13th day of March, 1902

Name of Father:	John Simmons	a citizen of the Creek	Nation.
Name of Mother:	Sarah Simmons	a citizen of the Creek	Nation.

Postoffice   Weleetka, Ind. Tery.

AFFIDAVIT OF MOTHER.

UNITED STATES OF AMERICA, Indian Territory,
Western Judicial   DISTRICT.

I, Sarah ~~Simmons~~ Asbury, on oath state that I am about 35 years of age and a citizen by birth, of the Creek Nation; that I am the lawful wife of George Asbury,

Applications for Enrollment of Creek Newborn
Act of 1905   Volume IV

who is a citizen, by birth of the Creek Nation; that a male child was born to me on the 13th day of March, 1902, that said child has been named Samuel Simmons, and was living March 4, 1905. I, also state that my former husband, John Simmons, acted as my physician and that he is now dead.

Sarah Asbury her x mark

Witnesses To Mark:
   { Joseph C. Ricketts
    Josiah Looney

Subscribed and sworn to before me this 20th day of March, 1905.

(Name Illegible)
Notary Public.

NC-292

Muskogee, Indian Territory, May 29, 1905.

John Simmons,
    Weleetka, Indian Territory.

Dear Sir:

    In the matter of the application for the enrollment of your minor child, Samuel Simmons, as a citizen of the Creek Nation, you are advised that the Commission requires the affidavit of the midwife or physician in attendance at the birth of said child; if same cannot be secured, the affidavits of two disinterested witnesses relative to its birth.

    There is herewith enclosed, for signature of midwife or physician, a blank form of birth affidavit. In executing same, care should be taken to see that all blanks are properly filled, all names spelled in full, and in the event that the person signing the affidavit is unable to write, signature by mark must be attested by two witnesses.

    The Commission is unable to identify the mother of said child on its rolls as Sarah Asbury; the name given in the affidavit on file. You are requested to furnish the Commission with the same under which said Sarah Asbury appears on the rolls, the

(The remainder of the letter is missing.)

Applications for Enrollment of Creek Newborn
Act of 1905   Volume IV

NC-292

Muskogee, Indian Territory, July 27, 1905.

Sarah Asbury,
    Weleetka, Indian Territory.

Dear Madam:

    In the matter of the application for the enrollment of your minor son Samuel Simmons, born March 13, 1902, as a citizen by blood of the Creek Nation, it appears from your affidavit on file with the records of this office as to the birth of said child that no physician or midwife attended you at his birth.

    You are advised that in lieu of the affidavit of the attending physician or midwife it will be necessary for you to furnish this office with the affidavits of two disinterested parties who know when said child was born, the names of his parents and whether or not he was living on March 4, 1905.

    This office has been unable to identify you upon the final roll of citizens by blood of the Creek Nation and in order that you may be identified on said roll you are requested to state the name under which you were enrolled, the names of your parents and other members of your family and to give your final roll number as the same appears upon your allotment certificate and deed.

    Please give this matter your immediate attention.

    Respectfully,

    Commissioner.

N.C. 295

DEPARTMENT OF THE INTERIOR,
COMMISSIONER TO THE FIVE CIVILIZED TRIBES.
Muskogee, Indian Territory, September 29, 1905.

    In the matter of the application for the enrollment of Roy Heneha and Ralph Heneha as citizens by blood of the Creek Nation.

    Michiley, being duly sworn, testified as follows:

Q What is your name? A Michiley.
Q What was the name of your father? A Artus Heneha.
Q What was the name of your mother? [sic] Lucy Anna

Applications for Enrollment of Creek Newborn
Act of 1905   Volume IV

Q What is the name of your wife? A Lucy.
Q What was her name before she was married? A Lucy Hill.
Q What was the name of her father? [sic] Hulbutta Fixico
Q What [sic] the name of her mother? A I dont[sic] know.
Q Was Lucy ever married to Jesse Hill? A Yes, sir.
Q Is Lucy the mother of your two children, Roy Henaha[sic] and Ralph Heneha?
A Yes, sir.

The mother of said children is identified as Lucy Hill on Creek Indian card field No. 2503 and her name is contained in a partial list of citizens by blood approved by the Secretary of the Interior March 28, 1902, roll No. 7446.

Q Are you ever called Mitchell Heneha? A That's what the white people call me.
Q But your right name is Michiley? A Yes, sir.
Q Do you want your two children Roy and Ralph Heneha or Roy and Ralph Michiley?
A I have no surname myself by my father's name was Artus Heneha and I prefer the name Heneha for my children.

Witness is identified as Michiley on Creek Indian card, field No. 7 and his name is contained in the partial list of citizens by blood approved by the Secretary of the Interior March 13, 1902, opposite roll No. 26. He is also identified as Mitchell Heneha, the father of Ralph and Roy Heneha.

Q What is your post office address? A Okemah.

I, Anna Garrigues, state on oath that the above and foregoing is a true and correct copy of my stenographic notes as taken in said cause on said date.

Anna Garrigues

Subscribed and sworn to before
me this 29th day of September 1905.

Edw C Griesel
Notary Public.

NC 305[sic].

Muskogee, Indian Territory, May 31, 1905.

Mitchell Heneha,
Castle, Indian Territory.

Dear Sir:

Applications for Enrollment of Creek Newborn
Act of 1905   Volume IV

In the matter of the application for the enrollment of your minor child, Ralph Heneha, you are advised that the Commission is unable to identify you or your wife, Lucy Heneha, on its rolls.

You are requested to advise the Commission as to any other name by which you and your wife may be known, the names of your parents, the Creek Indian Towns to which you belong, and if possible, the numbers which appear on your deeds to land in the Creek Nation.

There are herewith enclosed two blank forms of birth affidavits which you are requested to have signed by two disinterested parties, and in executing same care should be exercised to see that all blanks are properly filled, all names written in full and in the event that either of the persons signing the affidavits is unable to write, signature by mark must be attested by two witnesses. Each affidavit must be executed before a Notary Public and the notarial seal and signature of the officer must be attached to each separate affidavit.

Respectfully,

2BA   Chairman.

NC-295
31
Muskogee, Indian Territory, May 3̶0̶, 1905.

Lucy Heneha,
    Castle, Indian Territory.

Dear Madam:

There is on file with the Commission an affidavit executed by you relative to the birth of your minor child, Roy Heneha. The Commission is unable to identify you, or the father of said child, on its rolls.

You are requested to furnish the Commission with your maiden name, the names of your parents, the Creek Indian Town to which you belong, and, if possible, the number which appears on your deeds and the deeds of the father of said child to lands in the Creek Nation; also any other information which will identify you as a citizen of said Nation.

Respectfully,

Chairman.

Applications for Enrollment of Creek Newborn
Act of 1905 Volume IV

NC-355[sic]

Muskogee, Indian Territory, July 27, 1905.

Lucy Heneha,
    Castle, Indian Territory.

Dear Madam:

    In the matter of the application for the enrollment of your minor child, Ralph Heneha, as a citizen of the Creek Nation, you are advised that this office cannot identify you and Mitchell Heneha, the father of said child, as citizens of said Nation.

    You are requested to state your maiden name, the names of your parents, the Creek Indian Towns to which each of you belongs, and, if possible, the roll numbers as same appear on your and your husband's deeds to lands in the Creek Nation, which will help identify both of you as citizens thereof.

                  Respectfully,

                              Commissioner.

SUPPLEMENTAL PROOF.

DEPARTMENT OF THE INTERIOR,
COMMISSION TO THE FIVE CIVILIZED TRIBES.

    IN RE Application for Enrollment, as a citizen of the Creek (or Muskogee) Nation, of Ralph Heneha, born on the 16 day of Feb, 1905

Name of Father:	Michiley Heneha	a citizen of the	Creek	Nation.
Name of Mother:	Lucy Hill (nee Hill)	a citizen of the	Creek	Nation.

                    Postoffice   Okemah I T

                            <u>Acquaintance</u>
                    AFFIDAVIT OF ~~PARENT~~.
          (To be made if child is now living)

UNITED STATES OF AMERICA, ⎫
    Indian Territory,   ⎬
Western   DISTRICT. ⎭

    We   we are
    ~~I~~, Jackson Knight and Jas Scott, on oath state that ~~I am~~ *(blank)* ~~years of age and a~~ citizens by blood, of the Creek (or Muskogee) Nation; that ~~I am the~~ we are personally acquainted with Lucy Heneha ~~of~~ the lawful wife of Mitchell Heneha that there was born

Applications for Enrollment of Creek Newborn
Act of 1905   Volume IV

to her a female[sic] child who was born on the 5[sic] day of Oct.[sic] , 1902[sic], that said child is now living. also a male child born Feb 16, 1905 and said child is now living.

                                                      his
                                         Jackson x Knight
                                                    mark

Witnesses To Mark: his
{ W H Dill Okemah I.T.   Jas x Scott
  M.E. Dill   "   "   mark

Subscribed and sworn to before me this 8 *day of* Jany, *190*6.

    My Com Ex July 8 1906   WH Dill
                                                  Notary Public.

AFFIDAVIT OF PARENT.
(To be made if child is now living)

UNITED STATES OF AMERICA,
    Indian Territory,
 Western   DISTRICT.

    I, Michiley Heneha , on oath state that I am 26 years of age and a citizen by blood , of the Creek (or Muskogee) Nation; that I am the father of Ralph Heneha   a male   child who was born on the 16 day of Feby , 1905, that said child was living ~~died~~ on the 8th day of Jany , 1906

                                          Michiley Heneha

Witnesses To Mark:
{ WH Dill Okemah IT
  M.E. Dill   "   "

Subscribed and sworn to before me this 8 *day of* Jany, *190*6

    My Com Ex July 8 1906   WH Dill
                                                 Notary Public.

BIRTH AFFIDAVIT.

DEPARTMENT OF THE INTERIOR.
COMMISSION TO THE FIVE CIVILIZED TRIBES.

    IN RE APPLICATION FOR ENROLLMENT, as a citizen of the Creek Nation, of Ralph Heneha, born on the 24 day of Feby , 1905

Name of Father:	Mitchell Heneha	a citizen of the	Creek	Nation.
Name of Mother:	Lucy Heneha	a citizen of the	Creek	Nation.

Applications for Enrollment of Creek Newborn
Act of 1905   Volume IV

Postoffice   Castle, Indian Territory

AFFIDAVIT OF MOTHER.

UNITED STATES OF AMERICA, Indian Territory,
Western   DISTRICT.

I, Lucy Heneha , on oath state that I am about 30 years of age and a citizen by blood , of the Creek Nation; that I am the lawful wife of Mitchell Heneha , who is a citizen, by blood of the Creek Nation; that a male child was born to me on 24 day of February , 1905 , that said child has been named Ralph Heneha , and was living March 4, 1905.

            her
         Lucy x Heneha
Witnesses To Mark: mark
 { Alex Posey
  DC Skaggs

Subscribed and sworn to before me this 15 day of March , 1905.

        Drennan C Skaggs
         Notary Public.

        Husband
AFFIDAVIT OF ~~ATTENDING PHYSICIAN OR MID-WIFE.~~

UNITED STATES OF AMERICA, Indian Territory,
Western   DISTRICT.

                   my wife
I, Mitchell Heneha , a *(blank)* , on oath state that I attended on ~~Mrs~~. Lucy Heneha , ~~wife of~~ *(blank)* on the 24 day of February , 1905 ; that there was born to her on said date a male child; that said child was living March 4, 1905, and is said to have been named Ralph Heneha

        Mitchelly[sic] Heneha
Witnesses To Mark:

{

Subscribed and sworn to before me this 15 day of March, 1905.

        Drennan C Skaggs
         Notary Public.

Applications for Enrollment of Creek Newborn
Act of 1905   Volume IV

BIRTH AFFIDAVIT.

DEPARTMENT OF THE INTERIOR.
COMMISSION TO THE FIVE CIVILIZED TRIBES.

IN RE APPLICATION FOR ENROLLMENT, as a citizen of the Creek Nation, of Roy Heneha, born on the 5 day of October, 1902

Name of Father: Mitchell Heneha   a citizen of the   Creek   Nation.
Name of Mother: Lucy Heneha   a citizen of the   Creek   Nation.

Postoffice   Castle, Indian Territory

AFFIDAVIT OF MOTHER.

UNITED STATES OF AMERICA, Indian Territory,
Western   DISTRICT.

I, Lucy Heneha, on oath state that I am about 30 years of age and a citizen by blood, of the Creek Nation; that I am the lawful wife of Mitchell Heneha, who is a citizen, by blood of the Creek Nation; that a male child was born to me on 5 day of October, 1902, that said child has been named Roy Heneha, and was living March 4, 1905.

                                                her
                                     Lucy x Heneha
Witnesses To Mark: mark
  Alex Posey
  DC Skaggs

Subscribed and sworn to before me this 15" day of March, 1905.

                                Drennan C Skaggs
                                         Notary Public.

                                   Husband
AFFIDAVIT OF ~~ATTENDING PHYSICIAN OR MID-WIFE.~~

UNITED STATES OF AMERICA, Indian Territory,
Western   DISTRICT.

                                                                    my wife
I, Mitchell Heneha, a   *(blank)*, on oath state that I attended on ~~Mrs.~~ Lucy Heneha, ~~wife of~~ *(blank)* on the 5 day of October, 1902; that there was born to her on said date a male child; that said child was living March 4, 1905, and is said to have been named Roy Heneha

                                     Mitchelly[sic] Heneha

Witnesses To Mark:

Applications for Enrollment of Creek Newborn
Act of 1905 Volume IV

Subscribed and sworn to before me this 15 day of March, 1905.

> Drennan C Skaggs
> Notary Public.

N.C. 296

DEPARTMENT OF THE INTERIOR,
COMMISSIONER TO THE FIVE CIVILIZED TRIBES.
Muskogee, Indian Territory, January 3, 1906.

In the matter of the application for the enrollment of Lillie Murphy as a citizen by blood of the Creek Nation.

Joseph Harjo being duly sworn testified as follows through Jesse McDermott official interpreter.

Q What is your name? A Josie or Joseph Harjo
Q What was the name of your father? A Thulwar Harjo.
Q He is dead is he? A Yes, sir.
Q What was the name of your mother? A Tarye I have been told. She died when I was quite small.
Q To what Creek Indian town do you belong? A Thlopthlooo[sic].
Q How old are you? A About thirty.
Q What is your post office address? A Fentress.
Q Is your name Josie or Joseph? A Joseph. I am known among the Indians as Josie. I don't know how I am enrolled.
Q Have you received your land? A Yes, sir.
Q Didn't you ever look at the deed? A I never did examine the deed to see how the name was spelled although I have them at home.
Q Do you know the section, range and township in which the land described in that deed lies, if so state? A I dont[sic] know where the land is located but it is about six miles south of Okemah.

Witness is identified on Creek Indian card field No. 1478 under the name Joseph Harjo, opposite roll No. 4698.

Q Have you a child named Lilley? A Yes, sir
Q Is that child named Lilley Harjo? A Yes, sir.
Q When was Lilley born? A She was born in August 1904.
Q What day? A I am not positive but I think long about the 19th
Q Is she living? A No, she is dead.
Q When did she die? A I don't know
Q Don't you know about when she died? A I think she died in May.
Q Of 1905 or what year? A 1905.

Applications for Enrollment of Creek Newborn
Act of 1905   Volume IV

Q What is the name of her mother? A Mahala Harjo. That was her former name also. She was enrolled under the name of Mahala Harjo
Q To what Creek Indian town does she belong? A She belongs to the same town that I do.
Q What was the name of Mahala's father? A Temarheseh.
Q What was the name of her mother? A Lucy.
Q Do you know the name of her guardian that she was enrolled with? A No, sir. She used to live with Wicey Scott
Q Was Wicey ever known as Wicey Yahala? A She is now the wife of Chapley Yahola.

   Said Mahaley Harjo is identified on Creek Indian card field No. 1519, opposite roll No. 4858

Q The name of this child then is Lilly Harjo is it? A Yes, sir.

Witness is advised that this office has in its possession an affidavit signed by mark with the name Mahala Murphy, relative to the birth of Lilly Murphy born August 15, 1904 also the affidavit of Susie Davis a midwife to the same effect both these affidavits were executed before Tupper Dunn

Q Is this Lillie Murphy referred to your child? A Yes, sir.
Q How does it come that he got the name Murphy in there for you, for Mahala and for Lilly? A He is acquainted with me and I called my name Moffit and we came to him to take the application and thought he had it correct.
Q He probably thought you said Murphy? A Yes, sir.
Q And your name is Joseph Harjo? your wife's name is Mahaley Harjo and the child's name if Lillie Harjo, is that correct? A Yes, sir.
Q How did you get this name of Moffit that you gave Tupper Dunn? A I am known by the name of Moffit in the settlement where I live and I am enrolled as such on the 1895 tribal roll.
Q But your correct name is as you are enrolled, Joseph Harjo is it? A Yes, sir. My fathers[sic] name was Harjo.

   The witness is handed a blank birth affidavit for the mother and midwife with instructions to have same completed and executed before a notary public and returned to this office.

Q Are you sure that your child Lillie Harjo died in May? A Yes, sir.
Q Are you positive that she was living March 4th.[sic] A Yes, sir. We had the child with us when we made out those affidavits before Tupper Dunn March 15, 1905.
Q Your wife in the affidavit said the child was born August 16 and you said the 19th, do you think the 16th is about right? A Yes, sir.

   I, Anna Garrigues, on oath state that the above and foregoing is a true and correct transcript of my stenographic notes as taken in said cause on said date.

                              Anna Garrigues

Applications for Enrollment of Creek Newborn
Act of 1905   Volume IV

Subscribed and sworn to before me
this 6 day of January 1906.   J McDermott
                                           Notary Public.

COMMISSIONERS:
TAMS BIXBY,
THOMAS B. NEEDLES,
C.R. BRECKINBRIDGE.

DEPARTMENT OF THE INTERIOR,
COMMISSIONER TO THE FIVE CIVILIZED TRIBES.

WM. O. BEALL
Secretary

REFER IN REPLY TO THE FOLLOWING:

NC 296.

ADDRESS ONLY THE
COMMISSION TO THE FIVE CIVILIZED TRIBES.

Muskogee, Indian Territory, May 31, 1905.

Mahala Murphy,
    Fentress, Indian Territory.

Dear Madam:

    In the matter of the application for the enrollment of your minor child, Lilly Murphy, as a citizen of the Creek Nation, you are advised that the Commission cannot identify you or the father of said child on its rolls.

    You are requested to advise the Commission as to your maiden name, the names of your parents, the Creek Indian Towns to which you and your husband belong, and, if possible, the numbers of your deeds to land in the Creek Nation.

                               Respectfully,

                               Tams Bixby

                                         Chairman.

DEPARTMENT OF THE INTERIOR.
COMMISSION TO THE FIVE CIVILIZED TRIBES.

                                                                                     N.C. 296.

Muskogee, Indian Territory, July 7, 1905.

Joseph Murphy,
    Fentress, Indian Territory.

Dear Sir:

Applications for Enrollment of Creek Newborn
Act of 1905   Volume IV

In the matter of the application for the enrollment of your minor child, Lilly Murphy, as a citizen of the Creek Nation, you are advised that the Commission that this office cannot identify you or the mother of said child on its rolls.

You are requested to state the maiden name of your wife, the names of your parents, the Creek Indian towns to which you and your wife belong, and, if possible, the numbers of your deeds to land in the Creek Nation.

Respectfully,

Tams Bixby   Commissioner.

BIRTH AFFIDAVIT.

DEPARTMENT OF THE INTERIOR.
COMMISSION TO THE FIVE CIVILIZED TRIBES.

IN RE APPLICATION FOR ENROLLMENT, as a citizen of the Creek Nation, of Lilly Murphy, born on the 16 day of August, 1904

Name of Father: Joseph Murphy   a citizen of the   Creek   Nation.
Name of Mother: Mahala Murphy   a citizen of the   Creek   Nation.

Postoffice   Fentress Ind Ter.

AFFIDAVIT OF MOTHER.

UNITED STATES OF AMERICA, Indian Territory,
    Western   DISTRICT.

I, Mahala Murphy , on oath state that I am 19 years of age and a citizen by blood , of the Creek Nation; that I am the lawful wife of Joseph Murphy , who is a citizen, by blood of the Creek Nation; that a female child was born to me on 16 day of August , 1904 , that said child has been named Lilley Murphy , and was living March 4, 1905.

 her
Mahala x Murphy
 mark

Witnesses To Mark:
    RH Dill
    Tupper Dunn

Subscribed and sworn to before me this 15 day of March , 1905.

My Com Exp. Aug 19-1908   Tupper Dunn
                                Notary Public.

Applications for Enrollment of Creek Newborn
Act of 1905 Volume IV

AFFIDAVIT OF ATTENDING PHYSICIAN OR MID-WIFE.

UNITED STATES OF AMERICA, Indian Territory,
Western DISTRICT.

I, Susie Davis , a midwife , on oath state that I attended on Mrs. Mahala Murphy , wife of Joseph Murphy on the 16 day of August , 1904 ; that there was born to her on said date a female child; that said child was living March 4, 1905, and is said to have been named Lilley Murphy

                              her
                          Susie x Davis

Witnesses To Mark: mark
    RH Dill
    Tupper Dunn

Subscribed and sworn to before me this 15 day of March , 1905.

My Com Exp. Aug 19-1908   Tupper Dunn
                                      Notary Public.

BIRTH AFFIDAVIT.

DEPARTMENT OF THE INTERIOR.
COMMISSION TO THE FIVE CIVILIZED TRIBES.

IN RE APPLICATION FOR ENROLLMENT, as a citizen of the Creek Nation, of Lilley Harjo, born on the 16 day of August, 1904

Name of Father:	Joseph Harjo	a citizen of the	Creek	Nation.
Name of Mother:	Mehaley Harjo	a citizen of the	Creek	Nation.

                          Postoffice   Fentress I.T.

AFFIDAVIT OF MOTHER.

UNITED STATES OF AMERICA, Indian Territory,
Western DISTRICT.

I, Mehaley Harjo , on oath state that I am 19 years of age and a citizen by blood , of the Creek Nation; that I am the lawful wife of Joseph Harjo , who is a citizen, by blood of the Creek Nation; that a female child was born to me on 16 day of August , 1904 , that said child has been named Lilley Harjo , and was living March 4, 1905.

                                    her
                                Mehaley x Harjo
                                    mark

Applications for Enrollment of Creek Newborn
Act of 1905   Volume IV

Witnesses To Mark:
- *(Illegible)* Meaders
- J.C.F. Busey

    Subscribed and sworn to before me this 6th day of January, 1906.

Com Ex. Aug 2 1906   Jeff T Canard
                                      Notary Public.

AFFIDAVIT OF ATTENDING PHYSICIAN OR MID-WIFE.

UNITED STATES OF AMERICA, Indian Territory,
    Western   DISTRICT.

    I, Susie Davis, a midwife, on oath state that I attended on Mrs. Mehaley Harjo, wife of Joseph Harjo on the 16" day of August, 1904; that there was born to her on said date a female child; that said child was living March 4, 1905, and is said to have been named Lilley Harjo

                                          her
                                    Susie x Davis
Witnesses To Mark: mark
- W.W. Jimboy
- Sarfartcha

    Subscribed and sworn to before me this 30th day of January, 1906.

Com Ex. Aug 2, 1906   Jeff T Canard
                                      Notary Public.

DEPARTMENT OF THE INTERIOR.
COMMISSION TO THE FIVE CIVILIZED TRIBES.

    In the matter of the death of Lilly Harjo die *(Illegible)* a citizen of the Creek Nation, who formerly resided at or near Okemah, Ind. Ter., and died on the 19 day of March, 1905.

Applications for Enrollment of Creek Newborn
Act of 1905   Volume IV

DEPARTMENT OF THE INTERIOR,
COMMISSIONER TO THE FIVE CIVILIZED TRIBES.

REFER IN REPLY TO THE FOLLOWING:

NC-297

Muskogee, Indian Territory, **August 4, 1905.**

Barney Davis,
    Fentress, Indian Territory.

Dear Sir:

    You are hereby advised that on **July 28, 1905**, the Secretary of the Interior approved the enrollment of your minor child, **Lizzie Davis**, as a citizen by blood of the **Creek** Nation, and that the name of said child appears upon the roll of new born citizens of the **Creek** Nation as Number **175**.

    The child is now entitled to an allotment, and application therefor should be made without delay at the Land Office for the Nation in which the prospective allotment is located.

    An entire allotment for said child must be selected at the time of the original application.

                              Respectively,

                                          Commissioner.

BIRTH AFFIDAVIT.

DEPARTMENT OF THE INTERIOR.
COMMISSION TO THE FIVE CIVILIZED TRIBES.

    IN RE APPLICATION FOR ENROLLMENT, as a citizen of the Creek Nation, of Lizzie Davis, born on the 26 day of August, 1903

Name of Father:	Barney Davis	a citizen of the	Creek	Nation.
Name of Mother:	Susie Davis	a citizen of the	Creek	Nation.

                                Postoffice   Fentress, Ind. Ter.

AFFIDAVIT OF MOTHER.

UNITED STATES OF AMERICA, Indian Territory,
    Western   DISTRICT.

    I, Susie Davis, on oath state that I am 29 years of age and a citizen by blood, of the Creek Nation; that I am the lawful wife of Barney Davis, who is a citizen, by blood of the Creek Nation; that a female child was born to me on 26 day of

Applications for Enrollment of Creek Newborn
Act of 1905   Volume IV

August , 1903 , that said child has been named Lizzie Davis , and was living March 4, 1905.

Witnesses To Mark:
{ RH Dill
{ Tupper Dunn

Susie x Davis
her   mark

Subscribed and sworn to before me this 15 day of March , 1905.

my com. Exp. Aug 19-1908   Tupper Dunn
                                         Notary Public.

AFFIDAVIT OF ATTENDING PHYSICIAN OR MID-WIFE.

UNITED STATES OF AMERICA, Indian Territory,
       Western   DISTRICT.

I, Eliza Davis , a midwife , on oath state that I attended on Mrs. Susie Davis , wife of Barney Davis on the 26 day of August , 1903 ; that there was born to her on said date a *(blank)* child; that said child was living March 4, 1905, and is said to have been named Lizzie Davis

Witnesses To Mark:
{ RH Dill
{ Tupper Dunn

Eliza x Davis
her   mark

Subscribed and sworn to before me this 15 day of March , 1905.

my com. Exp. Aug 19-1908   Tupper Dunn
                                         Notary Public.

N.C. 298

DEPARTMENT OF THE INTERIOR,
COMMISSION TO THE FIVE CIVILIZED TRIBES.
MUSKOGEE, I.T. JUNE 10, 1905.

In the matter of the application for the enrollment of Roman and Nord Harjo as Creek citizens.

A.E. Harjo, being duly sworn, testified as follows:
Through Official Interpreter, Jesse McDermott.

Applications for Enrollment of Creek Newborn
Act of 1905   Volume IV

Examination by the Commission:
Q What is your name? A A.E. Harjo.
Q What is your age? A 32.
Q What is your post office address? A Arbeka
Q Are you a citizen of the Seminole Nation? A Yes sir.
Q Have you two children new born named Roman and Nord Harjo? A Yes sir.
Q Are those children living? A Yes sir.
Q Do you know when they were born? A Yes sir.
Q Give the dates? A Roman was born 30th of March.
Q How many years ago? A 1902.
Q Nord was born when? A (From a memorandum) December 29, 1903.
Q If it should be found that these two children have rights in both the Creek and Seminole Nations, in which Nation do you wish them to be enrolled and have them take allotments of land, Seminole or Creek? A In the Creek Nation.
Q You want to enrolled[sic] them as Creeks? A Yes sir.
Q What is the name of the midwife? A Lydia Frank.
Q Midwife in both cases? A Yes sir.

I, J.Y. Miller, a stenographer to the Commission to the Five Civilized Tribes, do hereby certify that the above and foregoing is a true and complete translation of my notes as same appear in my stenographic report of this case.

JY Miller

Subscribed and sworn to before me this 17th day of June, 1905.

Edw C Griesel
Notary Public.

BIRTH AFFIDAVIT.

DEPARTMENT OF THE INTERIOR.
COMMISSION TO THE FIVE CIVILIZED TRIBES.

IN RE APPLICATION FOR ENROLLMENT, as a citizen of the Creek Nation, of Roman Harjo, born on the 30 day of March, 1902

| Name of Father: | A.E. Harjo | a citizen of the | Seminole | Nation. |
| Name of Mother: | Arney Harjo | a citizen of the | Creek | Nation. |

Postoffice   Arbeka I.T.

Applications for Enrollment of Creek Newborn
Act of 1905 Volume IV

AFFIDAVIT OF MOTHER.

UNITED STATES OF AMERICA, Indian Territory, }
Western DISTRICT.

    I, Arney Harjo, on oath state that I am 34 years of age and a citizen by blood, of the Creek Nation; that I am the lawful wife of A. E. Harjo, who is a citizen, by blood of the Seminole Nation; that a male child was born to me on 30 day of March, 1902, that said child has been named Roman Harjo, and was living March 4, 1905.

                                                                                               her
                                                                                          Arney x Harjo

Witnesses To Mark: mark
{ E.D. Miles
  Tupper Dunn

    Subscribed and sworn to before me this 28 day of March, 1905.

    My Com Exp. Aug 19-1908   Tupper Dunn
                                                                    Notary Public.

AFFIDAVIT OF ATTENDING PHYSICIAN OR MID-WIFE.

UNITED STATES OF AMERICA, Indian Territory, }
Western DISTRICT.

    I, Liddie Frank, a midwife, on oath state that I attended on Mrs. Arney Harjo, wife of A. E. Harjo on the 30 day of March, 1902; that there was born to her on said date a *(blank)* child; that said child was living March 4, 1905, and is said to have been named Roman Harjo

                                                                      her
                                                                Lidda x Frank

Witnesses To Mark: mark
{ E.D. Miles
  Tupper Dunn

    Subscribed and sworn to before me this 28 day of March, 1905.

    My Commission Exp. Aug 19-1908   Tupper Dunn
                                                                    Notary Public.

BIRTH AFFIDAVIT.
DEPARTMENT OF THE INTERIOR.
COMMISSION TO THE FIVE CIVILIZED TRIBES.

    IN RE APPLICATION FOR ENROLLMENT, as a citizen of the Creek Nation, of Mord Harjo, born on the 29 day of December, 1903

Applications for Enrollment of Creek Newborn
Act of 1905   Volume IV

Name of Father: A.E. Harjo   a citizen of the   Seminole   Nation.
Name of Mother: Arney Harjo   a citizen of the   Creek   Nation.

Postoffice   Arbeka I.T.

AFFIDAVIT OF MOTHER.

UNITED STATES OF AMERICA, Indian Territory,
Western   DISTRICT.

I, Arney Harjo , on oath state that I am 34 years of age and a citizen by blood , of the   Creek   Nation; that I am the lawful wife of A. E. Harjo , who is a citizen, by blood of the Seminole   Nation; that a female   child was born to me on   29 day of December , 1903 , that said child has been named Mord Harjo , and was living March 4, 1905.

                              her
                              Arney x Harjo

Witnesses To Mark: mark
{ E.D. Miles
{ Tupper Dunn

Subscribed and sworn to before me this 28 day of March, 1905.

My Com Exp. Aug 19-1908   Tupper Dunn
                                              Notary Public.

AFFIDAVIT OF ATTENDING PHYSICIAN OR MID-WIFE.

UNITED STATES OF AMERICA, Indian Territory,
Western   DISTRICT.

I, Lidda Frank , a midwife , on oath state that I attended on Mrs. Arney Harjo , wife of A. E. Harjo on the 29 day of December , 1903 ; that there was born to her on said date a   *(blank)*   child; that said child was living March 4, 1905, and is said to have been named Mord Harjo

                              her
                            Lidda x Frank
                              mark

Witnesses To Mark:
{ E.D. Miles
{ Tupper Dunn

Subscribed and sworn to before me this 28 day of March, 1905.

My Com Exp. Aug 19-1908   Tupper Dunn
                                              Notary Public.

Applications for Enrollment of Creek Newborn
Act of 1905 Volume IV

NC 298.

Muskogee, Indian Territory, May 31, 1905.

Arney Harjo,
    Arbeka, Indian Territory.

Dear Madam:

In the matter of the application for the enrollment of your minor children, Roman and Mord Harjo, as citizens of the Creek Nation, you are advised that you will be allowed twenty days from date hereof within which to appear before the Commission at its office in Muskogee, Indian Territory, for the purpose of being examined under oath.

Respectfully,

Chairman.

NC. 298.

Muskogee, Indian Territory, July 14, 1905.

Commissioner to the Five Civilized Tribes,
    Seminole Enrollment Division,
        Muskogee, Indian Territory.

Gentlemen:

March 23, 1905, application was made to the Commission to the Five Civilized Tribes for the enrollment of Roman Harjo, born March 30, 1902, and Mord Harjo, born December 29, 1903, as citizens by blood of the Creek Nation. It is stated in said application that the father of said children is A.E. Harjo, a citizen of the Seminole Nation, and that the mother is Arney Harjo, identified as Arney Hill, a citien of the Creek Nation.

You are requested to inform the Creek Enrollment Division as to whether an application was made for the enrollment of said children, as citizens of the Seminole Nation, and if so, what disposition has been made of the same.

Respectfully,

Commissioner.

Applications for Enrollment of Creek Newborn
Act of 1905   Volume IV

DEPARTMENT OF THE INTERIOR.
COMMISSION TO THE FIVE CIVILIZED TRIBES.
Muskogee, Indian Territory, July 18, 1905.

Chief Clerk,
    Creek Enrollment Division.

Dear Sir:

    Receipt is acknowledged of your letter of July 14, 1905 (NC-298) stating that an application was made to the Commission to the Five Civilized Tribes for the enrollment of Roman Harjo, born March 30, 1902, and Mord Harjo, born December 29, 1903, children of A. E. Harjo, a citizen of the Seminole Nation, and Arney Harjo (identified as Arney Hill), a citizen of the Creek Nation, as citizens by blood of the Creek Nation and requesting to be informed as to whether application has been made for the enrollment of said children as citizens of the Seminole Nation

    In reply to your letter you are advised that the Commission that it does not appear from an examination of the records of this office that any application was made to the Commission to the Five Civilized Tribes for the enrollment of said Roman Harjo and Mord Harjo as citizens of the Seminole Nation.

Respectfully,

Tams Bixby   Commissioner.

NC 298

Muskogee, Indian Territory, November 12, 1906.

Chief Clerk,
    Seminole Enrollment Division.
        General Office.

Dear Sir:

    You are hereby advised that the names of roman and Mord Harjo, children of A. E. Harjo, an alleged citizen of the Seminole Nation, and Arney Harjo, a citizen by blood of the Creek Nation, are contained in the schedule of new Born citizens by blood of the Creek Nation, approved by the Secretary of the Interior August 11, 1905, opposite Nos. 291 and 292.

Respectfully,

Commissioner.

Applications for Enrollment of Creek Newborn
Act of 1905   Volume IV

NC-299.

Muskogee, Indian Territory, July 27, 1905.

Jennie Cherry,
    c/o Joe Cherry,
        Morse, Indian Territory.

Dear Madam:

    In the matter of the application for the enrollment of your minor child[sic] Colona Blanche Cherry and Francis Doyle Cherry as a citizen of the Creek Nation there are on file your affidavits only as to the birth of said children.

    It will be necessary for you to furnish this office with proper proof of the birth of said children and for that purpose two blanks, partially filled out are inclosed[sic] herewith. Care should be taken to sign the affidavits as the name of the affiant appears in the body thereof and in case any signature is by mark the same must be attested by two disinterested witnesses.

    Please give this matter your prompt attention.

        Respectfully,

            Commissioner.

BIRTH AFFIDAVIT.

DEPARTMENT OF THE INTERIOR.
COMMISSION TO THE FIVE CIVILIZED TRIBES.

IN RE APPLICATION FOR ENROLLMENT, as a citizen of the Creek Nation, of Francis Doyle Cherry , born on the 22 day of September , 1904

Name of Father: Joe Cherry   a citizen of the United States Nation.
Name of Mother: Jennie Pitman (nee) Cherry   a citizen of the   Creek   Nation.

        Postoffice   Morse I.T.

Applications for Enrollment of Creek Newborn
Act of 1905 Volume IV

AFFIDAVIT OF MOTHER.

UNITED STATES OF AMERICA, Indian Territory,
Western DISTRICT.

I, Jennie Pitman (nee) Cherry , on oath state that I am 35 years of age and a citizen by blood , of the Creek Nation; that I am the lawful wife of Joe Cherry , who is a citizen, by blood of the United States Nation; that a male child was born to me on 22 day of September , 1904 , that said child has been named Francis Doyle Cherry, and was living March 4, 1905.

Jennie Pitman nee Cherry

Witnesses To Mark: midwife left the country

Subscribed and sworn to before me this 16 day of March , 1905.

my com. exp Aug. 19-1908   Tupper Dunn
                                                 Notary Public.

BIRTH AFFIDAVIT.

DEPARTMENT OF THE INTERIOR.
COMMISSION TO THE FIVE CIVILIZED TRIBES.

IN RE APPLICATION FOR ENROLLMENT, as a citizen of the Creek Nation, of Francis Doyle Cherry, born on the 22nd day of September , 1904

Name of Father: Joe Cherry   a citizen of the United States Nation.
Name of Mother: Jennie Cherry   a citizen of the Creek Nation.
                       (formerly Pittman)
                                     Postoffice   Morse I.T.

AFFIDAVIT OF MOTHER.

UNITED STATES OF AMERICA, Indian Territory,
Western DISTRICT.

I, Jennie Cherry , on oath state that I am 35 years of age and a citizen by blood, of the Creek Nation; that I am the lawful wife of Joe Cherry , who is a citizen, by *(blank)* of the United States Nation; that a male child was born to me on 22nd day of September , 1904 , that said child has been named Francis Doyle Cherry, and was living March 4, 1905.

Jennie Cherry

Witnesses To Mark:

Applications for Enrollment of Creek Newborn
Act of 1905   Volume IV

Subscribed and sworn to before me this 31 day of July, 1905.

My Commission Expires Aug. 2 1906   Geo. H. Harrison
                                                                                  Notary Public.

AFFIDAVIT OF ATTENDING PHYSICIAN OR MID-WIFE.

UNITED STATES OF AMERICA, Indian Territory,
Western   DISTRICT.

I, Amalie Schoenecke, a midwife, on oath state that I attended on Mrs. Jennie Cherry, wife of Joe Cherry on the 22nd day of September, 1904; that there was born to her on said date a male child; that said child was living March 4, 1905, and is said to have been named Francis Doyle Cherry

                                                                  Amalie Schoenecke
Witnesses To Mark:

Subscribed and sworn to before me this 31 day of July, 1905.

My Commission Expires Aug. 2 1906   Geo. H. Harrison
                                                                                  Notary Public.

BIRTH AFFIDAVIT.

DEPARTMENT OF THE INTERIOR.
COMMISSION TO THE FIVE CIVILIZED TRIBES.

IN RE APPLICATION FOR ENROLLMENT, as a citizen of the Creek Nation, of Colona Blanche Cherry, born on the 25th day of October, 1903

Name of Father: Joe Cherry   a citizen of the United States Nation.
Name of Mother: Jennie Cherry   a citizen of the   Creek   Nation.
                              (formerly Pittman)
                                              Postoffice   Morse I.T.

AFFIDAVIT OF MOTHER.

UNITED STATES OF AMERICA, Indian Territory,
Western   DISTRICT.

I, Jennie Cherry, on oath state that I am 35 years of age and a citizen by blood, of the Creek Nation; that I am the lawful wife of Joe Cherry, who is a citizen, by *(blank)* of the United States ~~Nation~~; that a female child was born to me on 25th

Applications for Enrollment of Creek Newborn
Act of 1905 Volume IV

day of October, 1903, that said child has been named Colona Blanche Cherry, and was living March 4, 1905.

Jennie Cherry

Witnesses To Mark:
{

Subscribed and sworn to before me this 31 day of July, 1905.

MY COMMISSION EXPIRES AUG. 2 1906   Geo. H. Harrison
                                         Notary Public.

AFFIDAVIT OF ATTENDING PHYSICIAN OR MID-WIFE.

UNITED STATES OF AMERICA, Indian Territory,
    Western   DISTRICT.

I, Lee Cherry, an eye witness, on oath state that I attended on Mrs. Jennie Cherry, wife of Joe Cherry on the 25th day of October, 1903; that there was born to her on said date a female child; that said child was living March 4, 1905, and is said to have been named Colona Blanche Cherry

                                her
                         Lee x Cherry
Witnesses To Mark: mark
 { J O *(Illegible)*
   Jep Smith

Subscribed and sworn to before me this 4th day of August, 1905.

                         Frank J Smith
                         Notary Public.

BIRTH AFFIDAVIT.

DEPARTMENT OF THE INTERIOR.
COMMISSION TO THE FIVE CIVILIZED TRIBES.

IN RE APPLICATION FOR ENROLLMENT, as a citizen of the Creek Nation, of Colona Blanche Cherry, born on the 25 day of October, 1903

Name of Father: Joe Cherry   a citizen of the United States Nation.
Name of Mother: Jennie Pitman (nee) Cherry   a citizen of the Creek   Nation.

                    Postoffice   Morse I.T.

Applications for Enrollment of Creek Newborn
Act of 1905 Volume IV

AFFIDAVIT OF MOTHER.

UNITED STATES OF AMERICA, Indian Territory,
Western DISTRICT.

I, Jennie Pitman (nee) Cherry, on oath state that I am 35 years of age and a citizen by blood, of the Creek Nation; that I am the lawful wife of Joe Cherry, who is a citizen, by blood of the United States Nation; that a female child was born to me on 25 day of October, 1903, that said child has been named Colona Blanche Cherry, and was living March 4, 1905.

Jennie Pitman nee Cherry
Witnesses To Mark: midwife left the country

Subscribed and sworn to before me this 16 day of March, 1905.

my com. exp Aug. 19-1908   Tupper Dunn
Notary Public.

BIRTH AFFIDAVIT.

DEPARTMENT OF THE INTERIOR.
COMMISSION TO THE FIVE CIVILIZED TRIBES.

IN RE APPLICATION FOR ENROLLMENT, as a citizen of the Creek Nation, of Charlie Berryhill, born on the 26 day of January, 1904

Name of Father: Sam Berryhill   a citizen of the   Creek   Nation.
Name of Mother: Sophia Berryhill   a citizen of the   Creek   Nation.

Postoffice   Fentress Ind Ter.

AFFIDAVIT OF MOTHER.

UNITED STATES OF AMERICA, Indian Territory,
Western DISTRICT.

I, Sophia Berryhill, on oath state that I am 27 years of age and a citizen by blood, of the Creek Nation; that I am the lawful wife of Sam Berryhill, who is a citizen, by blood of the Creek Nation; that a male child was born to me on 26 day of January, 1904, that said child has been named Charlie Berryhill, and was living March 4, 1905.

her
Sophia x Berryhill
mark

Applications for Enrollment of Creek Newborn
Act of 1905   Volume IV

Witnesses To Mark:
{ E. D. Miles
{ R D Dill

Subscribed and sworn to before me this 15 day of March, 1905.

my com. exp Aug. 19-1908   Tupper Dunn
                                              Notary Public.

AFFIDAVIT OF ATTENDING PHYSICIAN OR MID-WIFE.

UNITED STATES OF AMERICA, Indian Territory,
  Western   DISTRICT.

I, Eliza Davis, a midwife, on oath state that I attended on Mrs. Sophia Berryhill, wife of Sam Berryhill on the 26 day of January, 1904; that there was born to her on said date a male child; that said child was living March 4, 1905, and is said to have been named Charlie Berryhill
                                              her
                              Eliza x Davis
                                              mark

Witnesses To Mark:
{ E. D. Miles
{ R D Dill

Subscribed and sworn to before me this 15 day of March, 1905.

my com. exp Aug. 19-1908   Tupper Dunn
                                              Notary Public.

Muskogee, Indian Territory, August 12, 1905.

Tupper Dunn,
    Okemah, Indian Territory.

Dear Sir:

Receipt is acknowledged of your letter of August 8, 1905, in which you ask when you can file for Charley and Clent Berryhill in the Creek Nation.

In reply you are advised that the Commission that the name of said Charley Berryhill is contained in a partial list of new-born Creeks by blood which is now pending before the Secretary of the Interior. When same is finally approved the parties in interest will be duly notified.

Applications for Enrollment of Creek Newborn
Act of 1905 Volume IV

In the matter of the application for the enrollment of said Clent Berryhill, you are informed that the parent of said child have been repeatedly advised that this office requires the affidavit of the midwife in attendance at its birth, or if there was no midwife in attendance, the affidavit of two dis-interested witnesses.

You are requested to inform Sophia Berryhill, the mother of said Clent Berryhill, that said affidavit is required and have same forwarded to this office at an early date.

Respectfully,

Acting Commissioner.

BIRTH AFFIDAVIT.

DEPARTMENT OF THE INTERIOR.
COMMISSION TO THE FIVE CIVILIZED TRIBES.

IN RE APPLICATION FOR ENROLLMENT, as a citizen of the Creek Nation, of Leah Frank, born on the 3 day of July, 1903

Name of Father: Barney Frank a citizen of the Creek Nation.
Name of Mother: Lidda Frank   a citizen of the Creek Nation.

Postoffice   Arbeka I.T.

AFFIDAVIT OF MOTHER.

UNITED STATES OF AMERICA, Indian Territory,
Western   DISTRICT.

I, Lidda Frank, on oath state that I am 27 years of age and a citizen by blood, of the Creek Nation; that I am the lawful wife of Barney Frank, who is a citizen, by blood of the Creek Nation; that a female child was born to me on 3 day of July, 1903, that said child has been named Leah Frank, and was living March 4, 1905.

        her
     Lidda x Frank
Witnesses To Mark: mark
 { E.D. Miles
   Tupper Dunn

Subscribed and sworn to before me this 15 day of March, 1905.

my com. exp Aug. 19-1908   Tupper Dunn
             Notary Public.

Applications for Enrollment of Creek Newborn
Act of 1905 Volume IV

AFFIDAVIT OF ATTENDING PHYSICIAN OR MID-WIFE.

UNITED STATES OF AMERICA, Indian Territory, }
    Western   DISTRICT.

I, Arney Harjo, a midwife, on oath state that I attended on Mrs. Lidda Frank, wife of Barney Frank on the 3 day of July, 1903; that there was born to her on said date a female child; that said child was living March 4, 1905, and is said to have been named Leah Frank

                        her
              Arney x Harjo
                  mark

Witnesses To Mark:
{ E.D. Miles
  Tupper Dunn

Subscribed and sworn to before me this 15 day of March, 1905.

my com. exp Aug. 19-1908   Tupper Dunn
                                      Notary Public.

BIRTH AFFIDAVIT.

DEPARTMENT OF THE INTERIOR.
COMMISSION TO THE FIVE CIVILIZED TRIBES.

IN RE APPLICATION FOR ENROLLMENT, as a citizen of the Creek Nation, of California Fixico, born on the 2nd day of June, 1902

Name of Father: Cano Fixico   a citizen of the   Creek   Nation.
Name of Mother: Lucy Fixico   a citizen of the Creek   Nation.

                        Postoffice   Paden, I. T.

AFFIDAVIT OF MOTHER.

UNITED STATES OF AMERICA, Indian Territory, }
    Western   DISTRICT.

I, Lucy Fixico, on oath state that I am about 22 years of age and a citizen by blood, of the Creek Nation; that I am the lawful wife of Cano Fixico (by Indian custom), who is a citizen, by blood of the Creek Nation; that a boy child was born

Applications for Enrollment of Creek Newborn
Act of 1905 Volume IV

to me on 2nd day of June, 1902, that said child has been named California Fixico, and was living March 4, 1905.

Her
Lucy x Fixico
mark

Witnesses To Mark:
{ Minnie Willingham
{ Fannie Herring

Subscribed and sworn to before me this 17th day of June, 1905.

J.L. Bruce
Notary Public.

AFFIDAVIT OF ATTENDING PHYSICIAN OR MID-WIFE.

UNITED STATES OF AMERICA, Indian Territory, }
Western DISTRICT.

I, Bessie Foster, a Mid-wife, on oath state that I attended on Mrs. Lucy Fixico, wife of Cano Fixico on the 2nd day of June, 1902; that there was born to her on said date a boy child; that said child was living March 4, 1905, and is said to have been named California Fixico

Her
Bessie x Foster
mark

Witnesses To Mark:
{ Minnie Willingham
{ Fannie Herring

Subscribed and sworn to before me this 17th day of June, 1905.

J.L. Bruce
Notary Public.

BIRTH AFFIDAVIT.

DEPARTMENT OF THE INTERIOR.
COMMISSION TO THE FIVE CIVILIZED TRIBES.

IN RE APPLICATION FOR ENROLLMENT, as a citizen of the Creek Nation, of California Fixico, born on the 2 day of June, 1902

Name of Father: Kano Fixico a citizen of the Creek Nation.
Name of Mother: Lucy Fixico (nee Kernells) a citizen of the Creek Nation.

Postoffice Paden, Indian Territory

Applications for Enrollment of Creek Newborn
Act of 1905 Volume IV

AFFIDAVIT OF MOTHER.

UNITED STATES OF AMERICA, Indian Territory,
Western DISTRICT.

I, Lucy Fixico, on oath state that I am about 22 years of age and a citizen by blood, of the Creek Nation; that I am the lawful wife of Kano Fixico, who is a citizen, by blood of the Creek Nation; that a male child was born to me on 2 day of June, 1902, that said child has been named California Fixico, and was living March 4, 1905. That Ladia Harjo attended on me at the birth of the child, but I have not been able to have her appear in person to corroborate this affidavit.

                                      her
                                Lucy x Fixico
Witnesses To Mark: mark
  Alex Posey
  DC Skaggs

Subscribed and sworn to before me this 15 day of March, 1905.

                                Drennan C Skaggs
                                Notary Public.

                                                Cr NC-302

Muskogee, Indian Territory, June 9, 1905.

Lucy Fixico,
    Paden, Indian Territory.

Dear Madam:

In the matter of the application for the enrollment of your minor child, California Fixico, as a citizen of the Creek Nation, you are advised that the Commission requires the affidavit of the midwife or physician in attendance at its birth.

For this purpose, there is herewith enclosed a blank form of birth affidavit. In having same executed, care should be taken to see that all blanks are properly filled, all names written in full and in the event that the person signing the affidavit is unable to write, signature by mark must be attested by two witnesses.

                            Respectfully,

1 B A   Chairman.

Applications for Enrollment of Creek Newborn
Act of 1905 Volume IV

BIRTH AFFIDAVIT.

DEPARTMENT OF THE INTERIOR.
COMMISSION TO THE FIVE CIVILIZED TRIBES.

IN RE APPLICATION FOR ENROLLMENT, as a citizen of the Creek Nation, of Herold D. Musgrove, born on the 13 day of December, 1904

Name of Father: George Musgrove   a citizen of the United States Nation.
(nee Fipps)
Name of Mother: Myrta May Musgrove   a citizen of the Creek Nation.

Postoffice   Paden, Indian Territory

AFFIDAVIT OF MOTHER.

UNITED STATES OF AMERICA, Indian Territory,
Western   DISTRICT.

I, Myrta May Musgrove, on oath state that I am 18 years of age and a citizen by blood, of the Creek Nation; that I am the lawful wife of George Musgrove, who is a citizen, by *(blank)* of the United States Nation; that a male child was born to me on 13 day of December, 1904, that said child has been named Herold D. Musgrove, and was living March 4, 1905.

Myrta May Musgrove

Witnesses To Mark:

{

Subscribed and sworn to before me this 15 day of March, 1905.

Drennan C Skaggs
Notary Public.

AFFIDAVIT OF ATTENDING PHYSICIAN OR MID-WIFE.

UNITED STATES OF AMERICA, Indian Territory,
Western   DISTRICT.

I, Alice M Fipps, a midwife, on oath state that I attended on Mrs. Myrta May Musgrove, wife of George Musgrove on the 13 day of December, 1904; that there was born to her on said date a male child; that said child was living March 4, 1905, and is said to have been named Herold D. Musgrove

Alice M Fipps

Witnesses To Mark:

{

Applications for Enrollment of Creek Newborn
Act of 1905   Volume IV

Subscribed and sworn to before me this 15 day of March , 1905.

                         Drennan C Skaggs
                         Notary Public.

BIRTH AFFIDAVIT.

DEPARTMENT OF THE INTERIOR.
COMMISSION TO THE FIVE CIVILIZED TRIBES.

IN RE APPLICATION FOR ENROLLMENT, as a citizen of the Creek Nation, of Eva Fipps , born on the 19 day of October , 1902

Name of Father:	Sam Fipps	a citizen of the United States Nation.
Name of Mother:	Alice M. Fipps	a citizen of the Creek Nation.

                 Postoffice   Okemah, Indian Territory

AFFIDAVIT OF MOTHER.

UNITED STATES OF AMERICA, Indian Territory,
     Western   DISTRICT.

     I, Alice M. Fipps , on oath state that I am 40 years of age and a citizen by blood , of the Creek Nation; that I am the lawful wife of Sam Fipps , who is a citizen, by *(blank)* of the United States Nation; that a female child was born to me on 19 day of October , 1902 , that said child has been named Eva Fipps , and was living March 4, 1905.

                         Alice M Fipps

Witnesses To Mark:

     Subscribed and sworn to before me this 15 day of March , 1905.

                         Drennan C Skaggs
                         Notary Public.

AFFIDAVIT OF ATTENDING PHYSICIAN OR MID-WIFE.

UNITED STATES OF AMERICA, Indian Territory,
     Western   DISTRICT.

     I, Nancy Fipps , a midwife , on oath state that I attended on Mrs. Alice M. Fipps , wife of Sam Fipps on the 19 day of October , 1902 ; that there was born to her

Applications for Enrollment of Creek Newborn
Act of 1905 Volume IV

on said date a female child; that said child was living March 4, 1905, and is said to have been named Eva Fipps

her
Nancy x Fipps
mark

Witnesses To Mark:
  { Alex Posey
    DC Skaggs

Subscribed and sworn to before me this 15 day of March, 1905.

Drennan C Skaggs
Notary Public.

NC 305.

Muskogee, Indian Territory, May 21, 1905.

Rhoda Spencer,
    Keokuk Falls, Oklahoma Territory.

Dear Madam:

In the matter of the application for the enrollment of your minor children, Lanah and Loma Spencer, as citizens of the Creek Nation, you are advised that you will be allowed thirty days from date within which to appear before the Commission at its office in Muskogee, Indian Territory, for the purpose of being examined under oath.

Respectfully,

Chairman.

N.C. 305.

Muskogee, Indian Territory, July 7, 1905.

Ramsey Spencer,
    Keokuk Falls, Oklahoma Territory.

Dear Sir:

In the matter of the application for the enrollment of your minor children, Lanah and Loma Spencer, as citizens of the Creek Nation, you are advised that you will be allowed a reasonable time within which to appear before this office for the purpose of electing in which nation, Creek or Seminole, you desire to have said children take their allotments of land.

Applications for Enrollment of Creek Newborn
Act of 1905   Volume IV

This office is unable to identify Rhoda Spencer, the mother of said children, as a citizen of the Creek Nation, and you are requested to state her maiden name, the names of her parents, the Creek Nation town to which she belongs, and, if possible, the number which appears on her deeds to land in the Creek Nation.

Yours truly,

Commissioner.

N C 305

Okemah I T   July 21, 1905

Hon Daws[sic] Commission
Muskogee, I T

Gentleman:

Enclosed find a list of my enrollment as Bank Chief Co-lah-yah of the Thle-wal-le Town Creek Nation I T

Name of Father   Ramsey Spencer
Name of Mother   Rhoda Spencer

names of children entirled[sic] to enrollment children of Rhoda Spencer a creek[sic] citizen

name of children   Lanah Spencer   aged 5 years
name 2nd child   Loma Spencer   aged one year

and i[sic] wish to have these allotments made in the creek[sic] nation[sic] and would like for you to take this matter up and have it adjusted

Yours truly

(signed) Rhoda Spencer
Keokuk Falls O[sic] T

NC 305.

Muskogee, Indian Territory, July 14, 1905.

Commissioner to the Five Civilized Tribes,
   Seminole Enrollment Division,
      Muskogee, Indian Territory.

Applications for Enrollment of Creek Newborn
Act of 1905 Volume IV

Gentlemen:

March 23, 1905, application was made to the Commission to the Five Civilized Tribes for the enrollment of Lanah Spencer, born July 18, 1901, and Loma Spencer, born May 12, 1904, as citizens by blood of the Creek Nation. It is stated in said application that the father of said children is Ramsey Spencer, a citizen of the Seminole Nation, and that the mother if Rhoda Spencer, an alleged citizen of the Creek Nation.

You are requested to inform the Creek Enrollment Division as to whether application has been made for the enrollment of said children, as citizens of the Seminole Nation, and if so, what disposition has been made of the same.

Respectfully,

Commissioner.

DEPARTMENT OF THE INTERIOR.
COMMISSION TO THE FIVE CIVILIZED TRIBES.

Muskogee, Indian Territory, July 18, 1905.

Chief Clerk,
Creek Enrollment Division.

Dear Sir:

Receipt is acknowledged of your letter of July 14, 1905 (NC-305) stating that application was made to the Commission to the Five Civilized Tribes for the enrollment of Lanah Spencer, born July 18, 1901, and Loma Spencer, born May 12, 1904, children of Ramsey Spencer, a citizen of the Seminole Nation, and Rhoda Spencer, an alleged citizen of the Creek Nation, as citizens by blood of the Creek Nation and requesting to be informed as to whether application has been made for the enrollment of said children as citizens of the Seminole Nation.

In reply to your letter you are advised that the Commission that it does not appear from an examination of the records of this office that any application was made to the Commission to the Five Civilized Tribes for the enrollment of said Lanah Spencer and Loma Spencer as citizens of the Seminole Nation.

Respectfully,

Tams Bixby   Commissioner.

Applications for Enrollment of Creek Newborn
Act of 1905   Volume IV

N.C. 305

Muskogee, Indian Territory, October 20, 1905.

Ludie Spencer,
    Care Ramsey Spencer,
        Keokuk Falls, Oklahoma Territory.

Dear Madam:

    In the matter of the application for the enrollment of your minor children, Lanah Spencer, born July 18, 1901, and Loma Spencer, born May 12, 1904, as citizens by blood of the Creek Nation, it will be necessary for you to file with this office the affidavit of the midwife or physician in attendance at the birth of said children.

    In the event that there was no physician or midwife in attendance when said children were born, this office desires the affidavits of two disinterested witnesses relative to the birth of each of said children. Said affidavits must set forth the names of said children, the dates of their birth, the names of their parents and whether or not they were living on March 4, 1905.

    In your affidavit of March 17, 1905 relative to the birth of the younger of said children, you give the name of said child as Loma Spencer, and in the affidavit of yourself and husband executed October 24, 1905, you spell the name of said child Lomah Spencer. Your name is signed to the affidavits of March 17, 1905, relative to the birth of said Loma and Lanah, Rhoda Spencer, and to your affidavit executed October 24, 1905, your named is signed Ludie Spencer.

    Your given name appears on the final roll of citizens by blood of the Creek Nation as Ludie.

    There are herewith enclosed forms of birth affidavits which have been partially filled out; you are requested to fill in the blank spaces in said affidavits, giving the correct name of said child, Loma or Lomah Spencer, in the affidavit relating to her birth, and to sign both of said affidavits with your correct name as the same appears in the boyd[sic] of the affidavit.

Respectfully,

AG-305   Commissioner.

NC-305

Muskogee, Indian Territory, July 26, 1905.

Rhoda Spencer,
    Keokuk Falls, Oklahoma Territory.

Applications for Enrollment of Creek Newborn
Act of 1905   Volume IV

Dear Madam:

In the matter of the application for the enrollment of your minor children, Lanah and Lomah Spencer, as citizens of the Creek Nation, you are advised that it is impossible, without further information, to identify you as a citizen of the Creek Nation.

You are requested to state your maiden name, the names of your parents, the Creek Indian Town to which you belong, and if possible, the roll number as same appears on your deeds to land in the Creek Nation which will help identify you as a citizen thereof.

This matter should receive your prompt attention.

       Respectfully,

              Commissioner.

(The above letter given again.)

(The letter below typed as given.)

      COPY.   NC 305

      Okemah, I.T.   August 23, 1905

Hon Daws Commission To Five Civilized Tribes
    Muskogee, I.T.

Gentleman:

In reply to your letter of the July 26th 1905 in regard the enrollment of my minor children Lanah and Lomah Spencer would state that my fathers name is Chisse Micco my mothers name is Sissie Micco my town king name Co-lah-yah of the Thle-wah-le Town. I made my fileing june 20th 1899 the name that i filed by was Ludie King selection of land SE 1/4 section 20 township 11 north range 17 160 A in the Muskogee land office. these children are entitled to land and i am anxious to get them filed before all the good land is taken up

since i filed i married Ramsey Spencer a Seminole indian and for the reason i have been writing as Rhoda Spencer Please report at once and oblige your truly

    (signed) Ludie King nee. (her x mark) Spencer

Witness to mark
Lamsey Spencer
H G Malat

Applications for Enrollment of Creek Newborn
Act of 1905 Volume IV

NC-305

Muskogee, Indian Territory, August 26, 1905.

Ludie Spencer,
    Okemah, Indian Territory.

Dear Madam:

    Receipt is acknowledged of your communication of August 23, 1905, giving information which enables this Office to identify you as a citizen of the Creek Nation; you state that you are anxious to get your minor children, Lanah and Lomah Spencer, filed before all the good land is taken up.

    You are advised that before the matter of the enrollment of your said children can be finally determined, it will be necessary that you file with this Office the joint affidavit of yourself and the Seminole father of said children, electing in which Nation you desire to have them enrolled and take their allotments of land.

    This matter should receive your prompt attention.

Respectfully,

Commissioner.

(The above letter given again.)

Muskogee, Indian Territory, December 13, 1905.

Rhoda Spencer (or Ludie King),
    Care Ramsey Spencer,
        Keokuk Falls, Oklahoma.

Dear Madam:

    In the matter of the application for the enrollment of your minor children, Lanah and Loma Spencer, as a citizen of the Creek Nation, you are advised that this office requires the affidavits of two disinterested witnesses relative to their birth. Said affidavits must set forth the names of said children, the dates of their birth, and names of their parents and whether or not they were living on March 4, 1905.

    This matter should receive your prompt attention.

Applications for Enrollment of Creek Newborn
Act of 1905   Volume IV

Respectfully,

Acting Commissioner.

(The letter below typed as given.)

(Copy)

Okemah. I.T.
July 21, 1905.

Hon. Daws[sic] Commission
Muskogee, I. T.

Gentlemen:

Enclosed find a list of my enrollment as
Bank Chief - CO-lah-yah. of the Thle-wal-le. Town. Creek nation. I.T.

Name of Father.	Ramsey Spencer.
Name of Mother.	Rhoda Spencer.

names of children entitled to enrollment children of Rhoda Spencer a creek citizen

name of children	Lanah Spencer.	aged 5 years.
name 2nd child.	Loma Spencer.	aged one year.
and i wish to have these allotments made in the creek nation
and would like for you to take this matter up and have it adjusted

yours truly.

(signed)	RHODA SPENCER

Keo Kuk Falls OT.

(The letter below typed as given.)

(Copy)   NC. 305

Okemah I. T.   August 23 1905

Hon Daws Commission To Five Civilized Tribes

Muskogee, I.T.
Gentleman:

Applications for Enrollment of Creek Newborn
Act of 1905   Volume IV

In reply to your letter of the July 26th 1905 in regard the enrollment of my minor children Lanah and Lomah Spencer would state that my fathers name is Chisse Micco my mothers name is Sissie Micco my town king name Co-lah-yah of the Thle-wah-le Town. I made my fileing june 20th 1899 the name that i filed by was Ludie King selection of land SE 1/4 section 20 township 11 north range 17 160 A in the Muskogee land office. these children are entitled to land and i am anxious to get them filed before all the good land is taken up

since i filed i married Ramsey Spencer a seminole indian and for the reason i have been writeing as Rhoda Spencer

Please report at once and oblige yours truly

        (signed) LUDIE KING nee. (her x mark) SPENCER

Witness to mark
Lamsey Spencer
H G Malat

NC 305.

        Muskogee, Indian Territory, October 31, 1906.

Chief Clerk,
    Seminole Enrollment Division,
        Muskogee, Indian Territory.

Dear Sir:

There is on file in this office an application for the enrollment of Lanah Spencer, born July 18, 1901, and of Loma Spencer, born May 12, 1904; the parents of said children are given as Ramsey Spencer, a citizen of the Seminole nation, and Ludia Spencer, who is identified as a citizen by blood of the Creek Nation, opposite roll number 500.

You are advised that the Commission that the names of said children are contained in the list of new born citizens by blood of the Creek Nation (enrolled under the act of Congress approved March 3, 1905), approved by the Secretary of the Interior October 15, 1906, opposite roll numbers 1021 and 1022, respectively.

        Respectfully,

                              Commissioner.

Applications for Enrollment of Creek Newborn
Act of 1905 Volume IV

DEPARTMENT OF THE INTERIOR
COMMISSIONER TO THE FIVE CIVILIZED TRIBES.

IN THE MATTER OF THE ENROLLMENT OF Lanah Spencer and Lomah Spencer, as citizens by blood of the Creek Nation, Indian Territory: Father, Ramsey Spencer, a Seminole citizen; Mother, Ludie Spencer (or Rhoda Spencer), a citizen of the Creek Nation, P. O., Keokuk Falls, O.T.

United States of America, Indian Territory,
       Western Judicial District.

Affiants, Ludie Spencer (or Rhoda Spencer) and Ramsey Spencer, being first duly sworn, on their oaths depose and say that they are each above the age of twenty one years; that said Ludie Spencer is a citizen by blood of the Creek Nation, and the mother of said Lanah Spencer and Lomah Spencer, minor children; and that said Ramsey Spencer is a citizen by blood of the Seminole Nation, and the father of said Lanah Spencer and Lomah Spencer.

And affiants state that they desire to have said Lanah Spencer and Lomah Spencer enrolled as citizens of the Creek Nation, and that they be permitted to take allotment in said Nation.
                                her
                            Ludie Spencer x
                                 mark
Witnesses;   Ramsey Spencer
    John W Willmott
    A S McKennon

Subscribed and sworn to before me at Wewoka, I.T., this the 24th day of October, A.D., 1905. My com. expires Oct. 5, 1906.

                                John W. Willmott
                                Notary Public.

BIRTH AFFIDAVIT.

DEPARTMENT OF THE INTERIOR.
COMMISSION TO THE FIVE CIVILIZED TRIBES.

IN RE APPLICATION FOR ENROLLMENT, as a citizen of the Creek Nation, of Loma Spencer, born on the 12 day of May, 1904

Name of Father:	Ramsey Spencer	a citizen of the	Seminole	Nation.
Name of Mother:	Ludie Spencer	a citizen of the	Creek	Nation.

Applications for Enrollment of Creek Newborn
Act of 1905 Volume IV

Postoffice   Keokuk Falls, Oklahoma

AFFIDAVIT OF MOTHER.

UNITED STATES OF AMERICA, Indian Territory,
Western   DISTRICT.

I, Ludie Spencer , on oath state that I am 35 years of age and a citizen by blood , of the Creek Nation; that I am the lawful wife of Ramsey Spencer , who is a citizen, by blood of the Seminole Nation; that a male child was born to me on 12 day of May , 1904 , that said child has been named Loma Spencer , and was living March 4, 1905.

            her
            Ludie Spencer x
            mark

Witnesses To Mark:
{ A S McKennon
  Jno. W. Willmott

Subscribed and sworn to before me this 6" day of November , 1905.

My com exp Oct 5-1906   John W. Willmott
              Notary Public.

AFFIDAVIT OF ATTENDING PHYSICIAN OR MID-WIFE.

UNITED STATES OF AMERICA, Indian Territory,
Western   DISTRICT.

We   we   or visited
~~I~~, Nancy and Echoille Spencer , a *(blank)* , on oath state that ~~I~~ attended on ^ Mrs. Ludie Spencer , wife of Ramsey Spencer on the 15th day of May , 1904 ; that there was born to her a few days prior to ~~on~~ said date a male child; that said child was living March 4, 1905, and is said to have been named Loma Spencer

          her
          Nancy x
Witnesses To Mark: mark   his
{ Jno. W. Willmott   Echoille Spencer x
  A S McKennon   mark

Subscribed and sworn to before me this 14th day of November, 1905.

My com exp Oct 5-1906   John W. Willmott
              Notary Public.

Applications for Enrollment of Creek Newborn
Act of 1905   Volume IV

BIRTH AFFIDAVIT.

DEPARTMENT OF THE INTERIOR.
COMMISSION TO THE FIVE CIVILIZED TRIBES.

IN RE APPLICATION FOR ENROLLMENT, as a citizen of the Creek Nation, of Lanah Spencer, born on the 18 day of July, 1901

Name of Father:	Ramsey Spencer	a citizen of the Seminole	Nation.
Name of Mother:	Rhoda Spencer	a citizen of the Creek	Nation.

Postoffice   Keokuk Falls, Oklahoma

AFFIDAVIT OF MOTHER.

UNITED STATES OF AMERICA, Indian Territory,
Western   DISTRICT.

I, Rhoda Spencer, on oath state that I am about 35 years of age and a citizen by blood, of the Creek Nation; that I am the lawful wife of Ramsey Spencer, who is a citizen, by blood of the Seminole Nation; that a female child was born to me on 18 day of July, 1901, that said child has been named Lanah Spencer, and was living March 4, 1905.

           her
         Rhoda x Spencer
Witnesses To Mark: mark
{ Alex Posey
 DC Skaggs

Subscribed and sworn to before me this 17 day of March, 1905.

         Drennan C Skaggs
         Notary Public.

AFFIDAVIT OF ATTENDING PHYSICIAN OR MID-WIFE.

UNITED STATES OF AMERICA, Indian Territory,
Western   DISTRICT.

                my wife
I, Ramsey Spencer, ~~a~~ *(blank)*, on oath state that I attended ~~on~~ ^ Mrs. Rhoda Spencer, ~~wife of~~ *(blank)* on the 18 day of July, 1901; that there was born to her on said date a female child; that said child was living March 4, 1905, and is said to have been named Lanah Spencer

         Ramsey Spencer
Witnesses To Mark:
{

Applications for Enrollment of Creek Newborn
Act of 1905 Volume IV

Subscribed and sworn to before me this 17 day of March, 1905.

                        Drennan C Skaggs
                        Notary Public.

BIRTH AFFIDAVIT.

DEPARTMENT OF THE INTERIOR.
COMMISSION TO THE FIVE CIVILIZED TRIBES.

IN RE APPLICATION FOR ENROLLMENT, as a citizen of the Creek Nation, of Loma Spencer, born on the 12 day of May, 1904

Name of Father:	Ramsey Spencer	a citizen of the Seminole	Nation.
Name of Mother:	Rhoda Spencer	a citizen of the Creek	Nation.

                    Postoffice   Keokuk Falls, Oklahoma

AFFIDAVIT OF MOTHER.

UNITED STATES OF AMERICA, Indian Territory, ⎫
    Western   DISTRICT. ⎭

I, Rhoda Spencer, on oath state that I am about 35 years of age and a citizen by blood, of the Creek Nation; that I am the lawful wife of Ramsey Spencer, who is a citizen, by blood of the Seminole Nation; that a male child was born to me on 12 day of May, 1904, that said child has been named Loma Spencer, and was living March 4, 1905.

                                      her
                             Rhoda x Spencer
Witnesses To Mark: mark
  ⎰ Alex Posey
  ⎱ DC Skaggs

Subscribed and sworn to before me this 17 day of March, 1905.

                        Drennan C Skaggs
                        Notary Public.

AFFIDAVIT OF ATTENDING PHYSICIAN OR MID-WIFE.

UNITED STATES OF AMERICA, Indian Territory, ⎫
    Western   DISTRICT. ⎭

                                                my wife
    I, Ramsey Spencer, ~~a~~ *(blank)*, on oath state that I attended ~~on~~ ^ Mrs. Rhoda Spencer, ~~wife of~~ *(blank)* on the 12 day of May, 1904 ; that there was born to her on

Applications for Enrollment of Creek Newborn
Act of 1905 Volume IV

said date a   male   child; that said child was living March 4, 1905, and is said to have been named Loma Spencer

Ramsey Spencer

Witnesses To Mark:
{

Subscribed and sworn to before me this 17 day of March, 1905.

Drennan C Skaggs
Notary Public.

BIRTH AFFIDAVIT.

DEPARTMENT OF THE INTERIOR.
COMMISSION TO THE FIVE CIVILIZED TRIBES.

IN RE APPLICATION FOR ENROLLMENT, as a citizen of the Creek Nation, of Lanah Spencer, born on the 18 day of July, 1901

Name of Father: Ramsey Spencer   a citizen of the   Citizen[sic]   Nation.
Name of Mother: Ludie Spencer   a citizen of the   Creek   Nation.

Postoffice   Keokuk Falls, Oklahoma

AFFIDAVIT OF MOTHER.

UNITED STATES OF AMERICA, Indian Territory, }
     Western   DISTRICT.

I, Ludie Spencer, on oath state that I am 35 years of age and a citizen by blood, of the Creek Nation; that I am the lawful wife of Ramsey Spencer, who is a citizen, by blood of the Seminole Nation; that a female child was born to me on 18 day of July, 1901, that said child has been named Lanah Spencer, and was living March 4, 1905.

her
Ludie Spencer x
mark

Witnesses To Mark:
 { A S McKennon
   Jno W. Willmott

Subscribed and sworn to before me this 6" day of November, 1905.

My com exp Oct 5 1906   John W. Willmott
Notary Public.

Applications for Enrollment of Creek Newborn
Act of 1905 Volume IV

AFFIDAVIT OF ATTENDING PHYSICIAN OR MID-WIFE.

UNITED STATES OF AMERICA, Indian Territory, }
    Western   DISTRICT.

    I, Mahala Stidham , a Midwife , on oath state that I attended on Mrs. Ludie Spencer , wife of Ramsey Spencer on the 18" day of July , 1901 ; that there was born to her on said date a female child; that said child was living March 4, 1905, and is said to have been named Lanah Spencer

                                            her
                                   Mahala x Stidham
Witnesses To Mark: mark
 { A S McKinnon
   Jno. W. Willmott

    Subscribed and sworn to before me this 6" day of November, 1905.

    My com exp Oct 5 1906   John W. Willmott
                                              Notary Public.

BIRTH AFFIDAVIT.
DEPARTMENT OF THE INTERIOR.
COMMISSION TO THE FIVE CIVILIZED TRIBES.

    IN RE APPLICATION FOR ENROLLMENT, as a citizen of the Seminole Nation, of Senar Wolf , born on the 5 day of July , 1902

                                                                               #1728
Name of Father: Wallace Wolf   a citizen of the Seminole   Nation.
Name of Mother: Nancy Wolf   a citizen of the   Creek   Nation.

                              Postoffice   Little I.T.

AFFIDAVIT OF MOTHER.

UNITED STATES OF AMERICA, Indian Territory, }
    (blank)   DISTRICT.

    I, Nancy Wolf , on oath state that I am 38 years of age and a citizen by Birth , of the Creek Nation; that I am the lawful wife of Wallace Wolf , who is a citizen, by Birth of the Seminole Nation; that a Female child was born to me on 5 day of July , 1902 , that said child has been named Senar , and was living March 4, 1905.

                                                        her
                                                   Nancy x Wolf
                                                        mark

Applications for Enrollment of Creek Newborn
Act of 1905   Volume IV

Witnesses To Mark:
{ T H Smith
{ William Mitchell

    Subscribed and sworn to before me this 11" day of July , 1905.

                              WW Lucas
                                   Notary Public.

AFFIDAVIT OF ATTENDING PHYSICIAN OR MID-WIFE.

UNITED STATES OF AMERICA, Indian Territory,
   (blank)   DISTRICT.

    I, Mary Cosa , a midwife , on oath state that I attended on Mrs. Nancy Wolf , wife of Wallace Wolf on the 5th day of July , 1902 ; that there was born to her on said date a   Female   child; that said child was living March 4, 1905, and is said to have been named Senar

                              her
                        Mary x Cosa
Witnesses To Mark: mark
{ T H Smith
{ William Mitchell

    Subscribed and sworn to before me this 11" day of July , 1905.

                              WW Lucas
                                   Notary Public.

BIRTH AFFIDAVIT.
DEPARTMENT OF THE INTERIOR.
COMMISSION TO THE FIVE CIVILIZED TRIBES.

    IN RE APPLICATION FOR ENROLLMENT, as a citizen of the Creek Nation, of Seaner Wolf , born on the 5 day of July , 1902

Name of Father:	Wallace Wolf	a citizen of the Seminole	Nation.
Name of Mother:	Nancy Wolf	a citizen of the Creek	Nation.

                        Postoffice   Keokuk Falls, Oklahoma

Applications for Enrollment of Creek Newborn
Act of 1905 Volume IV

AFFIDAVIT OF MOTHER.

UNITED STATES OF AMERICA, Indian Territory, }
Western   DISTRICT.

I, Nancy Wolf , on oath state that I am about 38 years of age and a citizen by blood , of the Creek Nation; that I am the lawful wife of Wallace Wolf , who is a citizen, by blood of the Seminole Nation; that a female child was born to me on 5 day of July , 1902 , that said child has been named Seaner Wolf , and was living March 4, 1905.

                                          her
                                  Nancy x Wolf

Witnesses To Mark: mark
{ Alex Posey
{ DC Skaggs

Subscribed and sworn to before me this 17 day of March , 1905.

                                Drennan C Skaggs
                                Notary Public.

AFFIDAVIT OF ATTENDING PHYSICIAN OR MID-WIFE.

UNITED STATES OF AMERICA, Indian Territory, }
Western   DISTRICT.

                                                  my wife
I, Wallace Wolf , a ~~(blank)~~ , on oath state that I attended on ^ Mrs. Nancy Wolf , ~~wife of~~ (blank) on the 5 day of July , 1902 ; that there was born to her on said date a female child; that said child was living March 4, 1905, and is said to have been named Seaner Wolf
                                    his
                                Wallace x Wolf
Witnesses To Mark: mark
{ Alex Posey
{ DC Skaggs

Subscribed and sworn to before me this 17 day of March , 1905.

                                Drennan C Skaggs
                                Notary Public.

                                                   Cr NC-306

Muskogee, Indian Territory, June 9, 1905.

Nancy Wolf,
    Keokuk Falls, Oklahoma Territory.

Dear Madam:

Applications for Enrollment of Creek Newborn
Act of 1905   Volume IV

In the matter of the application for the enrollment of your minor child, Senar Wolf, as a citizen of the Creek Nation, you are advised that the Commission requires the affidavit of the midwife or physician in attendance at its birth. For this purpose, there is herewith enclosed a blank form of birth affidavit. In having same executed, same care should be exercised to see that all blanks are properly filled, all names written in full and in the event that the person signing the affidavit is unable to write, signature by mark must be attested by two witnesses.

You are further advised that it will be necessary for you and the Seminole father of said child to appear before the Commission, at its office, in Muskogee, Indian Territory, at an early date, to elect in which Nation you desire to have said child enrolled.

Respectfully,

1 B A   Chairman.

NC 306.

Muskogee, Indian Territory, July 15, 1905.

Chief Clerk,
    Seminole Enrollment Division,
        Muskogee, Indian Territory.

Dear Sir:

March 23, 1905, application was made to the Commission to the Five Civilized Tribes for the enrollment of Seaner Wolf, born July 5, 1902, as a citizen of the Creek Nation. It is stated in said application that the father of said child is Wallace Wolf, a citizen of the Seminole Nation, and that the mother is Nancy Wolf, a citizen of the Creek Nation.

You are requested to inform the Creek Enrollment Division as to whether application has been made for the enrollment of said Seaner Wolf, as a citizen of the Seminole Nation, and if so, what disposition has been made of the same.

Respectfully,

Commissioner.

Applications for Enrollment of Creek Newborn
Act of 1905 Volume IV

DEPARTMENT OF THE INTERIOR.
COMMISSION TO THE FIVE CIVILIZED TRIBES.

Muskogee, Indian Territory, July 19, 1905.

Chief Clerk,
    Creek Enrollment Division.

Dear Sir:

    Receipt is hereby acknowledged of your letter of July 15, 1905, (NC-306) stating that application was made to the Commission to the Five Civilized Tribes for the enrollment of Seaner Wolf, born July 5, 1902, child of Wallace Wolf, a citizen of the Seminole Nation, and Nancy Wolf. a citizen of the Creek Nation, as a citizen by blood of the Creek Nation and requesting to be informed as to whether application has been made for the enrollment of said child as a citizen of the Seminole Nation.

    In reply to your letter you are advised that the Commission that it does not appear from an examination of the records of this office that any application was made for the enrollment of the said Seaner Wolf as a citizen of the Seminole Nation.

Respectfully,

Tams Bixby   Commissioner.

NC 306.

Muskogee, Indian Territory, November 12, 1905.

Chief Clerk,
    Seminole Enrollment Division,
        General Office.

Dear Sir:

    You are hereby advised that the name of Seaner Wolf, born to Wallace Wolf, an alleged citizen of the Seminole Nation, and Nancie Wolf, a citizen by blood of the Creek Nation, is contained in the schedule of New Born citizens of the Creek Nation, approved by the Secretary of the Interior August 22, 1905, opposite Roll No. 298.

Respectfully,

Commissioner.

Applications for Enrollment of Creek Newborn
Act of 1905 Volume IV

BIRTH AFFIDAVIT.

DEPARTMENT OF THE INTERIOR.
COMMISSION TO THE FIVE CIVILIZED TRIBES.

IN RE APPLICATION FOR ENROLLMENT, as a citizen of the Creek Nation, of Oceola Foster, born on the 14 day of February, 1905

Name of Father: David Foster   a citizen of the   Creek   Nation.
Name of Mother: Melanie Foster   a citizen of the   Creek   Nation.

                  Postoffice   Paden, Indian Territory

AFFIDAVIT OF MOTHER.

UNITED STATES OF AMERICA, Indian Territory,
    Western   DISTRICT.

    I, Melanie Foster , on oath state that I am about 27 years of age and a citizen by blood , of the Creek Nation; that I am the lawful wife of David Foster , who is a citizen, by blood of the Creek Nation; that a male child was born to me on 14 day of February , 1905 , that said child has been named Osceola Foster , and was living March 4, 1905.

                                  her
                            Melanie x Foster
Witnesses To Mark: mark
  { Alex Posey
    DC Skaggs

    Subscribed and sworn to before me this 14" day of March , 1905.

                          Drennan C Skaggs
                              Notary Public.

AFFIDAVIT OF ATTENDING PHYSICIAN OR MID-WIFE.

UNITED STATES OF AMERICA, Indian Territory,
    Western   DISTRICT.

    I, Betsey London , a midwife , on oath state that I attended on Mrs. Melanie Foster , wife of David Foster on the 14 day of February , 1905 ; that there was born to her on said date a male child; that said child was living March 4, 1905, and is said to have been named Osceola Foster

                                  her
                            Betsy x London
Witnesses To Mark: mark
  { Alex Posey
    DC Skaggs

Applications for Enrollment of Creek Newborn
Act of 1905 Volume IV

Subscribed and sworn to before me this 14" day of March , 1905.

                                        Drennan C Skaggs
                                        Notary Public.

BIRTH AFFIDAVIT.

DEPARTMENT OF THE INTERIOR.
COMMISSION TO THE FIVE CIVILIZED TRIBES.

IN RE APPLICATION FOR ENROLLMENT, as a citizen of the Creek Nation, of Jimmie Foster, born on the 24 day of December , 1902

Name of Father:	David Foster	a citizen of the	Creek	Nation.
Name of Mother:	Melanie Foster	a citizen of the	Creek	Nation.

                             Postoffice   Paden, Indian Territory

---

AFFIDAVIT OF MOTHER.

UNITED STATES OF AMERICA, Indian Territory, }
     Western   DISTRICT.

    I, Melanie Foster , on oath state that I am about 27 years of age and a citizen by blood , of the Creek Nation; that I am the lawful wife of David Foster , who is a citizen, by blood of the Creek Nation; that a male child was born to me on 24 day of December , 1902 , that said child has been named Jimmie Foster , and was living March 4, 1905.

                                                  her
                                    Melanie x Foster
                                          mark

Witnesses To Mark:
  { Alex Posey
    DC Skaggs

        Subscribed and sworn to before me this 14 day of March , 1905.

                                        Drennan C Skaggs
                                        Notary Public.

Applications for Enrollment of Creek Newborn
Act of 1905 Volume IV

AFFIDAVIT OF ATTENDING PHYSICIAN OR MID-WIFE.

UNITED STATES OF AMERICA, Indian Territory, ⎱
    Western   DISTRICT. ⎰

I, Mesaley Foster , a midwife , on oath state that I attended on Mrs. Melanie Foster , wife of David Foster on the 24 day of December , 1902 ; that there was born to her on said date a male child; that said child was living March 4, 1905, and is said to have been named Jimmie Foster

                                her
                          Mesaley x Foster
Witnesses To Mark: mark
  ⎰ Alex Posey
  ⎱ DC Skaggs

Subscribed and sworn to before me this 14" day of March , 1905.

                            Drennan C Skaggs
                              Notary Public.

BIRTH AFFIDAVIT.

DEPARTMENT OF THE INTERIOR.
COMMISSION TO THE FIVE CIVILIZED TRIBES.

IN RE APPLICATION FOR ENROLLMENT, as a citizen of the Creek Nation, of Roland E. Kelly , born on the 14th day of March , 1903

Name of Father: Ferdinand Kelly   a citizen of the   Creek   Nation.
Name of Mother: Lizzie Moore Kelly   a citizen of the   CreekNation.

                      Postoffice   Haskell, I.T.

AFFIDAVIT OF MOTHER.

UNITED STATES OF AMERICA, Indian Territory, ⎱
    (blank)   DISTRICT. ⎰

I, Lizzie Moore Kelly , on oath state that I am 35 years of age and a citizen by blood , of the Creek Nation; that I am the lawful wife of Ferdinand Kelly , who is a citizen, by blood of the Creek Nation; that a Male child was born to me on 14th day of March , 1903 , that said child has been named Roland E. Kelly , and is now living.

                            Lizzie Moore Kelly
Witnesses To Mark:
  ⎰
  ⎱

Applications for Enrollment of Creek Newborn
Act of 1905 Volume IV

Subscribed and sworn to before me this 20th day of March, 1905.

           E.B. Harris
           Notary Public.

AFFIDAVIT OF ATTENDING PHYSICIAN OR MID-WIFE.

UNITED STATES OF AMERICA, Indian Territory, ⎫
  Western   DISTRICT. ⎬

  I, Phyllis Smith, a Mid-wife, on oath state that I attended on Mrs. Lizzie Moore Kelly, wife of Ferdinand Kelly on the 14th day of March, 1903; that there was born to her on said date a male child; that said child is now living and is said to have been named Roland E. Kelly

           her
Witnesses To Mark: Phyllis x Smith
 { Paul Crowder   mark
   Eli Combs

Subscribed and sworn to before me this 20th day of March, 1905.

           E.B. Harris
           Notary Public.

BIRTH AFFIDAVIT.

DEPARTMENT OF THE INTERIOR.
COMMISSION TO THE FIVE CIVILIZED TRIBES.

  IN RE APPLICATION FOR ENROLLMENT, as a citizen of the Creek Nation, of Elizabeth Kelly, born on the 12th day of January, 1905
Name of Father: Ferdinand Kelly   a citizen of the Creek Nation.
Name of Mother: Lizzie Moore Kelly   a citizen of the CreekNation.

         Postoffice Haskell, I.T.

AFFIDAVIT OF MOTHER.

UNITED STATES OF AMERICA, Indian Territory, ⎫
  (blank)   DISTRICT. ⎬

  I, Lizzie Moore Kelly, on oath state that I am 35 years of age and a citizen by blood, of the Creek Nation; that I am the lawful wife of Ferdinand Kelly, who is a citizen, by blood of the Creek Nation; that a female child was born to me on 12th

Applications for Enrollment of Creek Newborn
Act of 1905 Volume IV

day of January, 1905, that said child has been named Elizabeth Kelly, and is now living.

Lizzie Moore Kelly

Witnesses To Mark:
{

Subscribed and sworn to before me this 20th day of March, 1905.

E.B. Harris
Notary Public.

AFFIDAVIT OF ATTENDING PHYSICIAN OR MID-WIFE.

UNITED STATES OF AMERICA, Indian Territory, ⎱
   Western   DISTRICT.   ⎰

I, P.S. Mitchell, a Physician, on oath state that I attended on Mrs. Lizzie Moore Kelly, wife of Ferdinand Kelly on the 12th day of January, 1905; that there was born to her on said date a female child; that said child is now living and is said to have been named Elizabeth Kelly

P.S. Mitchell M.D.

Witnesses To Mark:
{

Subscribed and sworn to before me this 20th day of March, 1905.

E.B. Harris
Notary Public.

NC 309.

Muskogee, Indian Territory, June 5, 1905.

Sarah Harjo,
    Okemah, Indian Territory.

Dear Madam:

In the matter of the application for the enrollment of your minor child, Estella Smith, as a citizen of the Creek Nation, you are advised that the Commission requires the affidavits of two disinterested witnesses as to the birth of said child.

Applications for Enrollment of Creek Newborn
Act of 1905 Volume IV

There are herewith enclosed two blank forms of birth affidavits, and in executing same care should be exercised to see that all blanks are properly filled, all names written in full and in the event that the persons signing the affidavits are unable to write, signatures by mark must be attested by two witnesses. Each affidavit must be executed before a Notary Public and the notarial seal and signature of the officer must be attached to each separate affidavit.

Respectfully,

2 BA.   Commissioner in Charge.

N.C. 309.

Muskogee, Indian Territory, July 7, 1905.

Sarah Harjo,
    Okemah, Indian Territory.

Dear Madam:

In the matter of the application for the enrollment of Estella Smith, as a citizen of the Creek Nation, you are advised that this office requires the affidavits of two disinterested witnesses to the birth of said child.

There are herewith enclosed two blank forms of birth affidavits. In having same executed, same care should be exercised to see that all blanks are properly filled, all names written in full, and in the event that the persons signing the affidavits are unable to write, signatures by mark must be attested by two witnesses.

Respectfully,

2 B A   Commissioner in Charge.

AFFIDAVIT OF ATTENDING PHYSICIAN OR MID-WIFE.

UNITED STATES OF AMERICA, Indian Territory,
   Western Judicial   DISTRICT.

~~I,~~ We Wisey Solomon and Albert Harjo , ~~a~~ *(blank)* , on oath state that ~~I~~ we ~~attended on~~ are acquainted on Mrs. Sarah Harjo , wife of Huntie Harjo on the 14 day of January , 1903 ; that there was born to her on said date a male child; that said child was living March 4, 1905, and is said to have been named Estella Smith

her
Wisey x Solomon
mark
Albert Harjo

Applications for Enrollment of Creek Newborn
Act of 1905 Volume IV

Witnesses To Mark:
{ Albert Harjo
{ Tupper Dunn

Subscribed and sworn to before me this 11 day of September, 1905.

my com exp. Aug. 19-1908   Tupper Dunn
                                             Notary Public.

BIRTH AFFIDAVIT.

DEPARTMENT OF THE INTERIOR.
COMMISSION TO THE FIVE CIVILIZED TRIBES.

IN RE APPLICATION FOR ENROLLMENT, as a citizen of the Creek Nation, of Estella Smith, born on the 14th day of January, 1903
(Former Husband)
Name of Father: Belcher Smith   a citizen of the   Creek   Nation.
Name of Mother: Sarah Harjo   a citizen of the   Creek   Nation.

Postoffice   Okemah, I.T.

AFFIDAVIT OF MOTHER.

UNITED STATES OF AMERICA, Indian Territory, }
Western Judicial   DISTRICT. }

I, Sarah Harjo, on oath state that I am 23 years of age and a citizen by Blood, of the Creek Nation; that I am the lawful wife of Huntie Harjo, who is a citizen, by Blood of the Creek Nation; that a Female child was born to me on 14th day of January, 1903, that said child has been named Estella Smith, and was living March 4, 1905.

                                       Sarah Harjo

Witnesses To Mark:
{

Subscribed and sworn to before me this 3rd day of July, 1905.

My Commission Expires Sept 6th 1906   John H Phillips
                                                          Notary Public.

Applications for Enrollment of Creek Newborn
Act of 1905 Volume IV

AFFIDAVIT OF ATTENDING PHYSICIAN OR MID-WIFE.

UNITED STATES OF AMERICA, Indian Territory, ⎱
Western Judicial   DISTRICT. ⎰

    I, Huntie Harjo , a Witness , on oath state that I ~~attended on Mrs~~. know the fact that said , ~~wife of~~ child was born to Sarah Harjo on the 14th day of January , 1903 ; that there was born to her on said date a   Female   child; that said child was living March 4, 1905, and is said to have been named Estella Smith

                                           Huntie Harjo

Witnesses To Mark:
{

    Subscribed and sworn to before me this 3rd   day of July , 1905.

        My Commission Expires Sept 6th 1906   John H Phillips
                                                                   Notary Public.

(The above birth affidavit given again)

BIRTH AFFIDAVIT.

DEPARTMENT OF THE INTERIOR.
COMMISSION TO THE FIVE CIVILIZED TRIBES.

    IN RE APPLICATION FOR ENROLLMENT, as a citizen of the Creek Nation, of Estella Smith, born on the 14 day of January , 1903

| Name of Father: | Belcher Smith | a citizen of the Creek | Nation. |
| Name of Mother: | Sarah Harjo | a citizen of the   Creek | Nation. |

                                  Postoffice   Okemah, Ind.Ter.

AFFIDAVIT OF MOTHER.

UNITED STATES OF AMERICA, Indian Territory, ⎱
       Western   DISTRICT. ⎰

    I, Sarah Harjo , on oath state that I am about 23   years of age and a citizen by blood , of the Creek   Nation; that I ~~am~~   was formerly   the lawful wife of Belcher Smith, who is a citizen, by   blood of the Creek   Nation; that a female child was born to me on   14   day of January, 1903 , that said child has been named Estella Smith , and was living March 4, 1905. That no one attended on me as midwife or physician at the time the child was born.

Applications for Enrollment of Creek Newborn
Act of 1905 Volume IV

Sarah Harjo

Witnesses To Mark: {

Subscribed and sworn to before me this 16 day of March, 1905.

Drennan C Skaggs
Notary Public.

N.C. 310.

DEPARTMENT OF THE INTERIOR,
COMMISSION TO THE FIVE CIVILIZED TRIBES.
MUSKOGEE, I. T. JUNE 13, 1905.

In the matter of the application for the enrollment of Luther I. and Everett M. Baker, as Creek citizens.

Kinkehe M. Baker, being duly sworn, testified as follows, through official interpreter Jesse McDermott.

Examination by the Commission:
Q What is your name? A Kinkehe M. Baker.
Q What is your age? A About 55.
Q What is your post?[sic] office? A Irene.
Q Are you a citizen of the Seminole Nation? A Yes sir.
Q Are you the father of Luther I. and Everett M. Baker? A Yes sir.
Q What is the name of their mother? A Rebecca J. Baker.
Q Are those two children living? A Yes sir.
Q Which one ~~of~~ is the older? A Luther.
Q You remember the date of his birth? A September, 1902.
Q Do you remember when the other one was born? A February 3, 1904.

Q If it should be found that these children have rights in both the Creek and Seminole Nations, in which Nation do you elect to have them enrolled and take allotments of land? A In the Creek Nation.
Q Do you elect for them to be enrolled in the Creek Nation? A Yes sir.

Rebecca J. Baker, being duly sworn, testified as follows:

By Commission:
Q What is your name? A Rebecca J. Baker.
Q What is your age? A 35.
Q What is your post office address? A Irene.
Q When were these children born? A Born September 14, 1902.

Applications for Enrollment of Creek Newborn
Act of 1905 Volume IV

Q Which one? A Luther I.
Q Enverett[sic] M/[sic] was born when? A February 3, 1904.
Q Are these children living? A Yes sir.
Q If it should be found that these children have rights in either the Creek or Seminole Nations, which Nation do you elect to have them enrolled? A In the Creek Nation.
Q You want them to have their allotments of land in the Creek Nation? A Yes sir.

      I, J.Y. Miller, being duly sworn, states[sic] that as stenographer to the Commission to the Five Civilized Tribes, that the above and foregoing is a true and full transcript of his stenographic notes as taken in said cause on said date.

                               JY Miller

Subscribed and sworn to before me this 17th day of June, 1905.

                               Edw C Griesel
                                          Notary Public.

NC 314[sic].

Muskogee, Indian Territory, June 5, 1905.

Rebecca J. Baker,
    Irene, Indian Territory.

Dear Madam:

      In the matter of the application for the enrollment of your minor children, Luther I. and Everett M. Baker, as citizens of the Creek Nation, you are advised that you will be allowed fifteen days from date hereof within which to appear before the Commission at its office in Muskogee, Indian Territory, to give testimony tending to show which Nation you elect to have said children enrolled.

                             Respectfully,

                                            Commissioner in Charge.

NC. 310.

Muskogee, Indian Territory, July 15, 1905.

Chief Clerk,
    Seminole Enrollment Division,
        Muskogee, Indian Territory.

Applications for Enrollment of Creek Newborn
Act of 1905 Volume IV

Dear Sir:

March 23, 1905, application was made to the Commission to the Five Civilized Tribes for the enrollment of Luther I. Baker, born September 14, 1902, and Everett M. Baker, born February 3, 1904, as citizens by blood of the Creek Nation. It is stated in said application that the father of said children is Kinkehee N. Baker, a citizen of the Seminole Nation, and that the mother is Rebecca J. Baker, a citizen of the Creek Nation.

You are requested to inform the Creek Enrollment Division as to whether application has been made for the enrollment of said children as citizens of the Seminole Nation, and if so, what disposition has been made of the same.

Respectfully,

Commissioner.

DEPARTMENT OF THE INTERIOR.
COMMISSION TO THE FIVE CIVILIZED TRIBES.

Muskogee, Indian Territory, July 19, 1905.

Chief Clerk,
    Creek Enrollment Division.

Dear Sir:

Receipt is acknowledged of your letter of July 15, 1905, (NC-310) stating that application was made to the Commission to the Five Civilized Tribes for the enrollment of Luther I. Baker, born September 14, 1902, and Everett M. Baker, born February 3, 1904, children of Kinkehee N. Baker, a citizen of the Seminole Nation, and Rebecca J. Baker, a citizen of the Creek Nation, as citizens by blood of the Creek Nation and requesting to be informed as to whether application has been made for the enrollment is said children as citizens of the Seminole Nation.

In reply to your letter you are informed that it does not appear from an examination of the records of this office that application was made for the enrollment of the said Luther I. Baker and Everett M. Baker as citizens of the Seminole Nation.

Respectfully,

Tams Bixby   Commissioner.

Applications for Enrollment of Creek Newborn
Act of 1905 Volume IV

NC 310

Muskogee, Indian Territory, November 12, 1905.

Chief Clerk,
    Seminole Enrollment Division,
        General Office.

Dear Sir:

    You are hereby advised that the names of Luther I. and Everett M. Baker, children of Kinkehee N. Baker, a citizen of the Seminole Nation, and Rebecca J. Baker, a citizen by blood of the Creek Nation, are contained in the schedule of New Born citizens by blood of the Creek Nation, approved by the Secretary of the Interior August 22, 1905, opposite Roll Nos. 303 and 304.

        Respectfully,

                Commissioner.

BIRTH AFFIDAVIT.

DEPARTMENT OF THE INTERIOR.
COMMISSION TO THE FIVE CIVILIZED TRIBES.

    IN RE APPLICATION FOR ENROLLMENT, as a citizen of the Creek Nation, of Luther I. Baker, born on the 14 day of September, 1902.

Name of Father:	Kinkehee N. Baker	a citizen of the	Seminole Nation.
Name of Mother:	Rebecca J. Baker	a citizen of the Creek	Nation.

        Postoffice   Irene, Ind. Terr.

AFFIDAVIT OF MOTHER.

UNITED STATES OF AMERICA, Indian Territory,
    Western   DISTRICT.

    I, Rebecca J. Baker, on oath state that I am 35 years of age and a citizen by blood, of the Creek Nation; that I am the lawful wife of Kinkehee N. Baker, who is a citizen, by blood of the Seminole Nation; that a male child was born to me on 14 day of September, 1902, that said child has been named Luther I. Baker, and was living March 4, 1905.

                Rebecca J. Baker

Witnesses To Mark:

Applications for Enrollment of Creek Newborn
Act of 1905 Volume IV

Subscribed and sworn to before me this 16 day of March, 1905.

                        Drennan C Skaggs
                        Notary Public.

AFFIDAVIT OF ATTENDING PHYSICIAN OR MID-WIFE.

UNITED STATES OF AMERICA, Indian Territory, }
   Western   DISTRICT.

(illegible)

I, Susie Baker, a mid-wife, on oath state that I ^ attended on Mrs. Rebeca J. Baker, wife of Kinkehee N. Baker on the 14 day of September, 1902; that there was born to her on said date a male child; that said child was living March 4, 1905, and is said to have been named Luther I. Baker

                        Susie A Baker

Witnesses To Mark:
{

Subscribed and sworn to before me this 16 day of March, 1905.

                        Drennan C Skaggs
                        Notary Public.

BIRTH AFFIDAVIT.

DEPARTMENT OF THE INTERIOR.
COMMISSION TO THE FIVE CIVILIZED TRIBES.

IN RE APPLICATION FOR ENROLLMENT, as a citizen of the Creek Nation, of Everett M. Baker, born on the 3 day of February, 1904

Name of Father:	Kinkehee N. Baker	a citizen of the	Seminole	Nation.
Name of Mother:	Rebecca J. Baker	a citizen of the	Creek	Nation.

                      Postoffice   Irene, Ind. Terr.

AFFIDAVIT OF MOTHER.

UNITED STATES OF AMERICA, Indian Territory, }
   Western   DISTRICT.

I, Rebecca J. Baker, on oath state that I am 35 years of age and a citizen by blood, of the Creek Nation; that I am the lawful wife of Kinkehee N. Baker, who is a citizen, by blood of the Seminole Nation; that a male child was born to me on 3

Applications for Enrollment of Creek Newborn
Act of 1905   Volume IV

day of February, 1904, that said child has been named Everett M. Baker, and was living March 4, 1905.

Rebecca J. Baker

Witnesses To Mark:

{

Subscribed and sworn to before me this 16 day of March, 1905.

Drennan C Skaggs
Notary Public.

AFFIDAVIT OF ATTENDING PHYSICIAN OR MID-WIFE.

UNITED STATES OF AMERICA, Indian Territory,
    Western   DISTRICT.

I, Susie Baker, a mid-wife, on oath state that I assisted the doctor who attended on Mrs. Rebeca J. Baker, wife of Kinkehee N. Baker on the 3 day of February, 1904; that there was born to her on said date a male child; that said child was living March 4, 1905, and is said to have been named Everett M. Baker

Susie A Baker

Witnesses To Mark:

{

Subscribed and sworn to before me this 16 day of March, 1905.

Drennan C Skaggs
Notary Public.

Cr NC-311

Muskogee, Indian Territory, June 12, 1905.

Jennetta Asbury,
    Catoosa, Indian Territory.

Dear Madam:

In the matter of the application for the enrollment of your minor child, Sippie Asbury, as a citizen of the Creek Nation, you are advised that the Commission requires the affidavits of two disinterested witnesses relative to its birth.

For this purpose there are herewith enclosed two blank forms of birth affidavits. In having same executed, care should be taken to see that all blanks are

Applications for Enrollment of Creek Newborn
Act of 1905   Volume IV

properly filled, all names written in full and in the event that a person signing the affidavit is unable to write, signature by mark must be attested by two witnesses.

                Respectfully,

2 B A   Chairman.

NC-311

                Muskogee, Indian Territory, July 29, 1905.

Francis Asbury,
      Catoosa, Indian Territory.

Dear Sir:

      In the matter of the application for the enrollment of your minor son Sippie Asbury, born March 10, 1904, as a citizen of the Creek Nation, you are advised that this office requires the affidavits of two disinterested witnesses relative to his birth. Said affidavits must set forth the date of the birth of said child, the names of his parents and whether or not he was living March 4, 1905.

      Please give this matter your prompt attention.

                Respectfully,

                              Commissioner.

          Affidavit of Witnesses relative to the Birth of Sippie Asbury.

United States of America, Indian Territory,   )
) ss.
Western Judicial District.   )

      We, James Chealake and Nancy Chealake, citizens of the Creek Nation, first being duly sworn state on oath "That they were present at Jennetta Asbury's place on March 10th, 1904, and on that day was born to Jennetta Asbury a male child who is now living and was named Sippie Asbury.

                                    James Chalake

Witnesses:
                                    Nancy Chalake

Luther Opry

Applications for Enrollment of Creek Newborn
Act of 1905 Volume IV

Subscribed and sworn to before me this the 15th day of August A. D. 1905.

Com. Expires Jany 13, 1909   R.W. Lumpkin
                                    Notary Public.

BIRTH AFFIDAVIT.

DEPARTMENT OF THE INTERIOR.
COMMISSION TO THE FIVE CIVILIZED TRIBES.

IN RE APPLICATION FOR ENROLLMENT, as a citizen of the CREEK Nation, of Sippie Asbury, born on the 10 day of March, 1904

| Name of Father: | Francis Asbury | a citizen of the | Creek | Nation. |
| Name of Mother: | Jennetta " | a citizen of the | " | Nation. |

Postoffice   Catoosa

AFFIDAVIT OF ~~MOTHER~~. Father

UNITED STATES OF AMERICA, Indian Territory,
          WESTERN   DISTRICT.

I, Francis Asbury, on oath state that I am 49 years of age and a citizen by blood, of the Creek Nation; that I am the lawful ~~wife~~ husb of Jennetta Asbury, who is a citizen, by blood of the Creek Nation; that a male child was born to me on 10 day of March, 1904, that said child has been named Sippie Asbury, and is now living. There was no midwife.

                                    Francis Asbury
Witnesses To Mark:

Subscribed and sworn to before me this 21 day of March, 1905.

                                    Edw C Griesel
                                    Notary Public.

Applications for Enrollment of Creek Newborn
Act of 1905 Volume IV

AFFIDAVIT OF ATTENDING PHYSICIAN OR MID-WIFE.

UNITED STATES OF AMERICA, Indian Territory,
WESTERN DISTRICT.

I, ..., a ...., on oath state that I attended on Mrs. ...., wife of .... on the .... day of ...., 1......; that there was born to her on said date a .... child; that said child is now living and is said to have been named

No mid wife

Witnesses To Mark:
{ ....
....

Subscribed and sworn to before me this .... day of ...., 1.......

....
Notary Public.

BIRTH AFFIDAVIT.

DEPARTMENT OF THE INTERIOR.
COMMISSION TO THE FIVE CIVILIZED TRIBES.

IN RE APPLICATION FOR ENROLLMENT, as a citizen of the CREEK Nation, of Sippie Asbury, born on the 10" day of March, 1904

Name of Father:	Francis Asbury	a citizen of the	Creek Nation.
Name of Mother:	Jennetta "	a citizen of the	" Nation.

Postoffice Catoosa

(child present.)

AFFIDAVIT OF MOTHER.

UNITED STATES OF AMERICA, Indian Territory,
WESTERN DISTRICT.

I, Jennetta Asbury, on oath state that I am 32 years of age and a citizen by blood, of the Creek Nation; that I am the lawful wife of Francis Asbury, who is a citizen, by blood of the Creek Nation; that a male child was born to me on 10" day of March, 1904, that said child has been named Sippie Asbury, and is now living.

            her
          Jennetta x Asbury
            mark

Witnesses To Mark:
{ H.G. Hains
  Lona Merrick

Applications for Enrollment of Creek Newborn
Act of 1905   Volume IV

Subscribed and sworn to before me this 14" day of April, 1905.

My Com. expires Apr 11, 1909.　　　　Zera E. Parrish
　　　　　　　　　　　　　　　　　　　　　Notary Public.

BIRTH AFFIDAVIT.

DEPARTMENT OF THE INTERIOR.
COMMISSION TO THE FIVE CIVILIZED TRIBES.

IN RE APPLICATION FOR ENROLLMENT, as a citizen of the Creek Nation, of Sippie Asbury, born on the 10 day of March, 1904

Name of Father:	Francis Asbury	a citizen of the	Creek	Nation.
Name of Mother:	Jennetta　"	a citizen of the	" "	Nation.

　　　　　　　　　　Postoffice　　Catoosa I.T.

AFFIDAVIT OF MOTHER.

UNITED STATES OF AMERICA, Indian Territory, ⎫
　　Western　　　　　　　DISTRICT.　　　　⎭

　　I, Jennetta Asbury, on oath state that I am 35 years of age and a citizen by birth, of the Creek Nation; that I am the lawful wife of Francis Asbury, who is a citizen, by birth of the Creek Nation; that a male child was born to me on 10 day of March, 1904, that said child has been named Sippie Asbury, and is now living.

　　　　　　　　　　　　　　　　　　　　her
　　　　　　　　　　　　　　　　Jennetta x Asbury
Witnesses To Mark:　　　　　　　　　mark
　⎰ Nancy Chalakee
　⎱ Jimmy Chalakee

Subscribed and sworn to before me this 15 day of August, 1905.

Com. expires　　　　　　　R.W. Lumpkins
Jany 18-1909.　　　　　　　　　Notary Public.

Applications for Enrollment of Creek Newborn
Act of 1905   Volume IV

DEPARTMENT OF THE INTERIOR,
COMMISSION TO THE FIVE CIVILIZED TRIBES.
MUSKOGEE, INDIAN TERRITORY I.T. June 16, 1905.

NC 312.

In the matter of the application for the enrollment of Pauline E. and Inez W. Baker, as citizens by blood of the Creek Nation.

Susie Baker, being duly sworn, testified as follows:

Examination by the Commission:
Q What is your name? A Susie Baker.
Q What is your age? A 25.
Q What is your post office address? A Irene.
Q Are you a citizen of the Creek Nation? A Yes sir.
Q What is the name of the child in your arms? A Pauline E. Baker.
Q When will that child be a year old? A The 16th day of next month.
Q Have you another new-born child at home? A Yes, Inez W. Baker.
Q Is she living? A Yes sir.
Q When was she born? A September 5, 1902.
Q Three years old next September? A Yes sir.
Q What is the name of the father of these two children? A Billie Baker.
Q Is he a Creek citizen? A No, he is a Seminole.
Q Are you and he living together as husband and wife? A Yes sir.
Q Was there a midwife present when Pauline was born? A No, sir. that time he was the only midwife.
Q I hand you now the two affidavits and return envelope and that it will be necessary for you to get the affidavits of two disinterested witnesses as to the birth of this child? There being no midwife you must do this. If it should be found that these two children have rights in either the creek or Seminole Nations, in which Nation do you want them to have their land? A In the Creek Nation.
Q You choose the Creek Nation for both of them? A Yes sir.
Q Do you know in which Nation your Husband wants them to be enrolled.? A Yes He told me that. He wants it in the Creek nation.
Q You and he are living together[sic] A Yes.

E. C. GRIESEL, being duly sworn, states that the above and foregoing is a true and correct transcript of his stenographic notes as taken in said cause on said date.

Edw C Griesel

SUBSCRIBED and sworn to before me this 23rd day of June 1905.

J. McDermott
Notary Public.

Applications for Enrollment of Creek Newborn
Act of 1905 Volume IV

BIRTH AFFIDAVIT.

DEPARTMENT OF THE INTERIOR.
COMMISSION TO THE FIVE CIVILIZED TRIBES.

IN RE APPLICATION FOR ENROLLMENT, as a citizen of the Creek Nation, of Inez W. Baker, born on the 5 day of September, 1902

Name of Father:	Billy Baker	a citizen of the	Seminole	Nation.
Name of Mother:	Susie Baker	a citizen of the	Creek	Nation.

Postoffice   Irene, Ind. Terr.

AFFIDAVIT OF MOTHER.

UNITED STATES OF AMERICA, Indian Territory,
Western   DISTRICT.

I, Susie Baker, on oath state that I am 25 years of age and a citizen by blood, of the Creek Nation; that I am the lawful wife of Billy Baker, who is a citizen, by blood of the Seminole Nation; that a female child was born to me on 5 day of September, 1902, that said child has been named Inez W. Baker, and was living March 4, 1905.

Susie Baker

Witnesses To Mark:
{

Subscribed and sworn to before me this 16 day of March, 1905.

Drennan C Skaggs
Notary Public.

AFFIDAVIT OF ATTENDING PHYSICIAN OR MID-WIFE.

UNITED STATES OF AMERICA, Indian Territory,
Western   DISTRICT.

I, Rebecca J. Baker, a *(blank)*, on oath state that I assisted the midwife who attended on Mrs. Susie Baker, wife of Billy Baker on the 5 day of September, 1902; that there was born to her on said date a female child; that said child was living March 4, 1905, and is said to have been named Inez W. Baker

Rebecca J. Baker

Witnesses To Mark:
{

Applications for Enrollment of Creek Newborn
Act of 1905   Volume IV

Subscribed and sworn to before me this 16 day of March, 1905.

                           Drennan C Skaggs
                           Notary Public.

BIRTH AFFIDAVIT.

DEPARTMENT OF THE INTERIOR.
COMMISSION TO THE FIVE CIVILIZED TRIBES.

IN RE APPLICATION FOR ENROLLMENT, as a citizen of the Creek Nation, of Pauline E. Baker, born on the 16th day of July, 1904

Name of Father:	Billy Baker	a citizen of the	Seminole	Nation.
Name of Mother:	Susie Baker	a citizen of the	Creek	Nation.

                 Postoffice   Irene, I.T.

AFFIDAVIT OF MOTHER.

UNITED STATES OF AMERICA, Indian Territory,
     Western   DISTRICT.

I, Susie Baker, on oath state that I am 27 years of age and a citizen by Blood, of the Creek Nation; that I am the lawful wife of Billy Baker, who is a citizen, by Blood of the Seminole Nation; that a female child was born to me on 16th day of July, 1904, that said child has been named Pauline E. Baker, and was living March 4, 1905.

                           Susie Baker

Witnesses To Mark:

Subscribed and sworn to before me this 2th[sic] day of August, 1905.

                           H.C. Collier
                           Notary Public.
my commission expires July 13th 1908

AFFIDAVIT OF ATTENDING PHYSICIAN OR MID-WIFE.

UNITED STATES OF AMERICA, Indian Territory,
     Western   DISTRICT.

                                                       they
I, Zigler Wood and Eliza Wood, a *(blank)*, on oath state that I attended on Mrs. Susie Baker, wife of Billy Baker on the 16 day of July, 1904; that there was

Applications for Enrollment of Creek Newborn
Act of 1905 Volume IV

born to her on said date a female child; that said child was living March 4, 1905, and is said to have been named Pauline E. Baker

	his	her
	Zigler x Wood	Eliza x Wood
Witnesses To Mark:	mark	mark

{ Thos M. Collier
{ Lavonia Collier

Subscribed and sworn to before me this 2^{th[sic]} day of August, 1905.

H.C. Collier
Notary Public.

my commission expires July 13th 1908

BIRTH AFFIDAVIT.

DEPARTMENT OF THE INTERIOR.
COMMISSION TO THE FIVE CIVILIZED TRIBES.

IN RE APPLICATION FOR ENROLLMENT, as a citizen of the Creek Nation, of Pauline E. Baker, born on the 16 day of July, 1904

Name of Father:	Billy Baker	a citizen of the	Seminole	Nation.
Name of Mother:	Susie Baker	a citizen of the	Creek	Nation.

Postoffice Irene, Ind. Terr.

AFFIDAVIT OF MOTHER.

UNITED STATES OF AMERICA, Indian Territory, }
  Western   DISTRICT.

I, Susie Baker, on oath state that I am 25 years of age and a citizen by Blood, of the Creek Nation; that I am the lawful wife of Billy Baker, who is a citizen, by Blood of the Seminole Nation; that a female child was born to me on 16 day of July, 1904, that said child has been named Pauline E. Baker, and was living March 4, 1905.

Susie Baker

Witnesses To Mark:
{
{

Subscribed and sworn to before me this 16 day of March, 1905.

Drennan C Skaggs
Notary Public.

Applications for Enrollment of Creek Newborn
Act of 1905 Volume IV

AFFIDAVIT OF ATTENDING PHYSICIAN OR MID-WIFE.

UNITED STATES OF AMERICA, Indian Territory, }
  Western   DISTRICT.

                                                                            my wife

I, Billy Baker , a *(blank)* , on oath state that I attended on ^ Mrs. Susie Baker , wife of *(blank)* on the 16 day of July , 1904 ; that there was born to her on said date a   female   child; that said child was living March 4, 1905, and is said to have been named Pauline E. Baker

                                                  Billy Baker

Witnesses To Mark:
{

Subscribed and sworn to before me this 16 day of March , 1905.

                                          Drennan C Skaggs
                                          Notary Public.

NC 312.

Muskogee, Indian Territory, May 31, 1905.

Susie Baker,
       Irene, Indian Territory.

Dear Madam:

In the matter of the application for the enrollment of your minor children, Pauline E. and Inez W. Baker, you are advised that you will be allowed twenty days from date within which to appear before the Commission at its office in Muskogee, Indian Territory, for the purpose of being examined under oath.

                                    Respectfully,

                                                Chairman.

NC. 312.

Muskogee, Indian Territory, July 14, 1906.

Commissioner to the Five Civilized Tribes,
    Seminole Enrollment Division,
        Muskogee, Indian Territory.

Applications for Enrollment of Creek Newborn
Act of 1905   Volume IV

Gentlemen:

March 23, 1905, application was made to the Commission to the Five Civilized Tribes for the enrollment of Pauline E. Baker, born July 16, 1904, and Inez W. Baker, born September 5, 1902, as citizens by blood of the Creek Nation. It is stated in said application that the father of said children is Billie Baker, a citizen of the Seminole Nation, and that the mother is Susie Baker, a citizen of the Creek Nation.

You are requested to inform the Creek Enrollment Division as to whether application has been made for the enrollment of said children as citizens of the Seminole Nation, and if so, what disposition has been made of the same.

          Respectfully,

                   Commissioner.

DEPARTMENT OF THE INTERIOR.
COMMISSION TO THE FIVE CIVILIZED TRIBES.

Muskogee, Indian Territory, July 18, 1905

Chief Clerk,
    Creek Enrollment Division.

Dear Sir:

Receipt is acknowledged of your letter of July 14, 1905, (CN-312) stating that an application was made to the Commission to the Five Civilized Tribes for the enrollment of Pauline E. Baker, born July 16, 1904, and Inez W. Baker, born September 5, 1902, children of Billie Baker, a citizen of the Seminole Nation, and Susie Baker, a citizen of the Creek Nation, as citizens by blood of the Creek Nation and requesting to be informed as to whether application has been made for the enrollment of said children as citizens of the Seminole Nation.

In reply to your letter you are advised that it does not appear from an examination of the records of this office that any application was made to the Commission to the Five Civilized Tribes for the enrollment of said Pauline E. Baker and Inez W. Baker as citizens of the Seminole Nation.

          Respectfully,

               Tams Bixby   Commissioner.

Applications for Enrollment of Creek Newborn
Act of 1905   Volume IV

NC-312.

Muskogee, Indian Territory, July 29, 1905.

Billy Baker,
    Irene, Indian Territory.

Dear Sir:

In the matter of the application for the enrollment of your daughter Pauline E. Baker, born June 15, 1904, as a citizen by blood of the Creek Nation, you are advised that it will be necessary, before the rights of said child as a citizen of said nation can be finally determined, for you to file with this office the affidavits of two disinterested parties who are acquainted with said child, know when she was born and whether or not she was living March 4, 1905.

Respectfully,

Commissioner.

NC 312

Muskogee, Indian Territory, August 21, 1906.

Clerk in Charge,
    Seminole Enrollment Division,
        Muskogee, Indian Territory.

Dear Sir:

Application has been made for the enrollment of Pauline E. Baker, born July 16. 1904, to Billy Baker, a Seminole, and Susie Baker, a citizen of the Creek Nation.

You are requested to advise this office if application has been made for the enrollment of said child as a citizen of the Seminole Nation, and if so, please furnish the present status of said application.

Respectfully,

Commissioner.

Applications for Enrollment of Creek Newborn
Act of 1905 Volume IV

REFER IN REPLY TO THE FOLLOWING:

DEPARTMENT OF THE INTERIOR,
COMMISSIONER TO THE FIVE CIVILIZED TRIBES.

Muskogee, Indian Territory, August 24, 1906.

Chief Clerk,
    Creek Enrollment Division,
        Muskogee, Indian Territory.

Dear Sir:

    Receipt is hereby acknowledged of your letter of August 21, 1906, asking if application has been made for enrollment as a citizen of the Seminole Nation of Pauline E. Baker, child of Billy Baker, a citizen of the Seminole Nation and Susie Baker, a citizen of the Creek Nation.

    In reply you are advised that it does not appear from the records of this office that application has been made on behalf of Pauline E. Baker for enrollment as a new born citizen of the Seminole Nation, Act of Congress approved March 3, 1905.

                Respectfully,

                Wm. O. Beall

                      Acting Commissioner.

NC 312.

Muskogee, Indian Territory, October 31, 1906.

Chief Clerk,
    Seminole Enrollment Division,
        Muskogee, Indian Territory.

Dear Sir:

    There is on file in this office an application for the enrollment of Pauline E. Baker, born July 16, 1904, and Inez W. Baker, born September 15, 1902; the parents of said children are given as Billy Baker, a citizen of the Seminole Nation, and Susie Baker, who is identified as a citizen by blood of the Creek Nation, opposite roll number 6642.

    You are advised that the name of Inez W. Baker is contained in a partial list of new born citizens by blood of the Creek Nation, approved by the Secretary of the Interior August 22, 1905, opposite roll number 305, and that the name of Pauline E. Baker is contained in a similar list approved October 15, 1906, opposite roll number 1023.

Applications for Enrollment of Creek Newborn
Act of 1905 Volume IV

Respectfully,

Commissioner.

BIRTH AFFIDAVIT.

DEPARTMENT OF THE INTERIOR.
COMMISSION TO THE FIVE CIVILIZED TRIBES.

IN RE APPLICATION FOR ENROLLMENT, as a citizen of the Muskogee or Creek Nation, of Stella Childers, born on the 9 day of January, 1904

Name of Father: Anderson J. Childers   a citizen of the   Creek   Nation.
Name of Mother: Lydia Childers (Liddia Childers) a citizen of the   Creek   Nation.

Postoffice   Wagoner, I.T.

AFFIDAVIT OF MOTHER.

UNITED STATES OF AMERICA, Indian Territory,
Western Judicial   DISTRICT.

I, Lydia Childers (Liddia Childers), on oath state that I am 26 years of age and a citizen by birth, of the Creek Nation; that I am the lawful wife of Anderson J. Childers, who is a citizen, by birth of the Creek Nation; that a female child was born to me on 9th day of January, 1904, that said child has been named Stella Childers, and is now living.

Lydia Childers (Liddia Childers)

Witnesses To Mark:

Subscribed and sworn to before me this 25th day of March, 1905.

My Com expires May 7, 1908.   Signa L. Hadfield
Notary Public.

Applications for Enrollment of Creek Newborn
Act of 1905 Volume IV

AFFIDAVIT OF ATTENDING PHYSICIAN OR MID-WIFE.

UNITED STATES OF AMERICA, Indian Territory,
Western Judicial   DISTRICT.

I, Maggie Pea , a mid-wife , on oath state that I attended on Mrs. Lydia Childers (Liddia Childers) , wife of Anderson J. Childers on the 9th day of January , 1904 ; that there was born to her on said date a female child; that said child is now living and is said to have been named Stella Childers

her
Maggie x Pea
mark

Witnesses To Mark:
- *(Name Illegible)*
- S.L. Hadfield

Subscribed and sworn to before me this 25th day of March , 1905.

My Com expires May 7, 1908.   Signa L. Hadfield
                          Notary Public.

BIRTH AFFIDAVIT.

DEPARTMENT OF THE INTERIOR.
COMMISSION TO THE FIVE CIVILIZED TRIBES.

IN RE APPLICATION FOR ENROLLMENT, as a citizen of the CREEK Nation, of Stella Childers, born on the 9 day of Jan , 1904

Name of Father:	Anderson J. Childers	a citizen of the	Creek	Nation.
Name of Mother:	Lydia "	a citizen of the	"	Nation.

Postoffice   Wagoner

AFFIDAVIT OF ~~MOTHER~~. Father

UNITED STATES OF AMERICA, Indian Territory,
WESTERN   DISTRICT.

I, Anderson J. Childers , on oath state that I am 35 years of age and a citizen by blood, of the Creek Nation; that I am the lawful ~~wife~~ husb of Liddie Childers, who is a citizen, by blood of the Creek Nation; that a female child was born to me on 9 day of Jan. , 1904 , that said child has been named Stella Childers , and is now living.

Anderson J. Childers

Applications for Enrollment of Creek Newborn
Act of 1905 Volume IV

Witnesses To Mark:
{

    Subscribed and sworn to before me this 21 day of March, 1905.

                              Edw C Griesel
                              Notary Public.

NC-314.

                    Muskogee, Indian Territory, August 3, 1905.

Peggie Mitchell,
    Boley, Indian Territory.

Dear Madam:

    In the matter of the application for the enrollment of your minor son Albert Mitchell as a citizen by blood of the Creek Nation this office is unable to identify you upon the final roll of citizens by blood of the Creek Nation and you are therefore requested to inform this office as to the name under which you were finally enrolled, the names of your parents and other members of your family, the Creek town to which you belong and, if you have received your allotment certificate and deed, *(ink smudge)*inal roll number as the same appears thereon.

    You should give this matter your immediate attention.

                    Respectfully,

                                    Commissioner.

C314

                    Muskogee, Indian Territory, October 3, 1905.

Peggy Willior,
    Care Willie Mitchell,
        Boley, Indian Territory.

Dear Madam:

    Receipt is acknowledged of your communication of September 28, 1905, in which you ask when you will be allowed to file.

Applications for Enrollment of Creek Newborn
Act of 1905 Volume IV

    The records of this office have been examined and as it appears therefrom that you have already filed on your land, it is presumed that your inquiry relates to your minor child, Albert Mitchell.

    In reply you are advised that the matter of the application for the enrollment of said Albert Mitchell, as a citizen by blood of the Creek Nation, is pending before this office and that when final action is had in the matter, you will be duly notified.

                                          Respectfully,

                                                               Commissioner.

REFER IN REPLY TO THE FOLLOWING:

NC 314

DEPARTMENT OF THE INTERIOR,
COMMISSIONER TO THE FIVE CIVILIZED TRIBES.

                                  Muskogee, Indian Territory, July 28, 1906.

Peggy Mitchell (or Willior),
    c/o Willie Mitchell,
        Boley, Indian Territory.

Dear Madam:

    There is on file in this office a blank form of birth affidavit, in the caption of which, and in the affidavit of the midwife, the date of the birth of your minor child, Albert Mitchell, is given as October 7, 1903, whereas you swear that said child was born October 7, 1904. This discrepancy should be corrected at once, and there is herewith enclosed a blank form of birth affidavit. In the event that the date given by the midwife, October 7, 1903, is correct, you are requested to have the enclosed affidavit executed to that effect and return to this office in the enclosed envelope.

                                          Respectfully,

                                          Tams Bixby

                                                        Commissioner.

1 BA
Envelope.

Applications for Enrollment of Creek Newborn
Act of 1905   Volume IV

NC 314.

BK.

Muskogee, Indian Territory, March 1, 1907.

Peggie Mitchell,
    c/o Willie Mitchell,
        Baley[sic], Indian Territory.

Dear Madam:

    You are hereby advised that on February 15, 1907, the Secretary of the Interior approved the enrollment of your minor child, Albert Mitchell, as a citizen by blood of the Creek Nation, and that the name of said child appears upon the roll of New Born citizens by blood of the Creek Nation, enrolled Act of Congress approved March 3, 1905, as number 1132.

    The child is now entitled to allotment, and application therefor should be made without delay at the Creek Land Office, Muskogee, Indian Territory.

                Respectfully,

                            Commissioner.

BIRTH AFFIDAVIT.

DEPARTMENT OF THE INTERIOR.
COMMISSION TO THE FIVE CIVILIZED TRIBES.

    IN RE APPLICATION FOR ENROLLMENT, as a citizen of the Creek Nation, of Albert Mitchell, born on the 7 day of October, 1903

Name of Father: Willie Mitchell   a citizen of the United States Nation.
Name of Mother: Peggie Mitchell (nee Williya) a citizen of the   Creek   Nation.

                Postoffice   Boley, Indian Territory

AFFIDAVIT OF MOTHER.

UNITED STATES OF AMERICA, Indian Territory, ⎫
    Western   DISTRICT. ⎬

    I, Peggie Mitchell, on oath state that I am about 25 years of age and a citizen by blood, of the Creek Nation; that I am the lawful wife of Willie Mitchell, who is a citizen, by *(blank)* of the United States Nation; that a male child was born to me on

Applications for Enrollment of Creek Newborn
Act of 1905   Volume IV

7 day of October, 1904[sic], that said child has been named Albert Mitchell, and was living March 4, 1905.

Witnesses To Mark:
{ Alex Posey
{ DC Skaggs

         her
       Peggie x Mitchell
        mark

Subscribed and sworn to before me this 14" day of March, 1905.

           Drennan C Skaggs
           Notary Public.

AFFIDAVIT OF ATTENDING PHYSICIAN OR MID-WIFE.

UNITED STATES OF AMERICA, Indian Territory,
  Western DISTRICT.

  I, Almeda Cobb, a midwife, on oath state that I attended on Mrs. Peggie Mitchell, wife of Willie Mitchell on the 7 day of October, 1903; that there was born to her on said date a male child; that said child was living March 4, 1905, and is said to have been named Albert Mitchell

         her
       Almeda x Cobb
        mark

Witnesses To Mark:
{ Alex Posey
{ DC Skaggs

Subscribed and sworn to before me this 14" day of March, 1905.

           Drennan C Skaggs
           Notary Public.

BIRTH AFFIDAVIT.

DEPARTMENT OF THE INTERIOR,
COMMISSION TO THE FIVE CIVILIZED TRIBES.

ENROLLMENT OF MINORS.   ACT OF CONGRESS, APPROVED APRIL 26, 1906.

  IN RE APPLICATION FOR ENROLLMENT, as a citizen of the Creek Nation, of Albert Mitchell, born on the 7th day of October, 1903

		U.S. citizen		
Name of Father:	Willie Mitchell	a ~~citizen~~ of the	Creek	Nation.
Name of Mother:	Peggy Mitchell	a citizen of the	Creek	Nation.
Tribal enrollment of father	*(blank)*	Tribal enrollment of mother		By blood

      (Present) Postoffice Boley, I.T.

Applications for Enrollment of Creek Newborn
Act of 1905   Volume IV

AFFIDAVIT OF MOTHER.

UNITED STATES OF AMERICA, Indian Territory,
Western   District.

I, Peggy Mitchell , on oath state that I am *(blank)* years of age and a citizen by blood , of the Creek Nation; that I am the lawful wife of Willie Mitchell , who is a U. S. citizen, by *(blank)* of the Creek Nation; that a male child was born to me on 7th day of October , 1903 , that said child has been named Albert Mitchell , and was living March 4, 1906.

                                         her
                                  Peggy x Mitchell
WITNESSES TO MARK: mark
  { Fannie Wright
    M. J. *(Illegible)*

Subscribed and sworn to before me this 30th day of July , 1906.

                                   J. M. Haynes
                                         Notary Public.

My Commission Expires November 9, 1907

AFFIDAVIT OF ATTENDING PHYSICIAN OR MID-WIFE.

UNITED STATES OF AMERICA, Indian Territory,
Western   District.

I, Almetie Cobb , a midwife , on oath state that I attended on Mrs. Peggy Mitchell , wife of Willie Mitchell on the 7th day of October , 1903 ; that there was born to her on said date a male child; that said child was living March 4, 1906, and is said to have been named Albert Mitchell

                                         her
                                  Almetie x Cobb
WITNESSES TO MARK: mark
  { Fannie Wright
    M. J. *(Illegible)*

Subscribed and sworn to before me this 30th day of July , 1906.

                                   J. M. Haynes
                                         Notary Public.

My Commission Expires November 9, 1907

Applications for Enrollment of Creek Newborn
Act of 1905   Volume IV

NC 315.

Muskogee, Indian Territory, June 5, 1905.

Annie Hutton,
    Boynton, Indian Territory.

Dear Madam:

    In the matter of the application for the enrollment of your minor child, Iola Hutton, you are advised that the Commission requires the affidavit of the midwife or physician in attendance at the birth of said child.

    There is herewith enclosed a blank form of birth affidavit, and in executing same care should be exercised to see that all blanks are properly filled, all names written in full and in the event that the person signing the affidavit is unable to write, signature by mark must be attested by two witnesses. The affidavit must be executed before a Notary Public and the notarial seal and signature of the officer must be attached to the affidavit.

                    Respectfully,

1 BA   Commissioner in Charge.

BIRTH AFFIDAVIT.

DEPARTMENT OF THE INTERIOR.
COMMISSION TO THE FIVE CIVILIZED TRIBES.

    IN RE APPLICATION FOR ENROLLMENT, as a citizen of the Creek Nation, of Iola Hutton, born on the 28 day of Feb, 1903

Name of Father:	Henry Hutton	a citizen of the	Creek	Nation.
Name of Mother:	Annie "	a citizen of the	"	Nation.

                      Postoffice   Boynton

Child Present - MAR 31 1905 - Gr

AFFIDAVIT OF MOTHER.

UNITED STATES OF AMERICA, Indian Territory,
    Western   DISTRICT.

    I, Annie Hutton, on oath state that I am 33 years of age and a citizen by adoption, of the Creek Nation; that I am the lawful wife of Henry Hutton, who is a citizen, by adoption of the Creek Nation; that a female child was born to me on 28 day of Feb, 1903, that said child has been named Iola Hutton, and is now living.

Applications for Enrollment of Creek Newborn
Act of 1905 Volume IV

Annie Hutton

Witnesses To Mark:
{

Subscribed and sworn to before me this 31 day of March , 1905.

Edw C Griesel
Notary Public.

BIRTH AFFIDAVIT.

DEPARTMENT OF THE INTERIOR.
COMMISSION TO THE FIVE CIVILIZED TRIBES.

IN RE APPLICATION FOR ENROLLMENT, as a citizen of the CREEK Nation, of Iola Hutton , born on the 28 day of Feby , 1903

Name of Father:	Henry Hutton	a citizen of the	Creek	Nation.
Name of Mother:	Annie "	a citizen of the	"	Nation.

Postoffice   Boynton

AFFIDAVIT OF ~~MOTHER~~. Father

UNITED STATES OF AMERICA, Indian Territory,
WESTERN DISTRICT.

I, Henry Hutton , on oath state that I am 41 years of age and a citizen by Freedman , of the Creek Nation; that I am the lawful ~~wife~~ husband of Annie Hutton , who is a citizen, by Freedman of the Creek Nation; that a female child was born to me on 28 day of Feby , 1903 , that said child has been named Iola Hutton , and is now living.

Henry Hutton

Witnesses To Mark:
{

Subscribed and sworn to before me this 24" day of March, 1905.

Edw C Griesel
Notary Public.

Applications for Enrollment of Creek Newborn
Act of 1905 Volume IV

AFFIDAVIT OF ATTENDING PHYSICIAN OR MID-WIFE.

UNITED STATES OF AMERICA, Indian Territory, }
Western Judicial   DISTRICT.

I, S.D. Johnson , a midwife , on oath state that I attended on Mrs. Annie Hutton, wife of Henry Hutton on the 28 day of Feb. , 1903 ; that there was born to her on said date a female child; that said child was living March 4, 1905, and is said to have been named Iola Hutton

            her
          S.D. x Johnson
Witnesses To Mark: mark
 { *(Illegible)* Monday
  AW Whitfield

Subscribed and sworn to before me this 12 day of June, 1905.

My Com expires Oct. 11   Geo. L. Robinson
    1908   Notary Public.

BIRTH AFFIDAVIT.

DEPARTMENT OF THE INTERIOR.
COMMISSION TO THE FIVE CIVILIZED TRIBES.

IN RE APPLICATION FOR ENROLLMENT, as a citizen of the Creek Nation, of Ella Johnson , born on the 8 day of March , 1904

Name of Father: Paro Johnson   a citizen of the Creek Nation.
Name of Mother: Hannah Johnson a citizen of the Creek Nation.

         Postoffice Boley, Ind. Terr.

AFFIDAVIT OF MOTHER.

UNITED STATES OF AMERICA, Indian Territory, }
Western   DISTRICT.

I, Hannah Johnson , on oath state that I am 33 years of age and a citizen by blood , of the Creek Nation; that I am the lawful wife of Paro Johnson , who is a citizen, by adoption of the Creek Nation; that a female child was born to me on 8 day of March , 1904 , that said child has been named Ella Johnson , and was living March 4, 1905.   her
             Hannah x Johnson
               mark

Applications for Enrollment of Creek Newborn
Act of 1905   Volume IV

Witnesses To Mark:
{ DC Skaggs
  Alex Posey

    Subscribed and sworn to before me this 14" day of March, 1905.

                                Drennan C Skaggs
                                Notary Public.

AFFIDAVIT OF ATTENDING PHYSICIAN OR MID-WIFE.

UNITED STATES OF AMERICA, Indian Territory, }
    Western   DISTRICT.

    I, Katy McGirt, a mid-wife, on oath state that I attended on Mrs. Hannah Johnson, wife of Paro Johnson on the 8" day of March, 1904; that there was born to her on said date a female child; that said child was living March 4, 1905, and is said to have been named Ella Johnson

                                  her
                          Katy x McGirt
Witnesses To Mark: mark
{ DC Skaggs
   Alex Posey

    Subscribed and sworn to before me this 14" day of March, 1905.

                              Drennan C Skaggs
                              Notary Public.

BIRTH AFFIDAVIT.
DEPARTMENT OF THE INTERIOR.
COMMISSION TO THE FIVE CIVILIZED TRIBES.

    IN RE APPLICATION FOR ENROLLMENT, as a citizen of the Creek Nation, of Leora Johnson, born on the 20 day of May, 1902

Name of Father: Paro Johnson   a citizen of the   Creek   Nation.
Name of Mother: Hannah Johnson   a citizen of the   Creek   Nation.

                        Postoffice   Boley, Ind. Terr.

Applications for Enrollment of Creek Newborn
Act of 1905 Volume IV

AFFIDAVIT OF MOTHER.

UNITED STATES OF AMERICA, Indian Territory, }
    Western   DISTRICT.

I, Hannah Johnson , on oath state that I am 33 years of age and a citizen by blood , of the Creek Nation; that I am the lawful wife of Paro Johnson , who is a citizen, by adoption of the Creek Nation; that a female child was born to me on 20 day of May , 1902 , that said child has been named Leora Johnson , and was living March 4, 1905.

                                           her
                                Hannah x Johnson
                                     mark

Witnesses To Mark:
{ DC Skaggs
  Alex Posey

Subscribed and sworn to before me this 14" day of March , 1905.

                                    Drennan C Skaggs
                                    Notary Public.

AFFIDAVIT OF ATTENDING PHYSICIAN OR MID-WIFE.

UNITED STATES OF AMERICA, Indian Territory, }
    Western   DISTRICT.

I, Katy McGirt , a mid-wife , on oath state that I attended on Mrs. Hannah Johnson , wife of Paro Johnson ~~on the~~ sometime in the month of May *(blank)* day of *(blank)* , 1902 ; that there was born to her on said date a female child; that said child was living March 4, 1905, and is said to have been named Leora Johnson

                                           her
                                Katy x McGirt
Witnesses To Mark: mark
{ DC Skaggs
  Alex Posey

Subscribed and sworn to before me this 14" day of March , 1905.

                                    Drennan C Skaggs
                                    Notary Public.

Applications for Enrollment of Creek Newborn
Act of 1905 Volume IV

BIRTH AFFIDAVIT.

DEPARTMENT OF THE INTERIOR.
COMMISSION TO THE FIVE CIVILIZED TRIBES.

IN RE APPLICATION FOR ENROLLMENT, as a citizen of the CREEK Nation, of Wiley Murrell, born on the 13 day of April, 1903

Name of Father: Calhoun Murrell   a citizen of the   Creek   Nation.
Name of Mother: Lucy   "   a citizen of the   "   Nation.

Postoffice   Tallahassee

Child Present - Gr

AFFIDAVIT OF MOTHER.

UNITED STATES OF AMERICA, Indian Territory,
WESTERN DISTRICT.

I, Lucy Murrell, on oath state that I am 28 years of age and a citizen by blood, of the Creek Nation; that I am the lawful wife of Calhoun Murrell, who is a citizen, by Freedman of the Creek Nation; that a male child was born to me on 13 day of April, 1903, that said child has been named Wiley Murrell, and is now living.

Lucy Murrell

Witnesses To Mark:

Subscribed and sworn to before me this 21 day of March, 1905.

Edw C Griesel
Notary Public.

AFFIDAVIT OF ATTENDING PHYSICIAN OR MID-WIFE.

UNITED STATES OF AMERICA, Indian Territory,
WESTERN DISTRICT.

I, Martha Sukey, a Mid wife, on oath state that I attended on Mrs. Lucy Murrell, wife of Calhoun Murrell on the 13 day of April, 1903; that there was born to her on said date a male child; that said child is now living and is said to have been named Wiley Murrell

Martha Sukey

Witnesses To Mark:

Applications for Enrollment of Creek Newborn
Act of 1905   Volume IV

Subscribed and sworn to before me this 24 day of March, 1905.

Edw C Griesel
Notary Public.

(Copy) BA-2462-*(illegible)*

DEPARTMENT OF THE INTERIOR,
COMMISSION TO THE FIVE CIVILIZED TRIBES.

Near Senora, I. T.,   April 21, 1905.

In the matter of the application for the enrollment of certain new-born children of "Snake" parents.

Louie Lowe, being duly sworn, testified as follows (through Official Interpreter Alex Posey.)

EXAMINATION BY THE COMMISSION:
Q What is your name? A Louie Lowe.
Q What is your age? A 25.
Q What is your postoffice? A Henryetta.
Q Are you a citizen of the Creek Nation? A I am a member of the Okchiye Town and Fishpond Town.

Statement: Lijah Toney of Hickory Ground and Losanna Lowe of Kialigee Town have a child named Foley Toney living. It is two years, two months and twenty-five days old. Their Postoffice is Henryetta.

Peter Sloan, a Seminole and Lodie of Weogufky Town have a child near three years old, and the youngest about a year old. The older named Lillie and the other's name is not know[sic], but it is a boy, both are living. Their postoffice is Henryetta.

I think Cakochee of Thlewarthle and Lucinda of Eufaula, Indian Territory. Canadian have a child that hasn't been filed for yet. It is about a year old. Don't know its name. It is a boy and living. Their postoffice is Senora but he never goes after his mail. It is usually returned.

Lillie Harjo in Weogufky and Sukie Harjo of Kialigee have one child; was born in either January of[sic] February this year, and is now living. Its mother is dead. I don't know its name, but it is under the custody of Joe and Cinda Yahdihka, whose postoffice is Dustin.

Applications for Enrollment of Creek Newborn
Act of 1905   Volume IV

Letka Chupco and Jenely, Leetka is of Fishpond or Greenleaf and Jenely of Mialigee Town. They have three children; one set of twins, both boys, nearly three years old, and the youngest child is a girl born last October. The twins are named John and Johnson and I don't know the name of the little girl; all three are living. Postoffice Senora. I think you have now all the children in this neighborhood, except those that will be born tonight.

(The above testimony was partly given by Louis Harjo of Senora, about 35 years of age, who was duly sworn through Official Interpreter).

Henry G. Hains, being duly sworn, on his oath states that the above and foregoing is a true and correct transcript of his stenographic notes as taken in said cause on said date.
(signed) HENRY G. HAINS.
Subscribed and sworn to before me this 11th day of May, 1905.
(signed) DRENNAN C SKAGGS.
Notary Public.

BIRTH AFFIDAVIT.

DEPARTMENT OF THE INTERIOR.
COMMISSION TO THE FIVE CIVILIZED TRIBES.

IN RE APPLICATION FOR ENROLLMENT, as a citizen of the Creek Nation, of Jefferson Tiger, born on the 4th day of September, 1904

Name of Father: Lilly Tiger (or Kachoche)   a citizen of the   Creek   Nation.
   Thlewathle Town.
Name of Mother: Lucinda Tiger   a citizen of the   Creek   Nation.
   Eufaula Canadian Town.
                    Postoffice   Henryetta, I.T.

AFFIDAVIT OF MOTHER.

UNITED STATES OF AMERICA, Indian Territory, }
   Western   DISTRICT.

I, Lucinda Tiger, on oath state that I am about 39 years of age and a citizen by blood, of the Creek Nation; that I am the lawful wife of Lilly Tiger, who is a citizen, by blood of the Creek Nation; that a male child was born to me on 4th day of September, 1904, that said child has been named Jefferson Tiger, and was living March 4, 1905. That no one attended on me as physician or mid-wife at the birth of the child.

Applications for Enrollment of Creek Newborn
Act of 1905 Volume IV

                                                                         her
                                                                    Lucinda x Tiger

Witnesses To Mark: mark
  { DC Skaggs
    Alex Posey

Subscribed and sworn to before me this 21 day of June , 1905.

                                                    Drennan C Skaggs
                                                  Notary Public.

AFFIDAVIT OF ATTENDING PHYSICIAN OR MID-WIFE.

UNITED STATES OF AMERICA, Indian Territory,
    Western   DISTRICT.

                                                                   are acquainted with
I, We, the undersigned, , a *(blank)* , on oath state that I we attended on Mrs. Lucinda Tiger , wife of Lilly Tiger on the *(blank)* day of *(blank)* , 190 ; that there was born to her on or about the 4th day of September, 1904 a male said date a *(blank)* child; that said child was living March 4, 1905, and is said to have been named Jefferson Tiger
                                                  her
                                                Louisa x Riley
Witnesses To Mark: mark
  { DC Skaggs   her
    Alex Posey   Sarah x Riley
                                                mark
Subscribed and sworn to before me this 21 day of June, 1905.

                                                  Drennan C Skaggs
                                                 Notary Public.

BIRTH AFFIDAVIT.

                                     DEPARTMENT OF THE INTERIOR.
COMMISSION TO THE FIVE CIVILIZED TRIBES.

    IN RE APPLICATION FOR ENROLLMENT, as a citizen of the Creek Nation, of Albert John , born on or about the 10 day of October , 1903

Name of Father: Short John   a citizen of the   Creek   Nation.
Name of Mother: Winey John   a citizen of the   Creek   Nation.
                                           Postoffice   Dustin, Ind. Ter.

Applications for Enrollment of Creek Newborn
Act of 1905 Volume IV

AFFIDAVIT OF MOTHER.

UNITED STATES OF AMERICA, Indian Territory,
Western DISTRICT.

    I, Winey John , on oath state that I am about 26 years of age and a citizen by blood , of the Creek Nation; that I am the lawful wife of Short John , who is a citizen, by blood of the Creek Nation; that a male child was born to me on or about 10 day of October , 1903 , that said child has been named Albert John , and was living March 4, 1905.

                                                    her
                                         Winey x John
Witnesses To Mark: mark
    { Alex Posey
      DC Skaggs

    Subscribed and sworn to before me this 20 day of March , 1905.

                                      Drennan C Skaggs
                                              Notary Public.

AFFIDAVIT OF ATTENDING PHYSICIAN OR MID-WIFE.

UNITED STATES OF AMERICA, Indian Territory,
Western DISTRICT.

    I, Lucinda Scott , a midwife , on oath state that I attended on Mrs. Winey John , wife of Short John on or about the 10 day of October , 1903 ; that there was born to her on said date a male child; that said child was living March 4, 1905, and is said to have been named Albert John

                                                  her
                                       Lucinda x Scott
Witnesses To Mark: mark
    { Alex Posey
      DC Skaggs
Subscribed and sworn to before me this 20 day of March, 1905.

                                      Drennan C Skaggs
                                             Notary Public.

Applications for Enrollment of Creek Newborn
Act of 1905 Volume IV

NC 320.

Muskogee, Indian Territory, June 5, 1905.

Lizzie Brown,
    Dustin, Indian Territory.

Dear Madam:

    In the matter of the application for the enrollment of your minor child, Sandy Brown as a citizen of the Creek Nation, you are advised that the Commission requires the affidavits of two disinterested witnesses relative to the birth of said child.

    There are herewith enclosed two blank forms of birth affidavit, and in executing same care should be exercised to see that all blanks are properly filled, all names written in full and in the event that either of the persons signing the affidavits is unable to write, signatures by mark must be attested by two witnesses. Each affidavit must be executed before a Notary Public and the notarial seal and signature of the officer must be attached to each separate affidavit.

                      Respectfully,

2 BA   Commissioner in Charge.

BIRTH AFFIDAVIT.

DEPARTMENT OF THE INTERIOR.
COMMISSION TO THE FIVE CIVILIZED TRIBES.

    IN RE APPLICATION FOR ENROLLMENT, as a citizen of the Creek Nation, of Ada Brown, born on the 17 day of February , 1902

| Name of Father: | Joe Brown | a citizen of the | Creek | Nation. |
| Name of Mother: | Lizzie Brown | a citizen of the | Creek | Nation. |

                      Postoffice   Dustin, Ind Ter

AFFIDAVIT OF MOTHER.

UNITED STATES OF AMERICA, Indian Territory, }
     Western   DISTRICT.

    I, Lizzie Brown , on oath state that I am about 24 years of age and a citizen by blood , of the Creek Nation; that I am the lawful wife of Joe Brown , who is a citizen, by blood of the Creek Nation; that a female child was born to me on 17 day of

Applications for Enrollment of Creek Newborn
Act of 1905 Volume IV

February, 1902, that said child has been named Ada Brown, and was living March 4, 1905.

                                                       her
Witnesses To Mark: Lizzie x Brown
  { Alex Posey   mark
    DC Skaggs

Subscribed and sworn to before me this 21 day of March, 1905.

                                   Drennan C Skaggs
                                   Notary Public.

AFFIDAVIT OF ATTENDING PHYSICIAN OR MID-WIFE.

UNITED STATES OF AMERICA, Indian Territory,
    Western   **DISTRICT.**

I, Lizzie Winn, a midwife, on oath state that I attended on Mrs. Lizzie Brown, wife of Joe Brown on the ----- day of February, 1902; that there was born to her on said date a female child; that said child was living March 4, 1905, and is said to have been named Ada Brown

                                         her
Witnesses To Mark: Lizzie x Winn
  { Alex Posey   mark
    DC Skaggs

Subscribed and sworn to before me this 21 day of March, 1905.

                                   Drennan C Skaggs
                                   Notary Public.

BIRTH AFFIDAVIT.
                              DEPARTMENT OF THE INTERIOR.
COMMISSION TO THE FIVE CIVILIZED TRIBES.

       IN RE APPLICATION FOR ENROLLMENT, as a citizen of the Creek Nation, of Sandy Brown, born on or about the 8 day of May, 1904

Name of Father: Joe Brown   a citizen of the   Creek   Nation.
    Okchiye Town
Name of Mother: Lizzie Brown   a citizen of the   Creek   Nation.
    Okchiye Town
                                Postoffice   Dustin, Ind Ter

Applications for Enrollment of Creek Newborn
Act of 1905   Volume IV

Acquaintance
AFFIDAVIT OF ~~ATTENDING PHYSICIAN OR MID-WIFE~~.

UNITED STATES OF AMERICA, Indian Territory, ⎱
   Western   DISTRICT.   ⎰

                                                 am acquainted with
    I, Sandy Watson , a ----- , on oath state that I ~~attended on~~ Mrs. Lizzie Brown , wife of Joe Brown on the *(blank)* day of *(blank)* , 1----- ; that there was born to her on or about the 4 day of May, 1904, a male ~~said date a   (blank)~~ child; that said child was living March 4, 1905, and is said to have been named Sandy Brown

                                              Sandy Watson

Witnesses To Mark:
{

Subscribed and sworn to before me this 17 day of June, 1905.

                                             Drennan C Skaggs
                                             Notary Public.

BIRTH AFFIDAVIT.

DEPARTMENT OF THE INTERIOR.
COMMISSION TO THE FIVE CIVILIZED TRIBES.

    IN RE APPLICATION FOR ENROLLMENT, as a citizen of the Creek Nation, of Sandy Brown, born on or about the 8 day of May , 1904

Name of Father:	Joe Brown	a citizen of the	Creek	Nation.
Okchiye Town				
Name of Mother:	Lizzie Brown	a citizen of the	Creek	Nation.
Okchiye Town				

                                       Postoffice   Dustin, I.T.

Acquaintance
AFFIDAVIT OF ~~ATTENDING PHYSICIAN OR MID-WIFE~~.

UNITED STATES OF AMERICA, Indian Territory, ⎱
   Western   DISTRICT.   ⎰

                                                 am acquainted with
    I, Earl Wynn , a ----- , on oath state that I ~~attended on~~ Mrs. Lizzie Brown , wife of Joe Brown on the *(blank)* day of *(blank)* , 1----- ; that there was born to her on May 8, 1904 ~~said date~~ a   male   child; that said child was living March 4, 1905, and is said to have been named Sandy Brown

                                              Earl Wynn

Witnesses To Mark:
{

Applications for Enrollment of Creek Newborn
Act of 1905   Volume IV

Subscribed and sworn to before me this 17 day of June, 1905.

                                      Drennan C Skaggs
                                      Notary Public.

BIRTH AFFIDAVIT.

DEPARTMENT OF THE INTERIOR.
COMMISSION TO THE FIVE CIVILIZED TRIBES.

IN RE APPLICATION FOR ENROLLMENT, as a citizen of the Creek Nation, of Sandy Brown, born on or about the 8 day of May, 1904

Name of Father:	Joe Brown	a citizen of the	Creek	Nation.
Name of Mother:	Lizzie Brown	a citizen of the	Creek	Nation.

                          Postoffice   Dustin, I.T.

AFFIDAVIT OF MOTHER.

UNITED STATES OF AMERICA, Indian Territory,
      Western   DISTRICT.

I, Lizzie Brown, on oath state that I am about 24 years of age and a citizen by blood, of the Creek Nation; that I am the lawful wife of Joe Brown, who is a citizen, by blood of the Creek Nation; that a male child was born to me on 8 day of May, 1904, that said child has been named Sandy Brown, and was living March 4, 1905. That no one attended on me as midwife or physician at the birth of the child.

                                        her
                                Lizzie x Brown

Witnesses To Mark: mark
   { Alex Posey
   { DC Skaggs

Subscribed and sworn to before me this 21 day of March, 1905.

                                      Drennan C Skaggs
                                      Notary Public.

Applications for Enrollment of Creek Newborn
Act of 1905 Volume IV

BIRTH AFFIDAVIT.

DEPARTMENT OF THE INTERIOR.
COMMISSION TO THE FIVE CIVILIZED TRIBES.

    IN RE APPLICATION FOR ENROLLMENT, as a citizen of the Creek Nation, of Thomas Clifford Brooks, born on the 12 day of March , 1904

Name of Father: John Brooks   a citizen of the United States Nation.
Name of Mother: Bettie Brooks (nee Chisholm) a citizen of the Creek   Nation.

        Postoffice   Hanna[sic], Ind. Ter.

AFFIDAVIT OF MOTHER.

UNITED STATES OF AMERICA, Indian Territory, ⎫
    Western   DISTRICT.   ⎬

    I, Bettie Brooks , on oath state that I am 22 years of age and a citizen by blood, of the Creek Nation; that I am the lawful wife of John Brooks , who is a citizen, by *(blank)* of the United States Nation; that a male child was born to me on 12 day of March , 1904 , that said child has been named Thomas Clifford Brooks , and was living March 4, 1905.

                                    Bettie Brooks
Witnesses To Mark:
{

    Subscribed and sworn to before me this 21 day of March , 1905.

                              Drennan C Skaggs
                                Notary Public.

AFFIDAVIT OF ATTENDING PHYSICIAN OR MID-WIFE.

UNITED STATES OF AMERICA, Indian Territory, ⎫
    Western   DISTRICT.   ⎬

    I, Mattie Chisholm , a midwife , on oath state that I attended on Mrs. Bettie Brooks , wife of John Brooks on the ~~(blank) day of~~ March , 1904 ; that there was born to her on said date a male child; that said child was living March 4, 1905, and is said to have been named Thomas Clifford Brooks
                                  her
                         Mattie x Chisholm
Witnesses To Mark: mark
  { Alex Posey
    DC Skaggs

Applications for Enrollment of Creek Newborn
Act of 1905 Volume IV

Subscribed and sworn to before me this 21 day of March, 1905.

          Drennan C Skaggs
          Notary Public.

Indian Territory, I
      I ss.
Western District. I

  We, the undersigned, do hereby elect to have our child, Joseph Mitchell, born on the 22 day of February, 1905, enrolled as a citizen of the Creek Nation, and to have said child receive his allotment of land and distribution of moneys in said nation.

	his
Witness to mark:	Sam x Mitchell
J McDermott	mark
H.L. Fairfield	her
	Nellie x Mitchell
	mark

Subscribed and sworn to before me this 24 day of Nov, 1906.
My Commission
Expires July 25, 1907   J. McDermott
            Notary Public.

AFFIDAVIT OF DISINTERESTED WITNESS.

UNITED STATES OF AMERICA,
Western DISTRICT,   SS
 INDIAN TERRITORY.

  We, the undersigned, on oath state that we are personally acquainted with Nellie Mitchell, the wife of Sam Mitchell; that there was born to her a male child on or about the 22 day of February 1905; that the said child has been named Joseph Mitchell, and was living March 4, 1905, and is now living.

  We further state that we have no interest in this case.

	her
	Eliza x Stidham
Witnesses: J Mitchell	mark
	his
H.L. Fairfield	Timmy x Stidham
	mark

Applications for Enrollment of Creek Newborn
Act of 1905 Volume IV

Subscribed and sworn to before me this 24 day of November, 1906.

My Commission
Expires July 1907   J McDermott

BIRTH AFFIDAVIT.

DEPARTMENT OF THE INTERIOR.
COMMISSION TO THE FIVE CIVILIZED TRIBES.

IN RE APPLICATION FOR ENROLLMENT, as a citizen of the Creek Nation, of Joseph Mitchell , born on the 22 day of February , 1905

Name of Father:	Sam Mitchell	a citizen of the Creek	Nation.
Name of Mother:	Nellie Mitchell	a citizen of the Seminole	Nation.

Postoffice   Carson, Ind Ter

AFFIDAVIT OF MOTHER.

UNITED STATES OF AMERICA, Indian Territory,
Western   DISTRICT.

I, Nellie Mitchell , on oath state that I am about 30 years of age and a citizen by blood , of the Seminole Nation; that I am the lawful wife of Sam Mitchell , who is a citizen, by blood of the Creek Nation; that a male child was born to me on 22 day of February , 1905 , that said child has been named Joseph Mitchell , and was living March 4, 1905.

                                her
                        Nellie x Mitchell
Witnesses To Mark: mark
 { Alex Posey
   D C Skaggs

Subscribed and sworn to before me this 21 day of March , 1905.

                        Drennan C Skaggs
                        Notary Public.

Applications for Enrollment of Creek Newborn
Act of 1905   Volume IV

AFFIDAVIT OF ATTENDING PHYSICIAN OR MID-WIFE.

UNITED STATES OF AMERICA, Indian Territory,
Western DISTRICT.

my wife
I, Sam Mitchell , ~~a~~ *(blank)* , on oath state that I attended on ^ Mrs. Nellie Mitchell , ~~wife of~~ *(blank)* on the 22 day of February , 1905 ; that there was born to her on said date a *(blank)* child; that said child was living March 4, 1905, and is said to have been named Joseph Mitchell

Sam Mitchell

Witnesses To Mark:

Subscribed and sworn to before me this 21 day of March , 1905.

Drennan C Skaggs
Notary Public.

AFFIDAVIT OF ATTENDING PHYSICIAN OR MID-WIFE.

UNITED STATES OF AMERICA, Indian Territory,
Western DISTRICT.

visited
I, Solomon McGirt , a Witness , on oath state that I ~~attended~~ on Mrs. Nellie Mitchell , wife of Sam Mitchell on the 22 day of Feb , 1905 ; that there was born to her on said date a male child; that said child is now living and is said to have been named Joseph Mitchell

Solomon McGirt

Witnesses To Mark:
JS Swofford
Tim Stidham

Subscribed and sworn to before me this 11 day of Sept, 1905.

Barney C. Robison
Notary Public.

Applications for Enrollment of Creek Newborn
Act of 1905 Volume IV

BIRTH AFFIDAVIT.

DEPARTMENT OF THE INTERIOR.
COMMISSION TO THE FIVE CIVILIZED TRIBES.

IN RE APPLICATION FOR ENROLLMENT, as a citizen of the Creek Nation, of Joseph Mitchell, born on the 22 day of Feb, 1905

Name of Father:	Sam Mitchell	a citizen of the	Creek	Nation.
Name of Mother:	Nellie Mitchell	a citizen of the	Seminole	Nation.

Postoffice Carson, I.T.

AFFIDAVIT OF MOTHER.

UNITED STATES OF AMERICA, Indian Territory,
Western DISTRICT.

I, Nellie Mitchell, on oath state that I am 25 years of age and a citizen by Blood, of the Seminole Nation; that I am the lawful wife of Sam Mitchell, who is a citizen, by Blood of the Creek Nation; that a male child was born to me on 22 day of Feb, 1905, that said child has been named Joseph Mitchell, and was living March 4, 1905.

her
Nellie x Mitchell
mark

Witnesses To Mark:
- Tim Stidham
- Robert Bruner

Subscribed and sworn to before me this 11 day of Sept., 1905.

Barney C Robison
Notary Public.

AFFIDAVIT OF ATTENDING PHYSICIAN OR MID-WIFE.

UNITED STATES OF AMERICA, Indian Territory,
Western DISTRICT.

I, Sam Mitchell, a husband, on oath state that I attended on Mrs. Nellie Mitchell, wife of myself on the 22 day of Feb, 1905; that there was born to her on said date a male child; that said child was living March 4, 1905, and is said to have been named Joseph Mitchell

Sam Mitchell

Witnesses To Mark:

Applications for Enrollment of Creek Newborn
Act of 1905   Volume IV

Subscribed and sworn to before me this 11 day of Sept , 1905.

Com Ex Sept 4, 08

Barney C Robison
Notary Public.

AFFIDAVIT OF ATTENDING PHYSICIAN OR MID-WIFE.

UNITED STATES OF AMERICA,
INDIAN TERRITORY,
Western   District.

I, Solomon McGirt , a Witness , on oath state that I ~~attended on~~ visited Mrs. Nellie Mitchell , wife of Sam Mitchell on the 22 day of Feb , 1905 ; that there was born to her on said date a male child; that said child is now living and is said to have been named Joseph Mitchell

Solomon x McGirt
his mark

Subscribed and sworn to before me this 11 day of Spt, 1905.

Barney C Robison
Notary Public.

Witness to mark
J.S. Swofford
Tim Stidham

Com ex Sept. 4 08

BIRTH AFFIDAVIT.

DEPARTMENT OF THE INTERIOR.
COMMISSION TO THE FIVE CIVILIZED TRIBES.

IN RE APPLICATION FOR ENROLLMENT, as a citizen of the Creek Nation, of Joseph Mitchell , born on the 22 day of Feb , 1905

Name of Father:	Sam Mitchell	a citizen of the Creek	Nation.
Name of Mother:	Nellie Mitchell	a citizen of the Seminole	Nation.

Postoffice   Carson I.T.

Applications for Enrollment of Creek Newborn
Act of 1905 Volume IV

AFFIDAVIT OF MOTHER.

UNITED STATES OF AMERICA, Indian Territory, }
    Western   DISTRICT.

    I, Nellie Mitchell , on oath state that I am 25 years of age and a citizen by Blood , of the Seminole Nation; that I am the lawful wife of Sam Mitchell , who is a citizen, by Blood of the Creek Nation; that a male child was born to me on 22 day of Feb , 1905 , that said child has been named Joseph Mitchell , and was living March 4, 1905.

                                                                           her
                                                                      Nellie x Mitchell
                                                                        mark

Witnesses To Mark:
   { Tim Stidham
      Robert Bruner

    Subscribed and sworn to before me this 11 day of Sept. , 1905.

                                             Barney C Robison
                                             Notary Public.

AFFIDAVIT OF ATTENDING PHYSICIAN OR MID-WIFE.

UNITED STATES OF AMERICA, Indian Territory, }
    Western   DISTRICT.

    I, Sam Mitchell , a Husband , on oath state that I attended on Mrs. Sam Mitchell , wife of myself on the 22 day of Feb , 1905 ; that there was born to her on said date a male child; that said child was living March 4, 1905, and is said to have been named Joseph Mitchell

                                             Sam Mitchell

Witnesses To Mark:
   {

    Subscribed and sworn to before me this 11 day of Sept , 1905.

                                             Barney C Robison
Com Ex Sept 4, 08   Notary Public.

(The first Birth Affidavit was given again)

Applications for Enrollment of Creek Newborn
Act of 1905   Volume IV

Cr NC-322

Muskogee, Indian Territory, June 9, 1905.

Nellie Mitchell,
    Carson, Indian Territory.

Dear Madam:

    In the matter of the application for the enrollment of your minor child, Joseph Mitchell, as a citizen of the Creek Nation, you are advised that the Commission requires the affidavits of two disinterested witnesses relative to the date of its birth. For this purpose, there are herewith enclosed two blank forms of birth affidavit. In having same executed, care should be exercised to see that all blanks are properly filled, all names written in full and in the event that the person signing an affidavit is unable to write, signature by mark must be attested by two witnesses.

    You are hereby advised that you will be allowed fifteen days from date herein within which to appear before the Commission at its office in Muskogee, Indian Territory, for the purpose of electing in which Nation you desire to have said Joseph Mitchell enrolled, in case it should be found that he is entitled to enrollment in either the Creek or Seminole Nation.

                Respectfully,

                                  Chairman.

NC. 322.

Muskogee, Indian Territory, July 14, 1905.

Commissioner to the Five Civilized Tribes,
    Seminole Enrollment Division,
        Muskogee, Indian Territory.

Gentlemen:

    March 23, 1905, application was mad to the Commission to the Five Civilized Tribes for the enrollment of Joseph Mitchell, born February 22, 1905, as a citizen by blood of the Creek Nation. It is stated in said application that the father of said child is Sam Mitchell, a citizen of the Creek Nation, and that the mother is Nellie Mitchell, a citizen of the Seminole Nation.

    You are requested to inform the Creek Enrollment Division a to whether application has been made for the enrollment of said Joseph Mitchell, as a citizen of the Seminole Nation, and if so, what disposition has been made of the same.

Applications for Enrollment of Creek Newborn
Act of 1905 Volume IV

Respectfully,

Commissioner.

DEPARTMENT OF THE INTERIOR.
COMMISSION TO THE FIVE CIVILIZED TRIBES.

Muskogee, Indian Territory, July 18, 1905.

Chief Clerk,
    Creek Enrollment Division.

Dear Sir:

    Receipt is hereby acknowledged of your letter of July 14, 1905, (NC-322) stating that an application was made to the Commission to the Five Civilized Tribes for the enrollment of Joseph Mitchell, born February 22, 1905, child of Sam Mitchell, a citizen of the Creek Nation, and Nellie Mitchell, a citizen of the Seminole Nation, as a citizen by blood of the Creek Nation and requesting to be advised as to whether application has been made for the enrollment of said child as a citizen of the Seminole Nation.

    In reply to your letter you are advised that it does not appear from an examination of the records of this office that any application was made to the Commission to the Five Civilized Tribes for the enrollment of said Joseph Mitchell as a citizen of the Seminole Nation.

Respectfully,

Tams Bixby   Commissioner.

NC-322.

Muskogee, Indian Territory, July 29, 1905.

Sam Mitchell,
    Carson, Indian Territory.

Dear Sir:

    In the matter of the application for the enrollment of your son Joseph Mitchell, born February 22, 1905, as a citizen by blood of the Creek Nation, you are advised that it will be necessary for you to file with this office the affidavits of two disinterested persons who are acquainted with said child, know when he was born, the names of his parents and whether or not he was living March 4, 1905.

Applications for Enrollment of Creek Newborn
Act of 1905   Volume IV

You are also requested to file with this office the joint affidavit of yourself and wife, Nellie Mitchell, electing whether you will have the said Joseph Mitchell finally enrolled as a citizen by blood of the Creek Nation or the Seminole Nation.

Please give this matter your immediate attention.

Respectfully,

Commissioner.

NC 322.

Muskogee, Indian Territory, March 1, 1907.

Sam Mitchell,
    Carson, Indian Territory.

Dear Sir:

You are hereby advised that on   , the Secretary of the Interior approved the enrollment of your minor child, , as a citizen by blood of the Nation, and that the name of said child appears upon the roll of new born citizens of the Nation as Number   . February 15, 1907, the Secretary of the Interior approved the enrollment of your minor child, Joseph Mitchell, as a citizen by blood of the Creek Nation, and that the name of said child appears upon the roll of New Born citizens by blood of the Creek Nation, enrolled under the Act of Congress approved March 3, 1905, as number 1133.

The child is now entitled to an allotment, and application therefor should be made without delay at the Creek Land Office, Muskogee, Indian Territory.

Respectfully,

Commissioner.

Applications for Enrollment of Creek Newborn
Act of 1905   Volume IV

BIRTH AFFIDAVIT.

DEPARTMENT OF THE INTERIOR.
COMMISSION TO THE FIVE CIVILIZED TRIBES.

IN RE APPLICATION FOR ENROLLMENT, as a citizen of the Creek Nation, of Stella Sandy, born on the 15 day of May, 1904

Name of Father:	Jacob Sandy	a citizen of the	Creek	Nation.
Name of Mother:	Sophia Sandy	a citizen of the	Creek	Nation.

Postoffice   Wetumka, Ind. Ter.

AFFIDAVIT OF MOTHER.

UNITED STATES OF AMERICA, Indian Territory, ⎫
   Western   DISTRICT.   ⎬

I, Sophia Sandy, on oath state that I am about 28 years of age and a citizen by blood, of the Creek Nation; that I am the lawful wife of Jacob Sandy, who is a citizen, by blood of the Creek Nation; that a female child was born to me on 15 day of May, 1904, that said child has been named Stella Sandy, and was living March 4, 1905.

                                                            her
                                               Sophia x Sandy
Witnesses To Mark: mark
   { Alex Posey
     DC Skaggs

Subscribed and sworn to before me this 21 day of March, 1905.

                                             Drennan C Skaggs
                                             Notary Public.

AFFIDAVIT OF ATTENDING PHYSICIAN OR MID-WIFE.

UNITED STATES OF AMERICA, Indian Territory, ⎫
   Western   DISTRICT.   ⎬

I, Melia Fish, a midwife, on oath state that I attended on Mrs. Sophia Sandy, wife of Jacob Sandy on ~~the~~ Sunday ~~day of~~ May, 1904; that there was born to her on said date a female child; that said child was living March 4, 1905, and is said to have been named Stella Sandy

                                                   her
                                             Melia x Fish
Witnesses To Mark: mark
   { Alex Posey
     DC Skaggs

Applications for Enrollment of Creek Newborn
Act of 1905   Volume IV

Subscribed and sworn to before me this 21 day of March, 1905.

                     Drennan C Skaggs
                     Notary Public.

BIRTH AFFIDAVIT.

DEPARTMENT OF THE INTERIOR.
COMMISSION TO THE FIVE CIVILIZED TRIBES.

IN RE APPLICATION FOR ENROLLMENT, as a citizen of the Creek Nation, of Hugh Benjamin Key, born on the 29th day of January, 1904

Name of Father:	John E. Key	a citizen of the	*(blank)*	Nation.
Name of Mother:	Luella Key, (Nee Henry)	a citizen of the	Creek	Nation.

               Postoffice   Henryetta Ind Ter.

AFFIDAVIT OF MOTHER.

UNITED STATES OF AMERICA, Indian Territory,
     Western   DISTRICT.

I, Luella Key (Nee Henry), on oath state that I am 22 years of age and a citizen by blood, of the Creek Nation; that I am the lawful wife of John S. Key, who is a citizen, by *(blank)* of the *(blank)* Nation; that a Male child was born to me on 29th day of January, 1904, that said child has been named Hugh Benjamin Key, and is now living.

                     Luella Key

Witnesses To Mark:

Subscribed and sworn to before me this 20th day of March, 1905.

My commission expires January 18-1908   J.O. Hamilton
                                           Notary Public.

AFFIDAVIT OF ATTENDING PHYSICIAN OR MID-WIFE.

UNITED STATES OF AMERICA, Indian Territory,
     Western   DISTRICT.

I, Charles E. Scharnagel, a Physician, on oath state that I attended on Mrs. Luella Key (Nee Henry), wife of John E. Key on the 29th day of January, 1904;

Applications for Enrollment of Creek Newborn
Act of 1905 Volume IV

that there was born to her on said date a Male child; that said child is now living and is said to have been named Hugh Benjamin Key

                                                Chas E. Scharnagel M.D.

Witnesses To Mark:
{

    Subscribed and sworn to before me this 20th day of March , 1905.

My commission expires January 18-1908   J.O. Hamilton
                                                        Notary Public.

BIRTH AFFIDAVIT.

DEPARTMENT OF THE INTERIOR.
COMMISSION TO THE FIVE CIVILIZED TRIBES.

IN RE APPLICATION FOR ENROLLMENT, as a citizen of the Creek Nation, of Hillibe Micco Henry, born on the 4th day of February , 1902

Name of Father:	Hugh Henry	a citizen of the	Creek	Nation.
Name of Mother:	Mintie Henry	a citizen of the	*(blank)*	Nation.

                                    Postoffice   Henryetta Ind. Ter.

AFFIDAVIT OF MOTHER.

UNITED STATES OF AMERICA, Indian Territory, }
    Western   **DISTRICT.**

    I, Mintie Henry , on oath state that I am 38 years of age and a citizen by *(blank)* , of the *(blank)* Nation; that I am the lawful wife of Hugh Henry , who is a citizen, by blood of the Creek Nation; that a Male child was born to me on 4th day of February , 1902 , that said child has been named Hillibe Micco Henry , and was living March 4, 1905.

                                                          her
                                                Mintie x Henry
Witnesses To Mark: mark
   { Belle C. Scharnagel
     John E. Key

Applications for Enrollment of Creek Newborn
Act of 1905   Volume IV

Subscribed and sworn to before me this 20th day of March , 1905.

                                      Olin W. Meacham
                                      Notary Public.
My com expires Aug 30 1906

AFFIDAVIT OF ATTENDING PHYSICIAN OR MID-WIFE.

UNITED STATES OF AMERICA, Indian Territory,
    Western   DISTRICT.

    I, Charles E. Scharnagel , a Physician , on oath state that I attended on Mrs. Mintie Henry , wife of Hugh Henry on the 4th day of February , 1902 ; that there was born to her on said date a   Male   child; that said child was living March 4, 1905, and is said to have been named Hillibe Micco Henry

                                      Charles E. Scharnagel M.D.

Witnesses To Mark:

    Subscribed and sworn to before me this 20th day of March , 1905.

                                      Olin W. Meacham
                                      Notary Public.
My com expires Aug 30 1906

(The letter below typed as given on microfilm.)

Western District I.T.   HANNA, I. T.   MAR 20 1905

I, Mrs T.E. McCan the (under signed) Do soleny sware I was and assistant on Mrs C C Gatlin a Creek citizen/ formerly Miss Lucy Ann Byrd) on the 20 of January 1904 whin her Daughter Hellen Gatlin was borned the Phusuin that attended her was Dr J.P. Owen and he is now Dead   Mrs T E McCan

Notary Public. sworn to before   DM Crawford
me this the 20 Day of March 1905   Notary Publik
                                  Term expires
                                      Sept 19, 1907

Applications for Enrollment of Creek Newborn
Act of 1905   Volume IV

BIRTH AFFIDAVIT.

DEPARTMENT OF THE INTERIOR.
COMMISSION TO THE FIVE CIVILIZED TRIBES.

    IN RE APPLICATION FOR ENROLLMENT, as a citizen of the Creek Nation, of Hellen Gatlin, born on the 20 day of January , 1904

Name of Father:	C. C. Gatlin	a citizen of the United States Nation.
Name of Mother:	Lucile Gatlin	a citizen of the Creek Nation.

                        Postoffice   Hanna, Ind. Ter.

AFFIDAVIT OF MOTHER.

UNITED STATES OF AMERICA, Indian Territory, ⎫
      Western   DISTRICT.   ⎭

    I, Lucile Gatlin , on oath state that I am 22 years of age and a citizen by blood , of the Creek   Nation; that I am the lawful wife of   C. C. Gatlin , who is a citizen, ~~by~~ *(blank)* of the United States   Nation; that a female   child was born to me on 20   day of January , 1904 , that said child has been named Hellen Gatlin , and was living March 4, 1905.

                                                 Lucile Gatlin

Witnesses To Mark:

    Subscribed and sworn to before me this 20 day of   March , 1905.

                                        Drennan C Skaggs
                                            Notary Public.

NC-326.

                              Muskogee, Indian Territory, July 29, 1905.

Lucy Ann Gatlin,
    Hanna, Indian Territory.

Dear Madam:

    There is on file with the records of this office an application for the enrollment of your minor daughter Helen Gatlin as a citizen by blood of the Creek Nation. You have been identified upon the final roll of citizens by blood of the Creek Nation as Lucy Ann Byrd. It is noted that you signed the affidavit as to the birth of your said daughter as

Applications for Enrollment of Creek Newborn
Act of 1905 Volume IV

Lucile Gatlin. The affidavit of Mrs. T. E. McCan, who assisted at the birth of your child does not set forth whether or not your said daughter was living March 4, 1905.

For the purpose of correcting the various discrepancies which occur in the record there is inclosed[sic] herewith blank proof of birth which has been partially filled out which you are requested to have properly executed and return to this office in the inclosed[sic] envelope.

Be careful to sign your affidavit as to the birth of your said daughter as your name appears in the body of the affidavit "Lucy Ann Gatlin", and to see that the notary public before whom the affidavits are sworn to attaches his name and seal to each affidavit.

       Respectfully,

          Commissioner.

CTD-7

BIRTH AFFIDAVIT.

DEPARTMENT OF THE INTERIOR.
COMMISSION TO THE FIVE CIVILIZED TRIBES.

IN RE APPLICATION FOR ENROLLMENT, as a citizen of the Creek Nation, of Helen Gatlin, born on the 20th day of January, 1904

Name of Father:	C. C. Gatlin	a citizen of the United States	Nation.
Name of Mother:	Lucy Ann Gatlin	a citizen of the Creek	Nation.
	(nee Byrd)		
		Postoffice Hanna, Ind. Ter.	

AFFIDAVIT OF MOTHER.

UNITED STATES OF AMERICA, Indian Territory,
 Western   DISTRICT.

  I, Lucy Ann Gatlin, on oath state that I am 22 years of age and a citizen by blood, of the Creek Nation; that I am the lawful wife of C. C. Gatlin, who is a citizen, by *(blank)* of the United States ~~Nation~~; that a female child was born to me on 20th day of January, 1904, that said child has been named Helen Gatlin, and was living March 4, 1905.

         Lucy Ann Gatlin

Witnesses To Mark:

  Subscribed and sworn to before me this 1 day of Aug, 1905.

Applications for Enrollment of Creek Newborn
Act of 1905 Volume IV

My commission expires Aug 12/0.   H.T. Norman
                                                                    Notary Public.

AFFIDAVIT OF ATTENDING PHYSICIAN OR MID-WIFE.

UNITED STATES OF AMERICA, Indian Territory, ⎫
    Western   DISTRICT.   ⎬

I, Mrs. T.E. McCan , a mid-wife , on oath state that I attended on Mrs. Lucy Ann Gatlin , wife of C. C. Gatlin on the 20th day of January , 1904 ; that there was born to her on said date a female child; that said child was living March 4, 1905, and is said to have been named Helen Gatlin

                                            Mrs. T. E. McCan

Witnesses To Mark:
⎰
⎱

Subscribed and sworn to before me this 1 day of Aug , 1905.

My commission expires Aug 12/0.   H.T. Norman
                                                                    Notary Public.

Cr NC-327

Muskogee, Indian Territory, June 9, 1905.

Melvina Ditzler,
    Weleetka, Indian Territory.

Dear Madam:

    In the matter of the application for the enrollment of your minor child, James Albert Ditzler, as a citizen of the Creek Nation, you are advised that the Commission requires the affidavit of the midwife or physician in attendance at the birth of said child. If the same cannot be secured, the affidavits of two disinterested witnesses relative to the birth of said child should be supplied.

    For this purpose, there are herewith enclosed two blank forms of birth affidavit. In having same executed, care should be taken to see that all blanks are properly filled, all names written in full and in the event that the person signing an affidavit is unable to write, signatures by mark must be attested by two witnesses.

Applications for Enrollment of Creek Newborn
Act of 1905   Volume IV

Respectfully,

Chairman.

2 B A

NC-327.

Muskogee, Indian Territory, July 29, 1905.

Will Ditzler,
    Weleetka, Indian Territory.

Dear Sir:

    In the matter of the application for the enrollment of your minor son James Albert Ditzler, born January 12, 1905, as a citizen by blood of the Creek Nation, you are advised that it will be necessary for you to file with this office the affidavit of the attending physician or midwife at the birth of said child and a blank for that purpose is inclosed[sic] herewith.

    If there was no physician or midwife in attendance at the birth of said child it will be necessary for you to file the affidavit of two disinterested witnesses setting forth when said child was born, the names of his parents and whether or not he was living March 4, 1905.

Respectfully,

Commissioner.

BC
Env.

The United States of America,)
                                                    ss.
Indian Territory, Western District,)

    I, Rosie Fisher, being first duly sworn deposes and says, that I am over the age of twenty-two years, that I now do and have for the past six years resided near Bryant, Creek Nation, Indian Territory, that I am well acquainted with Wm. H. Ditzler and Melvina Ditzler and have known them for the past five years and that they reside about two and one half miles from where I reside. That they are husband and wife and the father and mother of a male child, named James Albert Ditzler, which child was born on the 12th day of January, 1905, and that the said child is now living.

Rosie Fisher

Subscribed and sworn to before me 17th day of August, 1905.

Applications for Enrollment of Creek Newborn
Act of 1905   Volume IV

Commission Expires May, 25, 1907.   W.D. Shallenberger
Notary Public.

The United States of America,   )
ss.
Indian Territory, Western District,   )

    I, Laura Howard, being first duly sworn, state that I am over 45 years of age. That I am well acquainted with Wm. H. Ditzler and Melvina Ditzler, that I live about one half mile of their residence, that they are husband and wife, and that they are the father and mother of a male child named James Albert Ditzler, which child was born in the month of January, 1905, and is now living.

                                                    Laura Howard

Subscribed and sworn to before me 17th day of August, 1905.

                                        W.D. Shallenberger
                                              Notary Public.
My Commission Expires May, 25, 1907

BIRTH AFFIDAVIT.

DEPARTMENT OF THE INTERIOR.
COMMISSION TO THE FIVE CIVILIZED TRIBES.

    IN RE APPLICATION FOR ENROLLMENT, as a citizen of the Creek Nation, of James Albert Ditzler, born on the 12 day of January, 1904

Name of Father:	W.H. Ditzler	a citizen of the U.S. States	Nation.
Name of Mother:	Melvina Ditzler	a citizen of the Creek	Nation.

                                      Postoffice   Weleetka I T

AFFIDAVIT OF MOTHER.

UNITED STATES OF AMERICA, Indian Territory,
    Western   DISTRICT.

    I, Melvina Ditzler , on oath state that I am Twenty years of age and a citizen by birt[sic] Blood , of the Creek   Nation; that I am the lawful wife of W.H. Ditzler , ~~who is a citizen, by~~ *(blank)*   of the *(blank)* ~~Nation~~; that a male   child was born to me on the Twelth[sic] 12   day of January , 1904 , that said child has been named   James Albert Ditzler , and was living March 4, 1905. That there was no physician or mid-wife present at the birth of said child

Applications for Enrollment of Creek Newborn
Act of 1905 Volume IV

                        her
                    Melvina x Ditzler
                        mark

Witnesses To Mark:
{ A A Hatch
{ Rosie Fisher

Subscribed and sworn to before me this 17 day of Aug , 1905.

                      W D Shallenberger
                      Notary Public.

BIRTH AFFIDAVIT.
DEPARTMENT OF THE INTERIOR.
COMMISSION TO THE FIVE CIVILIZED TRIBES.

IN RE APPLICATION FOR ENROLLMENT, as a citizen of the Creek Nation, of James Albert Ditzler, born on the 12 day of January, 1905

Name of Father: Will Ditzler   a citizen of the United States Nation.
Name of Mother: Melvina Ditzler (nee Barnett)   a citizen of the Creek Nation.

                Postoffice   Weleetka, I. T.

AFFIDAVIT OF MOTHER.

UNITED STATES OF AMERICA, Indian Territory, }
    Western   DISTRICT.

    I, Melvina Ditzler , on oath state that I am 21 years of age and a citizen by Blood , of the Creek Nation; that I am the lawful wife of Will Ditzler , who is a citizen, ~~by~~ *(blank)* of the United States ~~Nation~~; that a male child was born to me on the 12 day of January , 1905 , that said child has been named James Albert Ditzler , and was living March 4, 1905.
                            her
                    Melvina x Ditzler
                        mark

Witnesses To Mark:
{ DC Skaggs
{ Alex Posey

Subscribed and sworn to before me this 21 day of March , 1905.

                    Drennan C Skaggs
                      Notary Public.

Applications for Enrollment of Creek Newborn
Act of 1905 Volume IV

AFFIDAVIT OF ATTENDING PHYSICIAN OR MID-WIFE.

UNITED STATES OF AMERICA, Indian Territory, }
Western DISTRICT. }

my wife

I, Will Ditzler, a *(blank)*, on oath state that I attended on ^ Mrs. Melvina Ditzler, wife of *(blank)* on the 12 day of January, 1905 ; that there was born to her on said date a male child; that said child was living March 4, 1905, and is said to have been named James Albert Ditzler

Will Ditzler

Witnesses To Mark:
{

Subscribed and sworn to before me this 21 day of March, 1905.

Drennan C Skaggs
Notary Public.

NC 328.

DEPARTMENT OF THE INTERIOR,
COMMISSIONER TO THE FIVE CIVILIZED RTIBES[sic].
Arbeka, Indian Territory, October 18, 1906.

In the matter of the application for the enrollment of Lewis Davis as a citizen by blood of the Creek Nation.

ELLA DAVIS, being duly sworn, testified as follows:

BY COMMISSIONER:

Q What is your name? A Ella Davis.
Q What is your age? A Now 28.
Q What is your postoffice address? A Arbeka, I.T.
Q Are you a Creek citizen? A I am.
Q Hae you a child that you named Lewis? A I did have.
Q Is he living? A No, he died when he was only six months old. He died the 20th of June the same year that he was born.
Q What year was he born? A January 12, 1902.
Q Are you positive that Lewis was born in January 1902, and that he died the same year? A Yes, I know it.

There is an affidavit on file at the office of the Commissioner to the Five Civilized Tribes, executed by you on August 29, 1904, in which you state that Lewis

Applications for Enrollment of Creek Newborn
Act of 1905 Volume IV

Davis was born January 12, 1901, and that he was deat at the time of the execution of the affidavit.
Q Do you recollect signing such affidavit? A Yes, I recollect something about it but I don't think I told Harve Malot that Lewis was born 1901. If he has that way, it is a mistake.

There is also another affidavit on file at the same office, executed by you on March 15, 1905, before Drennan C Skaggs, a notary, that Lewis was born January 12, 1902, and that he was living March 4, 1905 March 4, 1905.

Q How do you account for that? A I remember going before the Dawes Commission at Okemah and making an affidavit but thy never asked me whether Lewis was living March 4, 1905. They just made out the papers and said for me to sign it and I did.
Q Who is the father of Lewis? A Jesse Davis.

---oooOOOooo---

I, Jesse McDermott, on oath state that the above and foregoing is a full and true transcript of my notes as taken in said cause on said date.

Jesse McDermott

Subscribed and sworn to before me this sworn to before me this 10th day of December, 1906.

Alex Posey
Notary Public.

N.C. 328. F.H.W.
DEPARTMENT OF THE INTERIOR,
COMMISSIONER TO THE FIVE CIVILIZED TRIBES.

In the matter of the application for the enrollment of Lewis Davis, deceased, as a citizen by blood of the Creek Nation.

DECISION.

The record in this case shows that on August 31, 1904, an application was filed, in affidavit form, for the enrollment of Lewis Davis, deceased, as a citizen by blood of the Creek Nation, under the provisions of the Act of Congress approved March 3, 1905. A supplemental affidavit filed March 23, 1905, is attached to and made a part of the record herein. Further proceedings were had before a Creek enrollment field party, at Arbeka, Indian Territory, October 18, 1906.
It appears from the evidence in this case that the said Lewis Davis was born January 12, 1902. There is an apparent conflict in the evidence as to the date of death of the said Lewis Davis but the weight of evidence clearly establishes the fact that the said Lewis David died prior to March 4, 1905.

Applications for Enrollment of Creek Newborn
Act of 1905 Volume IV

The act of Congress approved March 3, 1905, (33 Stats., 1048), provides in part as follows:

"That the Commission to the Five Civilized Tribes is authorized for sixty days after the date of the approval of this Act to receive and consider applications for enrollment, of children, born subsequent to May twenty five, nineteen hundred and one, and prior to March fourth, nineteen hundred and five, and living on said latter date, to citizens of the Creek tribe of Indians whose enrollment has been approved by the Secretary of the Interior prior to the approval of this act; and to enroll and make allotments to such children."

It is therefore, ordered and adjudged that under the provisions of the law above quoted said Lewis Davis, deceased, is not entitled to be enrolled as a citizen by blood of the Creek Nation and the application for his enrollment as such is accordingly denied.

Muskogee, Indian Territory.

Tams Bixby
Commissioner.

JAN 14 1907

BIRTH AFFIDAVIT.

DEPARTMENT OF THE INTERIOR.
COMMISSION TO THE FIVE CIVILIZED TRIBES.

IN RE APPLICATION FOR ENROLLMENT, as a citizen of the Creek Nation, of Eugene Davis, born on the 7 day of June, 1904

Name of Father:	Jess Davis	a citizen of the Seminole	Nation.
Name of Mother:	Ella Davis	a citizen of the Creek	Nation.

Postoffice   Arbeka Indian Territory

AFFIDAVIT OF MOTHER.

UNITED STATES OF AMERICA, Indian Territory,
    Western   DISTRICT.

I, Ella Davis, on oath state that I am 25 years of age and a citizen by blood, of the Creek Nation; that I am the lawful wife of Jess Davis, who is a citizen, by blood of the Seminole Nation; that a male child was born to me on 7 day of June, 1904, that said child has been named Eugene Davis, and was living March 4, 1905.

Ella Davis

Applications for Enrollment of Creek Newborn
Act of 1905 Volume IV

Witnesses To Mark:

{

Subscribed and sworn to before me this 15 day of March, 1905.

Drennan C Skaggs
Notary Public.

AFFIDAVIT OF ATTENDING PHYSICIAN OR MID-WIFE.

UNITED STATES OF AMERICA, Indian Territory,
Western   DISTRICT. }

I, Lucinda Lena, a midwife, on oath state that I attended on Mrs. Ella Davis, wife of Jess Davis on the 7 day of June, 1904; that there was born to her on said date a   male   child; that said child was living March 4, 1905, and is said to have been named Eugene Davis

her
Lucinda x Lena
mark

Witnesses To Mark:
{ Alex Posey
{ DC Skaggs

Subscribed and sworn to before me this 15 day of March, 1905.

Drennan C Skaggs
Notary Public.

Copy

BIRTH AFFIDAVIT.

DEPARTMENT OF THE INTERIOR.
COMMISSION TO THE FIVE CIVILIZED TRIBES.

IN RE APPLICATION FOR ENROLLMENT, as a citizen of the Creek Nation, of Lewis Davis, born on the 12 day of January, 1902

Name of Father:	Jess Davis	a citizen of the	Seminole	Nation.
Name of Mother:	Ella Davis	a citizen of the	Creek	Nation.

Postoffice   Arbeka Indian Territory

Applications for Enrollment of Creek Newborn
Act of 1905   Volume IV

AFFIDAVIT OF MOTHER.

UNITED STATES OF AMERICA, Indian Territory, }
  Western   DISTRICT.

I, Ella Davis , on oath state that I am 25 years of age and a citizen by blood , of the Creek Nation; that I am the lawful wife of Jess Davis , who is a citizen, by blood of the Seminole Nation; that a male child was born to me on 12 day of January , 1902 , that said child has been named Lewis Davis , and is now living.

Ella Davis

Witnesses To Mark:
{

Subscribed and sworn to before me this 15 day of March , 1905.

Drennan C Skaggs
Notary Public.

Copy
AFFIDAVIT OF ATTENDING PHYSICIAN OR MID-WIFE.

UNITED STATES OF AMERICA, Indian Territory, }
  Western   DISTRICT.

I, Lucinda Lena , a midwife , on oath state that I attended on Mrs. Ella Davis , wife of Jess Davis on the 12" day of January , 1902 ; that there was born to her on said date a male child; that said child ~~is now~~ was living March 4, 1905 and is said to have been named Lewis Davis

her
Lucinda x Lena
mark

Witnesses To Mark:
{ Alex Posey
  DC Skaggs

Subscribed and sworn to before me this 15" day of March, 1905.

Drennan C Skaggs
Notary Public.

CR.NC-329.

Muskogee, Indian Territory, June 9, 1905.

Ella Davis,
  Arbeka, Indian Territory.

Dear Madam:

Applications for Enrollment of Creek Newborn
Act of 1905   Volume IV

In the matter of the application for the enrollment of your minor children, Ross, Eugene and Lewis Davis, as citizens of the Creek Nation, you are advised that it will be necessary for the father of said children to appear before the Commission, at its office, on[sic] Muskogee, Indian Territory, at an early date, for the purpose of electing in which Nation, the Creek or Seminole, he desires to have said children enrolled and receive allotments of land.

Respectfully,

Chairman.

NC 328.

Muskogee, Indian Territory, July 29, 1905.

Ella Davis,
    c/o Jess Davis,
        Arbeka, Indian Territory.

Dear Madam:

You are hereby advised that it will be necessary for you and your husband, Jess Davis, to appear in person before this office at Muskogee, Indian Territory, for the purpose of testifying under oath relative to the rights of your children, Lewis Davis, Eugene Davis and Ross Davis, to enrollment[sic] as citizens by blood of the Creek Nation.

Such appearance should be made at as[sic] early a date as possible.

Respectfully,

Commissioner.

BIRTH AFFIDAVIT.

DEPARTMENT OF THE INTERIOR.
COMMISSION TO THE FIVE CIVILIZED TRIBES.

IN RE APPLICATION FOR ENROLLMENT, as a citizen of the Creek Nation, of Lewis Davis, born on the 12th day of January, 1901

| Name of Father: | Jesse E. Davis | a citizen of the | Seminole | Nation. |
| Name of Mother: | Ella S. Davis | a citizen of the | Creek | Nation. |

Postoffice   Arbeka Indian Territory

Applications for Enrollment of Creek Newborn
Act of 1905   Volume IV

AFFIDAVIT OF MOTHER.

UNITED STATES OF AMERICA, Indian Territory, }
    Western   DISTRICT.

    I, Ella S. Davis , on oath state that I am 24 years of age and a citizen by Blood, of the Creek Nation; that I am the lawful wife of Jesse E. Davis , who is a citizen, by Blood of the Seminole Nation; that a male child was born to me on 12th day of January , 1901 , that said child has been named Lewis Davis , and is now ~~living~~. Dead.

                                    Ella S. Davis

Witnesses To Mark:
{ M C Jones
  (Illegible) J Frank

    Subscribed and sworn to before me this 29" day of August , 1904.

                      (Signed) H G Malot
       My Commission Expires July 2^d 1906. Notary Public.

Copy
AFFIDAVIT OF ATTENDING PHYSICIAN OR MID-WIFE.

UNITED STATES OF AMERICA, Indian Territory, }
    Western   DISTRICT.

    I, Lucinda Lena , a Midwife , on oath state that I attended on Mrs. Ella S. Davis, wife of Jesse E. Davis on the 12th day of January , 1901 ; that there was born to her on said date a male child; that said child is now ~~living~~ dead and is said to have been named Lewis Davis

                                 her
                         Lucinda Lena x
Witnesses To Mark: mark
{ JR Ingram
  Robert *(Illegible)*

    Subscribed and sworn to before me this 29" day of August , 1904.

                            H G Malot
      My Commission Expires July 2^d 1906. Notary Public.

Applications for Enrollment of Creek Newborn
Act of 1905 Volume IV

BIRTH AFFIDAVIT.

DEPARTMENT OF THE INTERIOR.
COMMISSION TO THE FIVE CIVILIZED TRIBES.

  IN RE APPLICATION FOR ENROLLMENT, as a citizen of the Creek Nation, of Ross Davis, born on the 18 day of May, 1903

Name of Father:	Jess Davis	a citizen of the	Seminole	Nation.
Name of Mother:	Ella Davis	a citizen of the	Creek	Nation.

        Postoffice Arbeka Indian Territory

AFFIDAVIT OF MOTHER.

UNITED STATES OF AMERICA, Indian Territory, }
  Western   DISTRICT.

  I, Ella Davis, on oath state that I am 25 years of age and a citizen by blood, of the Creek Nation; that I am the lawful wife of Jess Davis, who is a citizen, by blood of the Seminole Nation; that a male child was born to me on 18 day of May, 1903, that said child has been named Ross Davis, and was living March 4, 1905.

            Ella Davis

Witnesses To Mark:
{

  Subscribed and sworn to before me this 15 day of March, 1905.

            Drennan C Skaggs
              Notary Public.

AFFIDAVIT OF ATTENDING PHYSICIAN OR MID-WIFE.

UNITED STATES OF AMERICA, Indian Territory, }
  Western   DISTRICT.

  I, Lucinda Lena, a midwife, on oath state that I attended on Mrs. Ella Davis, wife of Jess Davis on the 18 day of May, 1903; that there was born to her on said date a male child; that said child was living March 4, 1905, and is said to have been named Ross Davis

           her
        Lucinda x Lena
Witnesses To Mark: mark
 { Alex Posey
  DC Skaggs

Applications for Enrollment of Creek Newborn
Act of 1905 Volume IV

Subscribed and sworn to before me this 15 day of March , 1905.

Drennan C Skaggs
Notary Public.

Cr NC-328

Muskogee, Indian Territory, June 9, 1905.

Ella Davis,
    Arbeka, Indian Territory.

Dear Madam:

In the matter of the application for the enrollment of your minor children, Ross, Eugene and Lewis Davis, as citizens of the Creek Nation, you are advised that it will be necessary for the father of said children to appear before the Commission, at its office, in Muskogee, Indian Territory, at an early date, for the purpose of electing in which Nation, the Creek or Seminole, he desires to have said children enrolled and receive allotments of land.

Respectfully,

Chairman.

NC. 328.

Muskogee, Indian Territory, July 14, 1905.

Commissioner to the Five Civilized Tribes,
    Seminole Enrollment Division,
        Muskogee, Indian Territory.

Gentlemen:

March 23, 1905, application was made to the Commission to the Five Civilized Tribes for the enrollment of Lewis Davis, born January 19, 1902, Ross Davis, born May 18, 1903, and Eugene Davis, born June 7, 1904, as citizens by blood of the Creek Nation. It is stated in said application that the father of said children is Jess Davis, a citizen of the Seminole Nation, and that the mother is Ella Davis, a citizen of the Creek Nation.

You are requested to inform the Creek Enrollment Division as to whether application has been made for the enrollment of said children as citizens of the Seminole Nation, and if so, what disposition has been made of the same.

Applications for Enrollment of Creek Newborn
Act of 1905 Volume IV

Respectfully,

Commissioner.

DEPARTMENT OF THE INTERIOR.
COMMISSION TO THE FIVE CIVILIZED TRIBES.

Muskogee, Indian Territory, July 18, 1905.

Chief Clerk,
    Creek Enrollment Division.

Dear Sir:

    Receipt is acknowledged of your letter of July 14, 1905 (NC-328) stating that application was made to the Commission to the Five Civilized Tribes for the enrollment of Lewis Davis, born January 12, 1902, Ross Davis, born May 18, 1903, and Eugene Davis, born June 7, 1904, children of Jess Davis, a citizen of the Seminole Nation, and Ella Davis, a citizen of the Creek Nation, as citizens by blood of the Creek Nation and requesting to be advised as to whether application has been made for the enrollment of said children as citizens of the Seminole Nation.

    In reply to your letter you are advised that is does not appear from an examination of the records of this office that any application was made to the Commission to the Five Civilized Tribes for the enrollment of said Lewis Davis, Ross Davis and Eugene Davis as citizens of the Seminole Nation.

Respectfully,

Tams Bixby   Commissioner.

NC-328.

Muskogee, Indian Territory, July 29, 1905.

Ella Davis,
    c/o Jess Davis,
        Arbeka, Indian Territory.

Dear Madam:

    You are hereby advised that it will be necessary for you and your husband, Jess Davis, to appear in person before this office at Muskogee, Indian Territory, for the purpose of testifying under oath relative to the rights of your children, Lewis Davis, Eugene Davis and Ross Davis, to enrollment as citizens by blood of the Creek Nation.

Applications for Enrollment of Creek Newborn
Act of 1905   Volume IV

Such appearance should be made at as early a date as possible.

Respectfully,

Commissioner.

NC 328

Muskogee, Indian Territory, November 12, 1906.

Chief Clerk,
    Seminole Enrollment Division,
        General Office.

Dear Sir:

You are hereby advised that the names of Ross and Eugene Davis, children of Jess Davis, an alleged citizen of the Seminole Nation, and Ella Davis, a citizen by blood of the Creek Nation, are contained in a schedule of New Born citizens of the Creek Nation, approve d by the Secretary of the Interior July 28, 1905, opposite Roll No. 128.

Respectfully,

Commissioner.

NC 328

Muskogee, Indian Territory, January 28, 1907.

Ella Davis,
    Care of Jesse Davis,
        Arbeka, Indian Territory.

Dear Madam:

There is herewith inclosed[sic] one copy of the decision of the Commissioner to the Five Civilized Tribes in the matter of the application for the enrollment of Lewis Davis, deceased, as a citizen by blood of the Creek Nation, denying said application.

The decision, with a copy of the proceedings had in the case, is this day transmitted to the Secretary of the Interior for his review and decision. The final decision of the Secretary will be made known to you as soon as the commissioner is informed of the same.

Applications for Enrollment of Creek Newborn
Act of 1905   Volume IV

Respectfully,

Register.   Tams Bixby
                                                            Commissioner
CM-28-33

NC 328

Muskogee, Indian Territory, January 28, 1907.

M. L. Mott,
       Attorney for the Creek Nation,
           Muskogee, Indian Territory.

Dear Sir:

    There is herewith inclosed[sic] one copy of the decision of the Commissioner to the Five Civilized Tribes in the matter of the application for the enrollment of Lewis Davis, deceased, as a citizen by blood of the creek Nation.

    The decision, with a copy of the proceedings had in the case, is this day transmitted to the Secretary of the Interior for his review and decision. The final decision of the Secretary will be made known to you as soon as the commissioner is informed of the same.

Very respectfully,

Tams Bixby
Commissioner.

CM-28-34

NC 328

Muskogee, Indian Territory, January 28, 1907.

The Honorable,
       The Secretary of the Interior.

Sir:

    There is herewith transmitted the record of proceedings in the matter of the application for the enrollment of Lewis Davis, deceased, as a citizen by blood of the Creek Nation, including the decision of the Commissioner dated January 24, 1907.

Very respectfully,

Commissioner.

Applications for Enrollment of Creek Newborn
Act of 1905 Volume IV

Through the Commissioner
   of Indian Affairs.
Inc. CM-28-35.

NC 328

Muskogee, Indian Territory, January 28, 1907.

The Honorable,
   The Secretary of the Interior.

Sir:

There is herewith transmitted the record of proceedings in the matter of the application for the enrollment of Lewis Davis, deceased, as a citizen by blood of the Creek Nation, including the decision of the Commissioner dated January 24, 1907.

Very respectfully,

Commissioner.

Through the Commissioner
   of Indian Affairs.
Inc. CM-28-35.

Refer in reply to the following:

Land. 10235-1907.   COPY

DEPARTMENT OF THE INTERIOR,
OFFICE OF INDIAN AFFAIRS,
WASHINGTON.   February 23, 1907.

The Honorable,
   The Secretary of the Interior.

Sir:

There is enclosed a report from the Commissioner to the Five Civilized Tribes dated January 28, 1907, transmitting the record relative to the application of Lewis Davis, deceased, as a citizen by blood of the Creek Nation.

On August 31, 1904, application was made to the Commission to the Five Civilized Tribes for the enrollment of Lewis Davis deceased, as a citizen by blood.

Applications for Enrollment of Creek Newborn
Act of 1905   Volume IV

On January 24, 1907, the Commissioner held that the applicant was not entitled to enrollment.

The record shows that the applicant was born on January 12, 1902, and died prior to March 4, 1906.

By reason of the provisions of Section 2 of the Act of April 26, 1906, (34 Stat. L. 137), the decision of the Commissioner adverse to the applicant is recommended for approval.

Very respectfully,

C. F. Larrabee,

Acting Commissioner.

H.R.D. -NL

	DEPARTMENT OF THE INTERIOR,	JF
LRS	WASHINGTON.	FHE

I.T.D.   4850, 4890, 4904, 4960, 4962-07.   March 1, 1907.
4964, 5082, 5166, 5202, 5328- "
5342, 5374, 5376, 5378, 5380- "
~~5396~~, 5398, 5400, 5402, 5404- "
5410, ~~5414~~, 5418, 5424, 5428- "
5466, 5488, 5498, 5548,   - "
D.C. 12430 - 1907

<u>DIRECT.</u>

Commissioner to the Five Civilized Tribes,
   Muskogee, Indian Territory.

Sir:

Your decisions in the following Creek citizenship cases adverse to the applicants are hereby affirmed, viz:

Title of case.	Date of your letter of transmittal.
Rhoda Walker,	December 19, 1906
Josiah McIntosh,	January 18, 1907
Tony Harlings,	January 18, 1907
George Allen, (Freedman)	January 28, 1907
Henry Edwards, (Freedman)	January 28, 1907
Lewis Davis, deceased,	January 28, 1907

Applications for Enrollment of Creek Newborn
Act of 1905   Volume IV

Robert Scott, deceased,	October 19, 1907
Tom and Mattie Jeffries, deceased,	February 8, 1907
Emma Dodge, (Freedman)	February 8, 1907
Georgia Davis, deceased, (Freedman)	February 7, 1907
Thelma Maud Gibson	February 7, 1907
Magie Nola Poe (Freedman)	January 28, 1907
Nelson McIntosh,	January 19, 1907
Calley Ceasar, deceased,	January 28, 1907
Sarah Buck, deceased,	January 25, 1907
Willie Perryman, (Freedman)	January 28, 1907
Joshua Gentry et al.	January 28, 1907
Dennis Taylor, (Freedman)	January 22, 1907
Paul and Pauline Bruner,	January 25, 1907
Eddie Levi, (Freedman)	January 28, 1907
Gabriel Hawkins, (Freedman)	January 28, 1907
Lottie Dickson, (Freedman)	January 22, 1907
Charles Tiger, deceased,	January 29, 1907
Herford Burnett, deceased,	January 28, 1907
Coburn Holt, (Freedman)	February 7, 1907
Marguerite Scott, deceased, (Freedman)	January 31, 1907

Copies of Indian Office letters submitting your reports and recommending that the decisions be approved, are inclosed[sic].

A copy hereof and all the papers in the above-mentioned cases have been sent to the Indian office.

Respectfully,

(Signed) Jesse E. Wilson,
Assistant Secretary.

27 inc. and 61 for Ind. Of.

AFMc
3-1-07

JWH

N C 328

Muskogee, Indian Territory, March 9, 1907.

Ella Davis,
    c/o Jess Davis,
        Arbeka, Indian Territory.

Dear Madam:--

Applications for Enrollment of Creek Newborn
Act of 1905 Volume IV

You are hereby advised that under date of March 1, 1907, the Secretary of the Interior affirmed the decision of the Commissioner to the Five Civilized Tribes, denying the application for the enrollment of your minor child, Lewis Davis, as a citizen by blood of the Creek Nation.

Respectfully,

Commissioner.

N.C. 329

DEPARTMENT OF THE INTERIOR,
COMMISSIONER TO THE FIVE CIVILIZED TRIBES.
MUSKOGEE, INDIAN TERRITORY I.T. January 12, 1906.

In the matter of the application for the enrollment of Sallie Harjo as a citizen by blood of the Creek Nation.

Yahola Harjo being duly sworn testified as follows through Alex Posey official interpreter.

Q What is your name? A Yahola Harjo.
Q What is your age? A I think I am now about thirty seven years old.
Q What is your post office address? A Wetumka.
Q What was the name of your father? A Simbaly.
Q What was the name of your mother? A Janie.
Q Have you a child named Sallie Harjo? A Yes, sir.
Q Is she living? A Living and about that tall (measuring about three feet).
Q What is the name of the mother of this child? A Lucy Harjo.
Q You have a child named James by her enrolled here, have you not? A Yes sir I had one but he's dead/
Q What was the name of Lucy's father and mother? A Her mother is Susie and her father Hulbutta Harjo.

The parents of said Susie are identified opposite Nos. 7083 and 7084 respectively.

Q Now we have written several letters to you in which we called attention to the fact that you had made an affidavit that your child Sallie was born November 2, 1904 whereas the mother and the midwife say it was born October 1, 1903 and we ask you to give us the correct date? A I was mistaken in the date. The affidavit of the mother and the midwife is correct.
Q We not only had your affidavit executed March 20, 1905 stating the child was born November 2, 1904 but at the bottom of one of our letters you wrote that November 2 is the correct date of my child's birth, how did you come to say that? A I was mistaken in both instances.

Applications for Enrollment of Creek Newborn
Act of 1905 Volume IV

Q How old is your child Sallie now? A Something like two years old. Indians never count dates like white people do. We always fix the dates of our ages approximately and never exactly.
Q The date given by the mother and midwife which you now state is correct would make the child two years old last October, it would be three years old next October, is that correct? A That's correct.

I, Anna Garrigues, on oath state that the above and foregoing is a true and correct copy of my stenographic notes taken in said cause on said date.

                                                Anna Garrigues

Subscribed and sworn to before me this 12 day of January 1906.

                                                J McDermott
                                                Notary Public.

BIRTH AFFIDAVIT.

DEPARTMENT OF THE INTERIOR.
COMMISSION TO THE FIVE CIVILIZED TRIBES.

IN RE APPLICATION FOR ENROLLMENT, as a citizen of the Creek Nation, of Sallie Harjo, born on the 1st day of October , 1903

Name of Father: Yahola Harjo   a citizen of the   Creek   Nation.
Name of Mother: Lucy Harjo   a citizen of the   Creek   Nation.

                                    Postoffice   Wetumka I.T.

                        AFFIDAVIT OF ~~MOTHER~~. Father

UNITED STATES OF AMERICA, Indian Territory, ⎱
      Western   **DISTRICT.** ⎰

    I, Yahola Harjo , on oath state that I am about 37 years of age and a citizen by blood , of the Creek Nation; that I am the lawful ~~wife~~ husband of Lucy Harjo, who is a citizen, by blood of the Creek Nation; that a female child was born to ~~me~~ her on 1st day of October , 1903 , that said child has been named Sallie Harjo , and was living March 4, 1905.   his
                                                                 Yahola x Harjo
Witnesses To Mark: mark
    ⎰ Alex Posey
    ⎱ H.G. Hains

Applications for Enrollment of Creek Newborn
Act of 1905 Volume IV

Subscribed and sworn to before me this 12 day of January, 1906.

                                                  Alex Posey
                                                           Notary Public.

BIRTH AFFIDAVIT.

DEPARTMENT OF THE INTERIOR.
COMMISSION TO THE FIVE CIVILIZED TRIBES.

IN RE APPLICATION FOR ENROLLMENT, as a citizen of the Creek Nation, of Sallie Harjo, born on the 2 day of November, 1904

Name of Father:	Yahola Harjo	a citizen of the	Creek	Nation.
Name of Mother:	Lucy Harjo	a citizen of the	Creek	Nation.

                                    Postoffice   Wetumka Ind.Ter.

                         AFFIDAVIT OF ~~MOTHER~~. Father

UNITED STATES OF AMERICA, Indian Territory,
    Western   DISTRICT.

I, Yahola Harjo, on oath state that I am about 36 years of age and a citizen by blood, of the Creek Nation; that I am the lawful ~~wife~~ husband of Lucy Harjo, who is a citizen, by blood of the Creek Nation; that a female child was born to me on 2 day of November, 1904, that said child has been named Sallie Harjo, and was living March 4, 1905. That the mother is unable to appear to make affidavit on account of illness.

                                                     his
                                            Yahola x Harjo
Witnesses To Mark: mark
   Alex Posey
   DC Skaggs

Subscribed and sworn to before me this 20 day of March, 1905.

                                        Drennan C Skaggs
                                            Notary Public.

Applications for Enrollment of Creek Newborn
Act of 1905 Volume IV

BIRTH AFFIDAVIT.

DEPARTMENT OF THE INTERIOR.
COMMISSION TO THE FIVE CIVILIZED TRIBES.

IN RE APPLICATION FOR ENROLLMENT, as a citizen of the Creek Nation, of Sallie Harjo, born on the 1st day of October, 1903

Name of Father:	Yahola Harjo	a citizen of the	Creek	Nation.
Name of Mother:	Lucy Harjo	a citizen of the	Creek	Nation.

Postoffice   Wetumka Ind. Ter.

AFFIDAVIT OF MOTHER.

UNITED STATES OF AMERICA, Indian Territory,
Western   DISTRICT.

I, Lucy Harjo, on oath state that I am 27 years of age and a citizen by Birth, of the Creek Nation; that I am the lawful wife of Yahola Harjo, who is a citizen, by Birth of the Creek Nation; that a Female child was born to me on 1st day of October, 1903, that said child has been named Sallie Harjo, and was living March 4, 1905.

                                                her
                                        Lucy x Harjo
Witnesses To Mark: mark
{ S A Watson
{ George Fife

Subscribed and sworn to before me this 1st day of July, 1905.

My Commission expires 1/31-09   Dan Upton
                                                     Notary Public.

AFFIDAVIT OF ATTENDING PHYSICIAN OR MID-WIFE.

UNITED STATES OF AMERICA, Indian Territory,
Western   DISTRICT.

I, Nancy Deer, a Midwife, on oath state that I attended on Mrs. Lucy Harjo, wife of Yahola Harjo on the 1st day of Oct, 1903; that there was born to her on said date a Female child; that said child was living March 4, 1905, and is said to have been named Sallie Harjo

                                           her
                                      Nancy x Deer
Witnesses To Mark: mark
{ S A Watson
{ George Fife

Applications for Enrollment of Creek Newborn
Act of 1905 Volume IV

Subscribed and sworn to before me this 1st day of July, 1905.

My Commission expires 1/31-09   Dan Upton
                                                            Notary Public.

Cr. NC-329

Muskogee, Indian Territory, June 9, 1905.

Yahola Harjo,
     Wetumka, Indian Territory.

Dear Sir:

    In the matter of the application for the enrollment of your minor child, Sallie Harjo, as a citizen of the Creek Nation, you are advised that the Commission requires the affidavits of the mother and the midwife or physician in attendance at the birth of said child.

    For this purpose, there is herewith enclosed a blank form of birth affidavit. In executing same, care should be taken to see that all blanks are properly filled, all names written in full and in the event that the person signing an affidavit is unable to write, signature by mark must be attested by two witnesses.

Respectfully,

Chairman.

1 B A

N.C. 329

Muskogee, Indian Territory, July 7, 1905.

Lucy Harjo,
     Wetumka, Indian Territory.

Dear Madam:

    There are on file at this office, affidavits in which the date of the birth of your minor child, Sallie Harjo, is given as November 2, 1904 and October 1, 1904.

    You are requested to advise this office as to the correct date of birth of said child.

Applications for Enrollment of Creek Newborn
Act of 1905 Volume IV

Respectfully,

Commissioner.

N C 329 COPY

Muskogee, Indian Territory, July 29, 1905.

Yahola Harjo,
    Wetumka, Indian Territory.

Dear Sir:

    In the matter of the application for the enrollment of your minor daughter Sallie Harjo as a citizen by blood of the Creek Nation there are on file affidavits in which the date of the birth of your said daughter is given as November 2, 1904 and October,[sic] 1 1904.

    You are requested to immediately inform this office as to which of the above dates, if either of them, is the correct date of the birth of said child, and you are advised that until the information is supplied the rights of your said daughter as a citizen by blood of the Creek Nation can not be finally determined.

Respectfully,

(Signed) Tams Bixby

Commissioner.

This is to certify that Nov 2d 1904 is the correct date of my childs[sic] birth.

Yours truly

(Signed) Yahola Harjo

REFER IN REPLY TO THE FOLLOWING:
N.C. 329

DEPARTMENT OF THE INTERIOR,
COMMISSIONER TO THE FIVE CIVILIZED TRIBES.

Muskogee, Indian Territory, August 11, 1905.

Lucy Harjo,
    Care Yahola Harjo,
        Wetumka, Indian Territory.

Applications for Enrollment of Creek Newborn
Act of 1905   Volume IV

Dear Madam:

  There are on file at this office, affidavits in which the date of the birth of your minor child, Sallie Harjo, is given as November 2, 1904 and October 1, 1904.

  You are requested to advise this office as to the correct date of birth of said child.

      Respectfully,

            Wm. O. Beall
            Commissioner.

NC-329

      Muskogee, Indian Territory, December 11, 1905.

Yahola Harjo,
  Wetumka, Indian Territory.

Dear Sir:

  In the matter of the application for the enrollment of your minor child, Sallie Harjo, as a citizen of the Creek Nation, there are on file in this Office affidavits which give dates of the birth of said child as October 1, 1903 and November 2, 1904. For the purpose of correcting said discrepancy, you wrote this Office stating that said child was born November 2, 1904.

  You are advised that it will be necessary for the mother of said child and the midwife, Nancy Deer, to execute new affidavits, giving the correct date of the child's birth, and for this purpose a blank form of birth affidavit is herewith enclosed; or it will be necessary that said mother and midwife appear in person at the office of the Commissioner to the Five Civilized Tribes at an early date for the purpose of being examined under oath.

      Respectfully,

1 B A   Acting Commissioner.

Applications for Enrollment of Creek Newborn
Act of 1905 Volume IV

REFER IN REPLY TO THE FOLLOWING:
_____

DEPARTMENT OF THE INTERIOR,
COMMISSIONER TO THE FIVE CIVILIZED TRIBES.

Muskogee, Indian Territory, October 23, 1906.

Lucy Harjo,
    c/o Yahola Harjo,
        Wetumka, Indian Territory.

Dear Madam:

    You are hereby advised that the name of your minor child, Sallie Harjo, is contained in the partial list of citizens by blood of the Creek Nation, approved by the Secretary of the Interior October 15, 1906, and that a selection of land in the Creek Nation may now be made for said child at the Creek Land Office in Muskogee, Indian Territory.

    This matter should receive your prompt attention.

                Respectfully,

                      Tams Bixby

                              Commissioner.

BIRTH AFFIDAVIT.

DEPARTMENT OF THE INTERIOR.
COMMISSION TO THE FIVE CIVILIZED TRIBES.

IN RE APPLICATION FOR ENROLLMENT, as a citizen of the CREEK Nation, of Buford Newberry, born on the 5 day of April, 1902

Name of Father: John Newberry   a citizen of the   U. S.   Nation.
Name of Mother: Jennetta "   a citizen of the   Creek Nation.

                    Postoffice   Oktaha

Applications for Enrollment of Creek Newborn
Act of 1905   Volume IV

(Child present)

AFFIDAVIT OF MOTHER.

UNITED STATES OF AMERICA, Indian Territory, }
    WESTERN   DISTRICT.

I, Jennetta Newberry , on oath state that I am   30 years of age and a citizen by blood , of the Creek   Nation; that I am the lawful wife of John Newberry , who is a citizen, by ----- of the U. S. Nation; that a   male   child was born to me on 5   day of April , 1902 , that said child has been named Buford Newberry , and is now living.

Jeannetta Newberry

Witnesses To Mark:
{

Subscribed and sworn to before me this 22 day of March , 1905.

Edw C Griesel
Notary Public.

BIRTH AFFIDAVIT.

DEPARTMENT OF THE INTERIOR.
COMMISSION TO THE FIVE CIVILIZED TRIBES.

IN RE APPLICATION FOR ENROLLMENT, as a citizen of the *(blank)* Nation, of Buford Newberry , born on the *(blank)* day of *(blank)* , 1*(blank)*

Name of Father: John Newberry   a citizen of the   *(blank)*   Nation.
Name of Mother: Jennetta   "   a citizen of the   *(blank)*   Nation.

Postoffice   *(blank)*

AFFIDAVIT OF ATTENDING PHYSICIAN OR MID-WIFE.

UNITED STATES OF AMERICA, Indian Territory, }
    Western   DISTRICT.

I, Geo. W. McGuire , a Physician   , on oath state that I attended on Mrs. Jennetta Newberry , wife of John Newberry on the 5th day of April , 1902 ; that there was born to her on said date a   male   child; that said child is now living and is said to have been named Buford Newberry

Geo W. McGuire

Witnesses To Mark:
{

Applications for Enrollment of Creek Newborn
Act of 1905   Volume IV

Subscribed and sworn to before me this 23 day of March, 1905.

Ben D. Gross
Notary Public.

NC 331.

Muskogee, Indian Territory, May 31, 1905.

Eddie Cobb,
    Boley, Indian Territory.

Dear Madam:

    In the matter of the application for the enrollment of your minor child, Johnnie Cobb, as a citizen of the Creek Nation, you are advised that the Commission is unable to identify you on its rolls.

    You are requested to advise the Commission as to your maiden name, the names of your parents, the Creek Indian Town to which you belong, and, if possible, the numbers which appear on your deeds to land in the Creek Nation.

Respectfully,

Chairman.

N C 331   COPY   C 1389

Boley I T   June 6th 1905

Mr. Thams[sic] Bixby

    Sir

In reply to your question as to whom my people is my fathers name is Bonney Riley mothers name is Toche Darrsaw and the town to which I belong Cheaha and my name in which I file is Addie Mitchell I haven't got my deed yet I send for it but id hadn't come yet.

Resp.

(Signed) Addie Cobb.

Applications for Enrollment of Creek Newborn
Act of 1905 Volume IV

BIRTH AFFIDAVIT.

DEPARTMENT OF THE INTERIOR.
COMMISSION TO THE FIVE CIVILIZED TRIBES.

IN RE APPLICATION FOR ENROLLMENT, as a citizen of the Creek Nation, of Johnnie Cobb, born on the 16 day of June, 1904

Name of Father: John Cobb   a citizen of the   Creek   Nation.
Name of Mother: Addie Cobb   a citizen of the   Creek   Nation.

Postoffice   Boley, Indian Territory

AFFIDAVIT OF MOTHER.

UNITED STATES OF AMERICA, Indian Territory,
    Western   DISTRICT.

I, Addie Cobb, on oath state that I am 32 years of age and a citizen by blood, of the Creek Nation; that I am the lawful wife of John Cobb, who is a citizen, by adoption of the Creek Nation; that a male child was born to me on 16 day of June, 1904, that said child has been named Johnnie Cobb, and was living March 4, 1905.

                                      Addie Cobb

Witnesses To Mark:

Subscribed and sworn to before me this 14 day of March, 1905.

                                      Drennan C Skaggs
                                          Notary Public.

AFFIDAVIT OF ATTENDING PHYSICIAN OR MID-WIFE.

UNITED STATES OF AMERICA, Indian Territory,
    Western   DISTRICT.

I, Mandy Gardner, a midwife, on oath state that I attended on Mrs. Addie Cobb, wife of John Cobb on the 16 day of June, 1904; that there was born to her on said date a male child; that said child was living March 4, 1905, and is said to have been named Johnnie Cobb
                                     her
Witnesses To Mark: Mandy x Gardner
   Alex Posey   mark
   D C Skaggs

Applications for Enrollment of Creek Newborn
Act of 1905 Volume IV

Subscribed and sworn to before me this 14 day of March, 1905.

>Drennan C Skaggs
>Notary Public.

BIRTH AFFIDAVIT.

DEPARTMENT OF THE INTERIOR.
COMMISSION TO THE FIVE CIVILIZED TRIBES.

(Child present)

IN RE APPLICATION FOR ENROLLMENT, as a citizen of the CREEK Nation, of Ruthie Childers, born on the 13 day of July, 1902

Name of Father:	Ben Childers	a citizen of the	Creek	Nation.
Name of Mother:	Annie "	a citizen of the	Creek	Nation.

>Postoffice   Coweta I.T.

AFFIDAVIT OF MOTHER.

UNITED STATES OF AMERICA, Indian Territory,
WESTERN DISTRICT.

I, Annie Childers, on oath state that I am 35 years of age and a citizen by blood, of the Creek Nation; that I am the lawful wife of Ben Childers, who is a citizen, by blood of the Creek Nation; that a female child was born to me on 13 day of July, 1902, that said child has been named Ruthie Childers, and is now living.

>Mrs. Annie Childers

Witnesses To Mark:

Subscribed and sworn to before me this 22" day of Mar., 1905.

>Edw C Griesel
>Notary Public.

Applications for Enrollment of Creek Newborn
Act of 1905 Volume IV

United States of America,
Western District of the
Indian Territory.

    Annie B. Childers, first being duly sworn deposes and says that she and her husband were alone when her two children, Ruthie Childers and Mose Childers were born; that no physician or mid-wife attended her during her confinement; that her husband, Ben Childers, died December 17, 1904.

                                          Annie B. Childers

Subscribed and sworn to before me this March 25, 1905.

                                          R.C. Allen
                                                        Notary Public.
My commission expires March 15, 1908.

BIRTH AFFIDAVIT.

DEPARTMENT OF THE INTERIOR.
COMMISSION TO THE FIVE CIVILIZED TRIBES.

    IN RE APPLICATION FOR ENROLLMENT, as a citizen of the Creek Nation, of Ruthie Childers, born on the 13th day of July, 1902

Name of Father:	Ben Childers	a citizen of the	Creek	Nation.
Name of Mother:	Annie B. Childers	a citizen of the	Creek	Nation.

                                Postoffice   Coweta, Indian Territory.

AFFIDAVIT OF MOTHER.

UNITED STATES OF AMERICA, Indian Territory,
    Western   DISTRICT.

    I, Annie B. Childers, on oath state that I am 35 years of age and a citizen by blood, of the Creek Nation; that I am the lawful ~~wife~~ widow of Ben Childers, who ~~is~~ was a citizen, by blood of the Creek Nation; that a female child was born to me on 13th day of July, 1902, that said child has been named Ruthie Childers, and was living March 4, 1905.

                                        Mrs Annie B. Childers

Witnesses To Mark:

Applications for Enrollment of Creek Newborn
Act of 1905   Volume IV

Subscribed and sworn to before me this 25th day of March, 1905.

R. C. Allen
Notary Public.

My commission expires March 15, 1908.

AFFIDAVIT OF ATTENDING PHYSICIAN OR MID-WIFE.

UNITED STATES OF AMERICA, Indian Territory,
Western   DISTRICT.

I, E.N. Perryman, ~~a~~ *(blank)*, on oath state that I ~~attended on~~ know Mrs. Annie B. Childers, wife of Ben Childers on the 13th day of July, 1902; that there was born to her on said date a female child; that said child was living March 4, 1905, and is said to have been named Ruthie Childers

E.N. Perryman

Witnesses To Mark:

Subscribed and sworn to before me this 25th day of March, 1905.

R. C. Allen
Notary Public.

My commission expires March 15, 1908.

BIRTH AFFIDAVIT.

DEPARTMENT OF THE INTERIOR.
COMMISSION TO THE FIVE CIVILIZED TRIBES.

IN RE APPLICATION FOR ENROLLMENT, as a citizen of the Creek Nation, of Ruthie Childers, born on the 13 day of July, 1902

Name of Father:	Ben Childers	a citizen of the	Creek	Nation.
Name of Mother:	Annie B. Childers	a citizen of the	Creek	Nation.

Postoffice   Coweta, I.T.

AFFIDAVIT OF MOTHER.

UNITED STATES OF AMERICA, Indian Territory,
Western   DISTRICT.

I, Annie B. Childers, on oath state that I am 35 years of age and a citizen by blood, of the Creek Nation; that I am the lawful ~~wife~~ widow of Ben Childers, who ~~is~~ was a citizen, by blood of the Creek Nation; that a female child was born to me on

Applications for Enrollment of Creek Newborn
Act of 1905   Volume IV

13   day of   July , 1902 , that said child has been named   Ruthie Childers   , and was living March 4, 1905.

Mrs Annie B. Childers

Witnesses To Mark:
- Joe Fennell
- B. F. Hughes

Subscribed and sworn to before me this   24   day of   June , 1905.

R. C. Allen
Notary Public.

My Com. Ex. Mch 15, 1908.

AFFIDAVIT OF ATTENDING PHYSICIAN OR MID-WIFE.

UNITED STATES OF AMERICA, Indian Territory,
    Western   **DISTRICT.**

~~I~~ We   Sousa Childers   , and   Eunice Fisher   , on oath state that ~~I~~ we ~~attended on~~ personally know   Mrs. Annie B. Childers   , wife of   Ben Childers   on the   13th   day of   July , 1902 ; that there was born to her on said date a   female   child; that said child was living March 4, 1905, and is said to have been named Ruthie Childers

her
Eunice x Fisher
mark

Witnesses To Mark:
- Joe Fennell
- B. F. Hughes

his
Sousa x Childers
mark

Subscribed and sworn to before me this   24   day of   June , 1905.

R. C. Allen
Notary Public.

My Com. Ex. Mch 15, 1908.

Applications for Enrollment of Creek Newborn
Act of 1905   Volume IV

BIRTH AFFIDAVIT.

DEPARTMENT OF THE INTERIOR.
COMMISSION TO THE FIVE CIVILIZED TRIBES.

(Child present)

IN RE APPLICATION FOR ENROLLMENT, as a citizen of the CREEK Nation, of Mose Childers, born on the 6 day of June, 1904

Name of Father:	Ben Childers	a citizen of the	Creek	Nation.
Name of Mother:	Annie "	a citizen of the	Creek	Nation.

Postoffice   Coweta I.T.

AFFIDAVIT OF MOTHER.

UNITED STATES OF AMERICA, Indian Territory,
    WESTERN   DISTRICT.

I, Annie Childers, on oath state that I am 35 years of age and a citizen by blood, of the Creek Nation; that I am the lawful wife of Ben Childers, who is a citizen, by blood of the Creek Nation; that a male child was born to me on 6 day of June, 1904, that said child has been named Mose Childers, and is now living.

                                  Mrs. Annie Childers

Witnesses To Mark:

Subscribed and sworn to before me this 22" day of Mar., 1905.

                                  Edw C Griesel
                                        Notary Public.

BIRTH AFFIDAVIT.

DEPARTMENT OF THE INTERIOR.
COMMISSION TO THE FIVE CIVILIZED TRIBES.

IN RE APPLICATION FOR ENROLLMENT, as a citizen of the Creek Nation, of Mose Childers, born on the 6th day of June, 1904

Name of Father:	Ben Childers	a citizen of the	Creek	Nation.
Name of Mother:	Annie B. Childers	a citizen of the	Creek	Nation.

Postoffice   Coweta, Indian Territory.

Applications for Enrollment of Creek Newborn
Act of 1905   Volume IV

AFFIDAVIT OF MOTHER.

UNITED STATES OF AMERICA, Indian Territory,
    Western   DISTRICT.

    I, Annie B. Childers , on oath state that I am 35   years of age and a citizen by blood , of the Creek   Nation; that I am the lawful ~~wife~~ widow of Ben Childers , who ~~is~~ was a citizen, by blood of the Creek   Nation; that a male   child was born to me on 6th   day of June , 1904 , that said child has been named Mose Childers , and was living March 4, 1905.

                                      Mrs Annie B. Childers

Witnesses To Mark:
{

    Subscribed and sworn to before me this 25th day of March , 1905.

                                       R. C. Allen
                                              Notary Public.

My commission expires March 15, 1908.

AFFIDAVIT OF ATTENDING PHYSICIAN OR MID-WIFE.

UNITED STATES OF AMERICA, Indian Territory,
    Western   DISTRICT.

    I, E.N. Perryman , ~~a~~ *(blank)* , on oath state that I ~~attended on~~ know Mrs. Annie B. Childers , wife of Ben Childers on the 6th day of June , 1904 ; that there was born to her on said date a male   child; that said child was living March 4, 1905, and is said to have been named Mose Childers

                                      E.N. Perryman

Witnesses To Mark:
{

    Subscribed and sworn to before me this 25th day of March , 1905.

                                       R. C. Allen
                                              Notary Public.

My commission expires March 15, 1908.

Applications for Enrollment of Creek Newborn
Act of 1905 Volume IV

BIRTH AFFIDAVIT.

DEPARTMENT OF THE INTERIOR.
COMMISSION TO THE FIVE CIVILIZED TRIBES.

IN RE APPLICATION FOR ENROLLMENT, as a citizen of the Creek Nation, of Mose Childers, born on the 6th day of June, 1904

Name of Father: Ben Childers   a citizen of the   Creek   Nation.
Name of Mother: Annie B. Childers   a citizen of the   Creek   Nation.

Postoffice   Coweta, Indian Territory.

AFFIDAVIT OF MOTHER.

UNITED STATES OF AMERICA, Indian Territory,
Western Judicial   DISTRICT.

I, Annie B. Childers, on oath state that I am 35 years of age and a citizen by birth, of the Creek Nation; that I am the lawful ~~wife~~ widow of Ben Childers, who was a citizen, by birth of the Creek Nation; that a male child was born to me on 6th day of June, 1904, that said child has been named Mose Childers, and was living March 4, 1905.

Mrs Annie B. Childers

Witnesses To Mark:

Subscribed and sworn to before me this 1st day of April, 1905.

R. C. Allen
Notary Public.

My commission expires March 15, 1908.

AFFIDAVIT OF ATTENDING PHYSICIAN OR MID-WIFE.

UNITED STATES OF AMERICA, Indian Territory,
Western Judicial   DISTRICT.

I, E.N. Perryman, a neighbor, on oath state that I ~~attended on~~ personally know Mrs. Annie B. Childers, wife of Ben Childers on the 6th day of June, 1904; that there was born to her on said date a male child; that said child was living March 4, 1905, and is said to have been named Mose Childers

E.N. Perryman

Witnesses To Mark:

Applications for Enrollment of Creek Newborn
Act of 1905   Volume IV

Subscribed and sworn to before me this 1st day of April, 1905.

R. C. Allen
Notary Public.

My commission expires March 15, 1908.

BIRTH AFFIDAVIT.

DEPARTMENT OF THE INTERIOR.
COMMISSION TO THE FIVE CIVILIZED TRIBES.

IN RE APPLICATION FOR ENROLLMENT, as a citizen of the Creek Nation, of Mose Childers, born on the 6 day of June, 1904

Name of Father:	Ben Childers	a citizen of the	Creek	Nation.
Name of Mother:	Annie B. Childers	a citizen of the	Creek	Nation.

Postoffice   Coweta, I.T.

AFFIDAVIT OF MOTHER.

UNITED STATES OF AMERICA, Indian Territory,
Western   DISTRICT.

I, Annie B. Childers, on oath state that I am 35 years of age and a citizen by blood, of the Creek Nation; that I am the lawful wife of Ben Childers, who is a citizen, by blood of the Creek Nation; that a male child was born to me on 6 day of June, 1904, that said child has been named Mose Childers, and was living March 4, 1905.

Mrs Annie B. Childers

Witnesses To Mark:
{ Joe Fennell
{ B. F. Hughes

Subscribed and sworn to before me this 24 day of June, 1905.

R. C. Allen
Notary Public.

My Com. Ex. Mch 15, 1908.

Applications for Enrollment of Creek Newborn
Act of 1905 Volume IV

AFFIDAVIT OF ATTENDING PHYSICIAN OR MID-WIFE.

UNITED STATES OF AMERICA, Indian Territory,
Western DISTRICT.

I We Sousa Childers , and Eunice Fisher , on oath state that I ~~attended on~~ personally know Mrs. Annie B. Childers , wife of Ben Childers on the 6 day of June , 1904 ; that there was born to her on said date a male child; that said child was living March 4, 1905, and is said to have been named Mose Childers

Witnesses To Mark:
 { Joe Fennell
 { B. F. Hughes

Eunice x Fisher (her mark)
Sousa x Childers (his mark)

Subscribed and sworn to before me this 24 day of June , 1905.

R. C. Allen
Notary Public.

My Com. Ex. Mch 15, 1908.

BIRTH AFFIDAVIT.

DEPARTMENT OF THE INTERIOR.
COMMISSION TO THE FIVE CIVILIZED TRIBES.

IN RE APPLICATION FOR ENROLLMENT, as a citizen of the CREEK Nation, of Montie Perryman, born on the 28 day of Nov. , 1902

Name of Father:	Benjamin Perryman	a citizen of the	Creek	Nation.
Name of Mother:	Mary "	a citizen of the	U.S.	Nation.

Postoffice   Clarksville

Child Present - Gr

AFFIDAVIT OF ~~MOTHER~~. Father

UNITED STATES OF AMERICA, Indian Territory,
WESTERN DISTRICT.

I, Benjamin Perryman , on oath state that I am 25 years of age and a citizen by blood , of the Creek Nation; that I am the lawful ~~wife~~ husband of Mary Perryman , who is a citizen, by ----- of the U. S. Nation; that a male child was born to me on

293

Applications for Enrollment of Creek Newborn
Act of 1905   Volume IV

28 day of Nov. , 1902 , that said child has been named Montie Perryman , and is now living.

Benjamin Perryman

Witnesses To Mark:
{

Subscribed and sworn to before me this 22 day of March, 1905.

Edw C Griesel
Notary Public.

BIRTH AFFIDAVIT.

DEPARTMENT OF THE INTERIOR.
COMMISSION TO THE FIVE CIVILIZED TRIBES.

IN RE APPLICATION FOR ENROLLMENT, as a citizen of the Creek Nation, of Montie Perryman, born on the 28 day of Nov. , 1902

Name of Father:	Benjamin Perryman	a citizen of the	Creek	Nation.
Name of Mother:	Mary "	a citizen of the	U.S.	Nation.

Postoffice   Clarksville

(Child present)

AFFIDAVIT OF MOTHER.

UNITED STATES OF AMERICA, Indian Territory, }
   Western   DISTRICT.

I, Mary Perryman , on oath state that I am 21 years of age and a citizen by -----, of the U.S. Nation; that I am the lawful wife of Benjamin Perryman , who is a citizen, by blood of the Creek Nation; that a male child was born to me on 28 day of Nov., 1902 , that said child has been named Montie Perryman , and is now living.

Mary Perryman

Witnesses To Mark:
{

Subscribed and sworn to before me this 22 day of March , 1905.

Edw C Griesel
Notary Public.

Applications for Enrollment of Creek Newborn
Act of 1905   Volume IV

AFFIDAVIT OF ATTENDING PHYSICIAN ~~OR MID-WIFE~~.

UNITED STATES OF AMERICA, Indian Territory, }
    Western   DISTRICT.

I, M T Smith , a Physician , on oath state that I attended on Mrs. Mary Perryman , wife of Ben Perryman on the 28th day of November , 1902 ; that there was born to her on said date a male child; that said child is now living and is said to have been named Montie V. Perryman

                                          M. T. Smith

Witnesses To Mark:
{

Subscribed and sworn to before me this 20th day of March, 1905.

                                      Ralph Dresback
                                      Notary Public.

REFER IN REPLY TO THE FOLLOWING:
NC-334.

DEPARTMENT OF THE INTERIOR,
COMMISSIONER TO THE FIVE CIVILIZED TRIBES.

                            Muskogee, Indian Territory, July 29, 1905.

Millie Harjo,
    c/o Tom Harjo,
        Wetumka, Indian Territory.

Dear Madam:

In the matter of the application for the enrollment of your daughter Susie Harjo, born May 5, 1904, as a citizen by blood of the Creek Nation it will be necessary for you to furnish this office with the affidavits of two disinterested persons who are acquainted with said child, know when she was born, the names of her parents and whether or not she was living March 4, 1905.

                            Respectfully,

                                  Tams Bixby
                                      Commissioner.

Applications for Enrollment of Creek Newborn
Act of 1905   Volume IV

REFER IN REPLY TO THE FOLLOWING:

DEPARTMENT OF THE INTERIOR,
COMMISSIONER TO THE FIVE CIVILIZED TRIBES.

Muskogee, Indian Territory, October 23, 1906.

Millie Harjo,
   c/o Tom Harjo,
      Wetumka, Indian Territory.

Dear Madam:

You are hereby advised that the name of your minor child, Susie Harjo, deceased, is contained in the partial list of citizens by blood of the Creek Nation, approved by the Secretary of the Interior, October 15, 1906, and that a selection of land in the Creek Nation may now be made for him by the administrator, at the Creek Land Office in Muskogee, Indian Territory.

This matter should receive your prompt attention.

      Respectfully,

          Tams Bixby   Commissioner.

Indian Territory, I
         I ss.
Western District I

We, the undersigned, on oath state that we are personally acquainted with Millie Harjo wife of Tommache Harjo; that on or about the 5 day of May, 1904, a female child was born to them and has been named Susie Harjo; and that said child was living March 4, 1905.

We further state that we have no interest in the above case.

Witnesses to mark:	her Lucy x Harjo mark
Alex Posey	his Sousa x Harjo
D C Skaggs	mark

Applications for Enrollment of Creek Newborn
Act of 1905   Volume IV

Subscribed and sworn to before me this 30 day of March, 1906.

Alex Posey
Notary Public.

DEPARTMENT OF THE INTERIOR.
COMMISSION TO THE FIVE CIVILIZED TRIBES.

In the matter of the death of   Susie Harjo   a citizen of the Creek Nation, who formerly resided at or near   Wetumka   , Ind. Ter., and died on the   9   day of September   , 1905.

AFFIDAVIT OF RELATIVE.

UNITED STATES OF AMERICA, Indian Territory,
    Western   DISTRICT.

I, Millie Harjo , on oath state that I am about 28 years of age and a citizen by blood , of the Creek   Nation; that my postoffice address is   Wetumka , Ind. Ter.; that I am   mother   of Susie Harjo   who was a citizen, by blood , of the Creek   Nation and that said Susie Harjo   died on the   9   day of September , 1905.

her
Millie x Harjo
mark

Witnesses To Mark:
  Alex Posey
  D C Skaggs

Subscribed and sworn to before me this 30 day of March, 1906.

Alex Posey
Notary Public.

Applications for Enrollment of Creek Newborn
Act of 1905 Volume IV

BIRTH AFFIDAVIT.

DEPARTMENT OF THE INTERIOR.
COMMISSION TO THE FIVE CIVILIZED TRIBES.

IN RE APPLICATION FOR ENROLLMENT, as a citizen of the Creek Nation, of Susie Harjo, born on the 5 day of May, 1904

Name of Father:	Tom Harjo	a citizen of the Creek	Nation.
Name of Mother:	Millie Harjo	a citizen of the Creek	Nation.

Postoffice   Wetumka, Ind. Ter.

AFFIDAVIT OF MOTHER.

UNITED STATES OF AMERICA, Indian Territory,
Western   DISTRICT.

I, Millie Harjo, on oath state that I am about 25 years of age and a citizen by blood, of the Creek Nation; that I am the lawful wife of Tom Harjo, who is a citizen, by blood of the Creek Nation; that a female child was born to me on 5 day of May, 1904, that said child has been named Susie Harjo, and was living March 4, 1905.

                                                her
                                     Millie x Harjo

Witnesses To Mark: mark
  { Alex Posey
    D C Skaggs

Subscribed and sworn to before me this 21 day of March, 1905.

                                      Drennan C Skaggs
                                        Notary Public.

AFFIDAVIT OF ATTENDING PHYSICIAN OR MID-WIFE.

UNITED STATES OF AMERICA, Indian Territory,
Western   DISTRICT.

I, Tom Harjo, a———, on oath state that I attended on my wife Mrs. Millie Harjo, wife of——— on the 5 day of May, 1904; that there was born to her on said date a female child; that said child was living March 4, 1905, and is said to have been named Susie Harjo

                                       his
                                   Tom x Harjo
Witnesses To Mark: mark
  { Alex Posey
    D C Skaggs

Applications for Enrollment of Creek Newborn
Act of 1905   Volume IV

Subscribed and sworn to before me this 21 day of March, 1905.

Drennan C Skaggs
Notary Public.

COMMISSIONERS:
TAMS BIXBY,
THOMAS B. NEEDLES,
C.R. BRECKINRIDGE.

WM. O. BEALL
Secretary

DEPARTMENT OF THE INTERIOR,
COMMISSIONER TO THE FIVE CIVILIZED TRIBES.

HGH
REFER IN REPLY TO THE FOLLOWING:

Cr NC-335

ADDRESS ONLY THE
COMMISSION TO THE FIVE CIVILIZED TRIBES.

Muskogee, Indian Territory, June 9, 1905.

Eurania Smith,
    Dustin, Indian Territory.

Dear Madam:

    In the matter of the application for the enrollment of your minor child, Ester Smith, as a citizen of the Creek Nation, you are advised that the Commission requires the affidavits of two disinterested witnesses relative to the date of its birth.

    For this purpose, there are herewith enclosed two blank forms of birth affidavit. In having same executed, same care should be taken to see that all blanks are properly filled, all names written in full and in the event that the person signing an affidavit is unable to write, signatures by mark must be attested by two witnesses.

Respectfully,
(Name Illegible)

2 B A
                                          Commissioner in Charge.

Cr. NC. 335.

Muskogee, Indian Territory, July 13, 1905.

John Smith,
    Dustin, Indian Territory.

Dear Madam[sic]:

    In the matter of the application for the enrollment of your minor child, Ester Smith , as a citizen of the Creek Nation, you are advised that this office requires the

Applications for Enrollment of Creek Newborn
Act of 1905   Volume IV

affidavits of two disinterested witnesses relative to the date of its birth.

For this purpose there are herewith enclosed two blank forms of birth affidavit. In having same executed, same care should be taken to see that all blanks are properly filled, all names written in full and in the event that the person signing the affidavit is unable to write, signature by mark must be attested by two witnesses.

Respectfully,

2 BA   Commissioner.

BIRTH AFFIDAVIT.

DEPARTMENT OF THE INTERIOR.
COMMISSION TO THE FIVE CIVILIZED TRIBES.

IN RE APPLICATION FOR ENROLLMENT, as a citizen of the Creek Nation, of Ester Smith, born on the 26 day of February, 1905

Name of Father:	John F. Smith	a citizen of the Creek	Nation.
Name of Mother:	Eurania Smith	a citizen of the Creek	Nation.

Postoffice   Dustin, Ind. Ter.

AFFIDAVIT OF MOTHER.

UNITED STATES OF AMERICA, Indian Territory,
         Western   DISTRICT.

I, Eurania Smith, on oath state that I am 39 years of age and a citizen by blood, of the Creek Nation; that I am the lawful wife of John F. Smith, who is a citizen, by blood of the Creek Nation; that a female child was born to me on 26 day of February, 1905, that said child has been named Ester Smith, and was living March 4, 1905. That no one attended on me as midwife or physician in attendance at the birth of said child physician at the birth of the child.

                                                           Eurania Smith

Witnesses To Mark:

Subscribed and sworn to before me this 20 day of March, 1905.

                                                           Drennan C Skaggs
                                                           Notary Public.

Applications for Enrollment of Creek Newborn
Act of 1905 Volume IV

BIRTH AFFIDAVIT.

DEPARTMENT OF THE INTERIOR.
COMMISSION TO THE FIVE CIVILIZED TRIBES.

IN RE APPLICATION FOR ENROLLMENT, as a citizen of the Creek Nation, of Ester Smith, born on the 26 day of Feb, 1905

Name of Father: John F Smith   a citizen of the   Creek   Nation.
Name of Mother: Eurania Smith   a citizen of the   Creek   Nation.

Postoffice   Dustin I.T.

AFFIDAVIT OF MOTHER.

UNITED STATES OF AMERICA, Indian Territory,
     Western   DISTRICT.

I, Eurania Smith, on oath state that I am 40 years of age and a citizen by birth, of the Creek Nation; that I am the lawful wife of John F Smith, who is a citizen, by birth of the Creek Nation; that a female child was born to me on 26 day of February, 1905, that said child has been named Ester, and was living March 4, 1905.

                                               Eurania Smith

Witnesses To Mark:

Subscribed and sworn to before me this 24 day of July, 1905.

MY COMMISSION EXPIRES MAY 20, 1907   *(Name Illegible)*
                                               Notary Public.

AFFIDAVIT OF ATTENDING PHYSICIAN OR MID-WIFE.

UNITED STATES OF AMERICA, Indian Territory,
     Western   DISTRICT.

I, Sophuma E Berryhill, a midway[sic], on oath state that I attended on Mrs. Eurania Smith, wife of John F. Smith on the 26 day of February, 1905 ; that there was born to her on said date a female child; that said child was living March 4, 1905, and is said to have been named Ester   her
                                             Sophuma E   x   Berryhill
Witnesses To Mark: mark
     John F Smith
     (Name Illegible)

Applications for Enrollment of Creek Newborn
Act of 1905   Volume IV

Subscribed and sworn to before me this 24 day of July, 1905.

MY COMMISSION EXPIRES MAY 20, 1907

(Name Illegible)
Notary Public.

NC-336

DEPARTMENT OF THE INTERIOR,
COMMISSIONER TO THE FIVE CIVILIZED TRIBES.

Muskogee, Indian Territory, December 13, 1905.

In the matter of the application for the enrollment of Roley Long as a citizen by blood of the Creek Nation.

Jesse Long, being duly sworn, testified as follows (through Jesse McDermott, Official Interpreter):

EXAMINATION BY THE COMMISSIONER:

Q What is your name? A Jesse Long.
Q How old are you, about? A I don't know just how old I am; I am over 50, though.

The witness appears to be about 60 years old.

Q What Creek Indian Town to[sic] belong to? A Tullediga.

The witness is identified as Jessie Long on Creek Indian card, Field No. 2828, and his name is contained in the partial roll of citizens by blood of the Creek Nation approved by the Secretary of the Interior March 28, 1902, opposite Roll No. 8004.

Q You are the father or[sic] Roley Long, are you? A Yes sir.
Q Have you a child Lola Long? A In the Indian language "Lola" means the same as Roley in English.
Q You want us to call this child Roley or Lola? A Roley.
Q In one affidavit that you executed in this case, you state that Roley was born the 19th of August, 1901, and in another one you and Martha Haines, the midwife, said the child was born the 13th of August, 1901; which is the correct date? A The 19th is the correct date.
Q What is the name of Roley's mother? A Wiggie.
Q Are you married to Wiggie? A Yes sir.
Q What town did Wiggie belong to? A Tullediga.
Q Has Wiggie a sister named Sallie? A Yes sir.
Q Wiggie is dead, is she? A Yes sir.

Applications for Enrollment of Creek Newborn
Act of 1905   Volume IV

Wiggie Long, the mother of said child, is identified on Creek Indian card, Field No. 2826, and her name is contained in the partial list of citizens by blood of the Creek Nation approved by the Secretary of the Interior March 28, 1902, opposite Roll No. 7995, as Wiggie.

The witness is notified that this Office desires the affidavit of two disinterested witnesses relative to the birth of said child, Roley Long, and a blank for that purpose is furnished him.

He is further advised that Martha Haines, midwife, neglected to state the name of the child in her affidavit, and it will therefore be necessary for her to execute a new affidavit. A form for that purpose is handed him.

....

I, J. Y. Miller, a stenographer to the Commissioner to the Five Civilized Tribes, do hereby certify that the above and foregoing is a true and complete translation of my notes as same appear in my stenographic report of this case.

JY Miller

Sworn to and subscribed before me this the 19th day of December, 1905.

J McDermott   Notary Public.

AFFIDAVIT OF DISINTERESTED WITNESSES.

United States of America,
   Indian Territory,   ss.
   Western District.

were
We, the undersigned, on oath state that we ~~are~~ personally acquainted with Wiggie Long, wife of Jessie Long, and that there was born to her on or about the 19 day of August, 1901, a male child; that said child was living March 4, 1905, and is said to have been named Roley Long. We further state that we have no interest in this case.

W.E. McQueen

Charley Wesley

(2) Witnesses to mark:

_____

_____

Applications for Enrollment of Creek Newborn
Act of 1905   Volume IV

Subscribed and sworn to before me this 27 day of Dec 1905, ~~1905~~.

                        Dan Upton
                                  Notary Public.

BIRTH AFFIDAVIT.

DEPARTMENT OF THE INTERIOR.
COMMISSION TO THE FIVE CIVILIZED TRIBES.

IN RE APPLICATION FOR ENROLLMENT, as a citizen of the Creek Nation, of Roley Long, born on the 19 day of August, 1901

| Name of Father: | Jesse Long | a citizen of the | Creek | Nation. |
| Name of Mother: | Wiggie Long | a citizen of the | Creek | Nation. |

                      Postoffice   Dustin, Ind. Ter.

AFFIDAVIT OF MOTHER.

UNITED STATES OF AMERICA, Indian Territory,
    Western   DISTRICT.

    I, Jesse Long, on oath state that I am about 45 years of age and a citizen by blood, of the Creek Nation; that I am the lawful ~~wife~~ husband of Wiggie, who ~~is~~ was a citizen, by blood of the Creek Nation; that a male child was born to ~~me~~ her on 19 day of August, 1901, that said child has been named Roley Long, and is now living. That the mother Wiggie Long is now dead; that I attended on her at the birth of the child.

                              his
                        Jesse x Long
Witnesses To Mark: mark
   { Alex Posey
   { D.C. Skaggs

Subscribed and sworn to before me this 20 day of March, 1905.

                        Drennan C Skaggs
                              Notary Public.

Applications for Enrollment of Creek Newborn
Act of 1905   Volume IV

BIRTH AFFIDAVIT.

DEPARTMENT OF THE INTERIOR.
COMMISSION TO THE FIVE CIVILIZED TRIBES.

IN RE APPLICATION FOR ENROLLMENT, as a citizen of the Creek Nation, of Lolie Long, born on the 13 day of August, 1901

Name of Father:	Jesse Long	a citizen of the	Creek	Nation.
Name of Mother:	Wiggie Long	a citizen of the	Creek	Nation.

Postoffice   Spokogee

father
AFFIDAVIT OF ~~MOTHER~~.
Mother is dead

UNITED STATES OF AMERICA, Indian Territory, }
Western   DISTRICT.

I, Jesse Long, on oath state that I am 35 years of age and a citizen by birth, of the Creek Nation; that I am the lawful ~~wife~~ husband of Wiggie Long, who is a citizen, by birth of the Creek Nation; that a male child was born to me on 13th day of August, 1901, that said child has been named Lolie Long, and is now living.

                       his
                       Jesse x Long
Witnesses To Mark: mark
{ Jim Hill
{ Horace Wilson

Subscribed and sworn to before me this 2nd day of May, 1903.

My Com Exp Aug 16" 1906   J. P. Boyle
                                       Notary Public.

AFFIDAVIT OF ATTENDING PHYSICIAN OR MID-WIFE.

UNITED STATES OF AMERICA, Indian Territory, }
Western   DISTRICT.

I, Martha Haynes, a Midwife, on oath state that I attended on Mrs. Wiggie Long, wife of Jesse Long on the 13th day of August, 1901; that there was born to her on said date a male child; that said child is now living and is said to have been named *(blank)*
                                    her
                              Martha x Haynes
Witnesses To Mark: mark
{ Jim Hill
{ Horace Wilson

Applications for Enrollment of Creek Newborn
Act of 1905 Volume IV

Subscribed and sworn to before me this 2nd day of May, 1903.

My Com Exp Aug 16" 1906   J. P. Boyle
                                      Notary Public.

(The birth affidavit above is given again.)

BIRTH AFFIDAVIT.

DEPARTMENT OF THE INTERIOR.
COMMISSION TO THE FIVE CIVILIZED TRIBES.

IN RE APPLICATION FOR ENROLLMENT, as a citizen of the Creek Nation, of Roley Long, born on the 19 day of August, 1901

Name of Father:	Jesse Long	a citizen of the	Creek	Nation.
Name of Mother:	Wiggie Long	a citizen of the	Creek	Nation.

                                     Postoffice   Dustin, Ind. Ter.

AFFIDAVIT OF MOTHER.

UNITED STATES OF AMERICA, Indian Territory,
     Western   **DISTRICT.**

I, Wiggie Long, on oath state that I am 50[sic] years of age and a citizen by Birth, of the Creek Nation; that I am the lawful wife of Jessie Long, who is a citizen, by Birth of the Creek Nation; that a male child was born to me on 19 day of August, 1901, that said child has been named Roley Long, and was living March 4, 1905.

                                               her
                                   Wiggie x Long
Witnesses To Mark: mark
   { WE McQueen
     Charley Wesley

Subscribed and sworn to before me this 27" day of Dec., 1905.

                                         Dan Upton
                                              Notary Public.

Applications for Enrollment of Creek Newborn
Act of 1905 Volume IV

AFFIDAVIT OF ATTENDING PHYSICIAN OR MID-WIFE.

UNITED STATES OF AMERICA, Indian Territory, }
Western DISTRICT.

I, Martha Haynes, a midwife, on oath state that I attended on Mrs. Wiggie Long, wife of Jessie Long on the 19" day of August, 1901; that there was born to her on said date a male child; that said child was living March 4, 1905, and is said to have been named Roley Long

                                            her
                                  Martha x Haynes

Witnesses To Mark: mark
{ W E McQueen
{ Charley Wesley

Subscribed and sworn to before me this 27" day of Dec., 1905.

                                  Dan Upton
                                      Notary Public.

BIRTH AFFIDAVIT.

DEPARTMENT OF THE INTERIOR.
COMMISSION TO THE FIVE CIVILIZED TRIBES.

IN RE APPLICATION FOR ENROLLMENT, as a citizen of the Creek Nation, of Roley Long, born on the 19 day of August, 1901

Name of Father: Jessie Long   a citizen of the   Creek   Nation.
Name of Mother: Wiggie Long   a citizen of the   Creek   Nation.

                            Postoffice   Dustin, Ind. Ter.

AFFIDAVIT OF MOTHER.

UNITED STATES OF AMERICA, Indian Territory, }
Western DISTRICT.

I, Wiggie Long, on oath state that I am 30 years of age and a citizen by Birth, of the Creek Nation; that I am the lawful wife of Jessie Long, who is a citizen, by Birth of the Creek Nation; that a male child was born to me on 19 day of August, 1901, that said child has been named Roley Long, and was living March 4, 1905.

                                       her
                                Wiggie x Long

Witnesses To Mark: mark
{ W E McQueen
{ Charley Wesley

Applications for Enrollment of Creek Newborn
Act of 1905   Volume IV

Subscribed and sworn to before me this 27 day of Dec, 1905.

> Dan Upton
> Notary Public.

AFFIDAVIT OF ATTENDING PHYSICIAN OR MID-WIFE.

UNITED STATES OF AMERICA, Indian Territory, ⎱
    Western   DISTRICT.   ⎰

I, Martha Haynes , a midwife , on oath state that I attended on Mrs. Wiggie Long , wife of Jessie Long on the 19 day of August , 1901 ; that there was born to her on said date a male child; that said child was living March 4, 1905, and is said to have been named Roley Long

> her
> Martha x Haynes
> mark

Witnesses To Mark:
 { W E McQueen
   Charley Wesley

Subscribed and sworn to before me this 27 day of Dec., 1905.

> Dan Upton
> Notary Public.

BIRTH AFFIDAVIT.

DEPARTMENT OF THE INTERIOR.
COMMISSION TO THE FIVE CIVILIZED TRIBES.

IN RE APPLICATION FOR ENROLLMENT, as a citizen of the Creek Nation, of Roley Long , born on the 19 day of August , 1901

Name of Father:	Jesse Long	a citizen of the	Creek	Nation.
Name of Mother:	Wiggie Long	a citizen of the	Creek	Nation.

Postoffice   Dustin, Ind. Ter.

AFFIDAVIT OF MOTHER.

UNITED STATES OF AMERICA, Indian Territory, ⎱
    Western   DISTRICT.   ⎰

I, Jesse Long , on oath state that I am about 45 years of age and a citizen by blood, of the Creek Nation; that I am the lawful ~~wife~~ husband of Wiggie , who ~~is~~ was a

Applications for Enrollment of Creek Newborn
Act of 1905 Volume IV

citizen, by blood of the Creek Nation; that a male child was born to ~~me~~ her on 19 day of August , 1901 , that said child has been named Roley Long , and is now living. That the mother Wiggie Long is now dead; that I attended on her at the birth of the child.

his
Jesse x Long
mark

Witnesses To Mark:
{ Alex Posey
{ D.C. Skaggs

Subscribed and sworn to before me this 20 day of March, 1905.

Drennan C Skaggs
Notary Public.

NC 336.

Muskogee, Indian Territory, June 1, 1905.

Jesse Long,
    Dustin, Indian Territory.

Dear Sir:

    In the matter of the application for the enrollment of your minor child, Roley Long, there are herewith enclosed two blank forms of birth affidavit which you are requested to have signed by two disinterested witnesses relative who know the date of the birth of said child, and in executing same care should be exercised to see that all blanks are properly filled, all names written in full and in the event that either of the persons signing the affidavits is unable to write, signatures by mark must be attested by two witnesses. Each affidavit must be executed before a Notary Public and the notarial seal and signature of the officer must be attached to each separate affidavit.

    It is stated that the mother of said child, Wiggie Long is dead.

    There is herewith enclosed blank form of birth affidavit which you are requested to have filled out and executed before an officer authorized to administer oaths, and return it to the Commission in the enclosed envelope.

    For the purposes of identifying Wiggie Long, you are requested to furnish the Commission with her maiden name, the names of her parents, the Creek Indian Town to which she belonged, and if possible, the numbers which appear on her deeds to land in the Creek Nation.

Respectfully,

Com
Chairman.

1DA
2BA.

Applications for Enrollment of Creek Newborn
Act of 1905 Volume IV

Muskogee, Indian Territory, August 3, 1905.

Jesse Long,
    Dustin, Indian Territory.

Dear Sir:

    In the matter of the application for the enrollment of your minor child, Roley Long, as a citizen by blood of the Creek Nation, you are advised that this office is unable to identify you or Wiggie Long, deceased, on its rolls or citizens of the Creek Nation.

    You are requested to state the names of your parents and those of said Wiggie Long, the Creek Indian town to which each of you belongs, and, if possible, the numbers which appear on your deeds to land in the Creek Nation.

    There is also on file in this office an affidavit executed by you and Martha Haynes, a midwife, May 2, 1903, in which it is stated that your child Lolie Long was born August 13, 1901.

    In your latter affidavit it is stated that your child Roley Long was born August 19, 1901.

    It is presumed that Lolie Long is identical with Roley Long.

    For the correction of the discrepancy in dates there is herewith enclosed a blank form of birth affidavit which should be properly signed and executed by yourself and said midwife. Care should be taken that the names of affiants are signed as same appear in the body of the affidavit and that the notary public, before whom the affidavit is executed, affixes his signature and seal. Affidavits should then be returned to this office in enclosed envelope.

    Respectfully,

    Commissioner.

1 B A
Env.

NC 336.   EK.

Muskogee, Indian Territory, March 1, 1907.

Jesse Long,
    Dustin, Indian Territory.

Dear Sir:

Applications for Enrollment of Creek Newborn
Act of 1905   Volume IV

You are hereby advised that on February 15, 1907, the Secretary of the Interior approved the enrollment of your minor child, Roley Long, as a citizen by blood of the Nation, and that the name of said child appears upon the roll of New Born citizens by blood of the Creek Nation, enrolled under the Act of Congress approved March 3, 1905, as number 1134.

The child is now entitled to an allotment, and application therefor should be made without delay at the Creek Land Office, Muskogee, Indian Territory.

Respectfully,

Commissioner.

N.C. 337.

DEPARTMENT OF THE INTERIOR,
COMMISSIONER TO THE FIVE CIVILIZED TRIBES.
Wetumka, I. T., April 14, 1906.

In the matter of the application for the enrollment of Jennie Josie as a citizen by blood of the Creek Nation.

SOFLEY JOSIE, being duly sworn, testified as follows:

Through Alex Posey official interpreter:

BY THE COMMISSIONER:
Q What is your name? A Sofley Josie.
Q How old are you? A About thirty.
Q What is your post office address? A Wetumka.
Q Are you a citizen of the Creek Nation? A No, sir, Seminole.
Q Under what name are you enrolled in the Seminole Nation? A As John Tulmochussee.
Q Have you a child named Jennie? A Yes, sir.
Q What is the name of the child's mother? A Lena Josie.
Q Is Lena a citizen of the Creek Nation? A Yes, sir.
Q To what town does she belong? A Hutchechuppa.
Q What was her maiden name: A Lena Jack.
Q If it should be found that your child, Jennie Josie, is entitled to enrollment in either the Creek or Seminole Nation, in which nation do you elect to have her enrolled? A In the Creek Nation.

---oooOOOooo---

I, D. C. Skaggs, on oath state that the above and foregoing is a full and true transcript of my stenographic notes as taken in said cause on said date.

DC Skaggs

Applications for Enrollment of Creek Newborn
Act of 1905   Volume IV

Subscribed and sworn to before me this 20 day of April, 1906.

Alex Posey
Notary Public.

NC. 337.

Muskogee, Indian Territory, July 14, 1905.

Commissioner to the Five Civilized Tribes,
Seminole Enrollment Division,
Muskogee, Indian Territory.

Gentlemen:

March 23, 1905, application was made to the Commission to the Five Civilized Tribes for the enrollment of Jennie Josie, born September 12, 1903, as a citizen by blood of the Creek Nation. It is stated in said application that the father of said child is Sofley Josie, a citizen of the Seminole Nation, and that the mother is Lena Josie, identified as Lena Jack, a citizen of the Creek Nation.

You are requested to inform the Creek Enrollment Division as to whether application has been made for the enrollment of said Jennie Josie, as a citizen of the Seminole Nation, and if so, what disposition has been made of the same.

Respectfully,

Commissioner.

DEPARTMENT OF THE INTERIOR.
COMMISSION TO THE FIVE CIVILIZED TRIBES.

Muskogee, Indian Territory, July 18, 1905.

Chief Clerk,
Creek Enrollment Division.

Dear Sir:

Receipt is acknowledged of your letter of July 14, 1905 (NC-337) stating that application was made to the Commission to the Five Civilized Tribes for the enrollment of Jennie Josie, born September 12, 1903, child of Sofley Josie, a citizen of the Seminole Nation, and Lena Josie (identified as Lena Jack), a citizen of the Creek Nation, as a citizen by blood of the Creek Nation and requesting to be informed as to whether an

Applications for Enrollment of Creek Newborn
Act of 1905   Volume IV

application has been made for the enrollment of said child as a citizen of the Seminole Nation.

In reply to your letter you are advised that it does not appear from an examination of the records of this office that any application was made to the Commission to the Five Civilized Tribes for the enrollment of said Jennie Josie as a citizen of the Seminole Nation.

Respectfully,

Tams Bixby   Commissioner.

Indian Territory I
                I ss
Western District I

We, the undersigned, on oath state that we are personally acquainted with Lena Josie wife of Sofley Josie; that on or about the 12 day of September, 1903, a female child was born to them and has been named Jennie Josie; and that said child was living March 4, 1905.

We further state that we have no interest in the above case.

Witnesses to mark:　　　　　　　　　Amos King
　　　　　　　　　　　　　　　　　　　　　his
Alex Posey　　　　　　　　　　　　　Yahola x Harjo
　　　　　　　　　　　　　　　　　　　　mark
D C Skaggs

_____

_____

Subscribed and sworn to before me this 14 day of April, 1906.

Alex Posey
Notary public[sic].

Applications for Enrollment of Creek Newborn
Act of 1905   Volume IV

Indian Territory, I
        I ss:
Western District.I

    We, the undersigned, do hereby elect to have our child, Jennie Josie, born on the 12 day of September, 1903, enrolled as a citizen of the Creek Nation, and to have said child receive her allotment of land and distribution of moneys in said nation.

Witnesses to mark:

Alex Posey

D C Skaggs

          his
Sofley x Josie
          mark
          her
Lena x Josie
          mark

    Subscribed and sworn to before me this 14 day of April, 1906.

                Alex Posey
                      Notary public[sic].

BIRTH AFFIDAVIT.

DEPARTMENT OF THE INTERIOR.
COMMISSION TO THE FIVE CIVILIZED TRIBES.

    IN RE APPLICATION FOR ENROLLMENT, as a citizen of the Creek Nation, of Jennie Josie, born on the 12 day of September , 1903

Name of Father: Sofley Josie   a citizen of the   Seminole Nation.
Name of Mother: Lena Josie (nee Jack)   a citizen of the   Creek   Nation.

                Postoffice   Wetumka, Ind. Ter.

AFFIDAVIT OF MOTHER.

UNITED STATES OF AMERICA, Indian Territory,
    Western   **DISTRICT.**

    I, Lena Josie , on oath state that I am about 19 years of age and a citizen by blood , of the Creek Nation; that I am the lawful wife of Sofley Josie , who is a citizen, by blood of the Seminole Nation; that a female child was born to me on 12 day of September , 1903 , that said child has been named Jennie Josie , and was living March 4, 1905.
                                  her
                            Lena x Josie
                              mark

Applications for Enrollment of Creek Newborn
Act of 1905   Volume IV

Witnesses To Mark:
{ Alex Posey
{ D C Skaggs

Subscribed and sworn to before me this 21 day of March, 1905.

Drennan C Skaggs
Notary Public.

AFFIDAVIT OF ATTENDING PHYSICIAN OR MID-WIFE.

UNITED STATES OF AMERICA, Indian Territory,
Western   DISTRICT.

I, Sofley Josie, ~~a (blank)~~, on oath state that I attended on ^ my wife Mrs. Lena Josie, ~~wife of (blank)~~ on the 12 day of September, 1903 ; that there was born to her on said date a female child; that said child was living March 4, 1905, and is said to have been named Jennie Josie

his
Sofley x Josie
mark

Witnesses To Mark:
{ DC Skaggs
{ Alex Posey

Subscribed and sworn to before me this 21 day of March, 1905.

Drennan C Skaggs
Notary Public.

Cr NC-337

Muskogee, Indian Territory, June 8, 1905.

Lena Josie,
    Wetumka, Indian Territory.

Dear Madam:

    In the matter of the application for the enrollment of your minor child, Jennie Josie, you are advised that the Commission requires the affidavit of the midwife or physician in attendance at the birth of said child. For this purpose, there is herewith enclosed a blank form of birth affidavit. In having same executed, care should be taken to see that all blanks are properly filled, all names written in full, and in the event that the person signing the affidavit is unable to write, signature by mark must be attested by two witnesses.

Applications for Enrollment of Creek Newborn
Act of 1905 Volume IV

For the purpose of electing the Nation in which you desire to have said child enrolled, it will be necessary that its father, a citizen of the Seminole Nation, should appear before the Commission, as its office, in Muskogee, Indian Territory, at an early date.

Respectfully,

Chairman.

1 B A

Cr NC -337

Muskogee, Indian Territory, July 21, 1905.

Sofley Josie,
    Wetumka, Indian Territory.

Dear Sir:

In the matter of the application for the enrollment of your minor child, Jennie Josie, you are advised that this office requires the affidavit of the midwife or physician in attendance at the birth of said child. For this purpose, there is herewith enclosed a blank form of birth affidavit. In having same executed, care should be taken to see that all blanks are properly filled, all names written in full, and in the event that the person signing the affidavit is unable to write, signature by mark must be attested by two witnesses.

For the purpose of electing the Nation in which you desire to have said child enrolled, it will be necessary for you to appear before this office, in Muskogee, Indian Territory, at an early date.

Respectfully,

Commissioner.

1 B A

DEPARTMENT OF THE INTERIOR.
N.C. 337.   **COMMISSION TO THE FIVE CIVILIZED TRIBES.**

Wetumka, Indian Territory, April 20, 1906.

Commissioner to the Five Civilized Tribes,
    Muskogee, Indian Territory.

Sir:

There is enclosed herewith affidavits and testimony in the matter of the application for the enrollment of Jennie Josie as a citizen by blood of the Creek Nation.

Applications for Enrollment of Creek Newborn
Act of 1905   Volume IV

Respectfully,

Alex Posey
In Charge Creek Field Party.

NB 337.

Muskogee, Indian Territory, October 31, 1906.

Chief Clerk,
    Seminole Enrollment Division,
        Muskogee, Indian Territory.

Dear Sir:

    There is on file in this office an application for the enrollment of Jennie Josie, born September 12, 1903, to Sofley Josie, who is identified on the rolls of citizens by blood of the Seminole Nation, under the name of John Tulmochusee[sic], and Lena Josie, who is identified on the rolls of citizens by blood of the Creek Nation, opposite roll number 7130.

    You are advised that the name of said child is contained in a partial list of new born citizens by blood of the Creek Nation (enrolled under the act of Congress approved March 3, 1905) approved by the Secretary of the Interior October 15, 1905, opposite roll number 1026.

Respectfully,

Commissioner.

Applications for Enrollment of Creek Newborn
Act of 1905   Volume IV

NC 338.

DEPARTMENT OF THE INTERIOR,
COMMISSION TO THE FIVE CIVILIZED TRIBES.
MUSKOGEE, INDIAN TERRITORY I. T. JUNE 19, 1905.

In the matter of the application for the enrollment of Lizzie Reynolds, as a citizen by blood of the Creek Nation.

John R. Reynolds, being duly sworn, testified as follows:

Examination by the Commission:
Q What is your name? A John R. Reynolds.
Q How old are you? A 50.
Q What is your post office address? A Hanna.
Q Are you a citizen of the Creek Nation? A No sir.
Q Have you a child named Lizzie Reynolds? A Yes sir.
Q When was Lizzie born? A She was born the 3rd of March.
Q This year? A Yes sir.
Q Who was present when this child was born? A I was the only one present.
Q Is this child living? A Yes sir.
Q Is the mother of the child living? A Yes sir.
Q Di[sic] you act as midwife when this child was born? A Yes sir.
Q Are you familiar with the dates and the months and years? Do keep a record of any kind of the dates of the birth and death of your children? A Yes sir, I mark them all down.
Q Did you mark down the date of the birth of Lizzie Reynolds? A Yes. sir.
Q In what did you mark it? A In a Bible.
Q Have you that Bible with you? A No sir.
Q You have it at home? A Yes sir.
Q Do you remember with what you wrote that? A Lead pencil.
Q Did you write it yourself? A Yes sir.
Q Do you remember what you said --the words you used? A Lizzie Reynolds born March the 3rd, 1905, that is according to the way I marked all the ages of the children.
Q Well what child did you put down before Lizzie Reynolds? A Arthur Reynolds and William is ahead of him. He is done enrolled.
Q Well how long after the birth of the child did you put that down? A I think it was the next day. I put it down in order not to forget or make a mistake.
Q Well John do you remember what day of the week it was when you put down that entry i the Bible? About this child Lizzie? A I don't believe I can remember what day it was.
Q Do you know what day of the week it was that Lizzie was born? A It seems to me it was Wednesday or Thursday, somewhere about the middle of the week. I wouldn't be positive, I was kinder bothered I had several children to put down.
Q Do you take any newspaper? A Yes sir.
Q Do you remember hearing of the inauguration of President Roosevelt? A Yes sir.
Q You remember that? A Yes sir.

Applications for Enrollment of Creek Newborn
Act of 1905   Volume IV

Q Do you remember whether this child was born before or after that? A I think it was before as well as I remember.
Q How long before? A I guess ----seems to me it was about the same time of the inauguration.
Q What time of the day or the hour was this child Lizzie born? A In the night. About 11--between 10 and 11.
Q Well was it born between 10 and 1 P.M. of the 3rd of March of[sic] the 2nd or 4th, which? A 3rd of March.
Q You say nobody was present? A No sir.
Q Now did anyone come into the house shortly after the child was born? A No, not until the next day.
Q Name some of the people that came in the next day? A A couple of renters who lived about a quarter of a mile. They were Miss Wine and Mrs Slawson I think it was the first evening after the child was born that they came.
Q You think you can get those two people before the Commission? A Well people are so busy and money is scarce I don't know whether I can or not.
Q The witness is advised that it will be necessary for him to appear with these people and the mother of said child as soon as possible; The mother of said child has never testified; and it would be adviseable[sic] to have the affidavits of these two neighbors you mentioned and if possible to have them here in person to be examined under oath.

Lona Merrick, being duly sworn, states that the above and foregoing is a true and correct transcript of her stenographic notes as taken in said cause on said date.

Lona Merrick

Subscribed and sworn to before me this 20th day of June, 1905.

Edw C Griesel
Notary Public.

BIRTH AFFIDAVIT.

DEPARTMENT OF THE INTERIOR.
COMMISSION TO THE FIVE CIVILIZED TRIBES.

IN RE APPLICATION FOR ENROLLMENT, as a citizen of the Creek Nation, of Lizzie Reynolds, born on the 3d day of March , 1905

Name of Father: John R Reynolds	a citizen of the U. S.	Nation.
Name of Mother: Era Edna Reynolds	a citizen of the Creek	Nation.

Postoffice   Hanna, I.T.

Applications for Enrollment of Creek Newborn
Act of 1905   Volume IV

AFFIDAVIT OF ~~MOTHER~~ acquaintance.

UNITED STATES OF AMERICA, Indian Territory,　}
　Western　　　　　DISTRICT.

　　　　　　　　　　　　　　　　　　with Era Edna Reynolds
　　I, S.E. Waren , on oath state that I am acquainted ~~years of age and~~ a citizen by blood, of the Creek   Nation; ~~that I am~~ the lawful wife of John R Reynolds , who is a citizen, by ----- of the U.S. Nation; that a Female   child was born to ~~me~~ her on the 3d day of March , 1905 , that said child has been named Lizzie Reynolds , and was living March 4, 1905.

　　　　　　　　　　　　　　　　　　SE Waren

Witnesses To Mark:
{

　　Subscribed and sworn to before me this the 26 day of June , 1905.

　　　　　　　　　　　　　　T. T. Caves
　　　　　　　　　　　　　　　　Notary Public.

AFFIDAVIT OF ATTENDING PHYSICIAN OR MID-WIFE.

UNITED STATES OF AMERICA, Indian Territory,　}
　Western　　　　　DISTRICT.

　　　　　　　　　　　　　　　　　acquainted with
　　I, Alcy Slawson , a *(blank)* , on oath state that I was ~~attended on~~ Mrs. Era Edna Reynolds , wife of John R Reynolds on the 3d   day of March , 1905 ; that there was born to her on said date a Female   child; that said child was living March 4, 1905, and is said to have been named Lizzie Reynolds

　　　　　　　　　　　　　　　　　Mrs Alcy Slawson

Witnesses To Mark:
{

　　Subscribed and sworn to before me this the 26 day of June , 1905.

　　　　　　　　　　　　　　T. T. Caves
　　　　　　　　　　　　　　　　Notary Public.

Applications for Enrollment of Creek Newborn
Act of 1905   Volume IV

BIRTH AFFIDAVIT.

DEPARTMENT OF THE INTERIOR.
COMMISSION TO THE FIVE CIVILIZED TRIBES.

IN RE APPLICATION FOR ENROLLMENT, as a citizen of the Creek Nation, of Lizzie Reynolds, born on the 3 day of March , 1905

Name of Father: John R Reynolds   a citizen of the United States Nation.
Name of Mother: Era Edna Reynolds   a citizen of the   Creek   Nation.

Postoffice   Hanna, Ind.Ter.

AFFIDAVIT OF MOTHER.

UNITED STATES OF AMERICA, Indian Territory, ⎫
      Western   DISTRICT.   ⎭

I, Era Edna Reynolds , on oath state that I am 29 years of age and a citizen by blood , of the Creek Nation; that I am the lawful wife of John R. Reynolds , who is a citizen, by *(blank)* of the United States Nation; that a female child was born to me on 3 day of March , 1905 , that said child has been named Lizzie Reynolds , and was living March 4, 1905.
                                                              her
                                   Era Edna x Reynolds
Witnesses To Mark: mark
 ⎧ Alex Posey
 ⎩ DC Skaggs

Subscribed and sworn to before me this 20 day of March , 1905.

                                      Drennan C Skaggs
                                      Notary Public.

AFFIDAVIT OF ATTENDING PHYSICIAN OR MID-WIFE.

UNITED STATES OF AMERICA, Indian Territory, ⎫
      Western   DISTRICT.   ⎭
                                                               my wife
I, John R. Reynolds , ~~a~~ , on oath state that I attended on ^ Mrs. Era Edna Reynolds , wife of ~~John R. Reynolds~~ on the 3 day of March , 1905 ; that there was born to her on said date a *(blank)* child; that said child was living March 4, 1905, and is said to have been named Lizzie Reynolds
                                         John R. Reynolds
Witnesses To Mark:
 ⎧

Applications for Enrollment of Creek Newborn
Act of 1905   Volume IV

Subscribed and sworn to before me this 20 day of March , 1905.

Drennan C Skaggs
Notary Public.

BIRTH AFFIDAVIT.

DEPARTMENT OF THE INTERIOR.
COMMISSION TO THE FIVE CIVILIZED TRIBES.

IN RE APPLICATION FOR ENROLLMENT, as a citizen of the Creek Nation, of Arthur Leroy Reynolds, born on the about 9 day of June , 1902

Name of Father:	John R Reynolds	a citizen of the	U. S.	Nation.
Name of Mother:	Era Edna Reynolds	a citizen of the	Creek	Nation.

Postoffice   Hanna, I.T.

acquaintance
AFFIDAVIT OF ~~MOTHER~~.

UNITED STATES OF AMERICA, Indian Territory,
Western   DISTRICT.

with Era Edna Reynolds
I, Joe Smith , on oath state that I am acquainted ~~years of age and~~ a citizen by blood, of the   Creek   Nation; ~~that I am~~ the lawful wife of John R Reynolds , who is a citizen, by ----- of the U.S. Nation; that a male   child was born to ~~me~~ her on or about 9   day of June , 1902 , that said child has been named Arthur Leroy Reynolds , and was living March 4, 1905.

Joe Smith

Witnesses To Mark:

Subscribed and sworn to before me this the 27 day of June , 1905.

T. T. Caves
Notary Public.

AFFIDAVIT OF ATTENDING PHYSICIAN OR MID-WIFE.

UNITED STATES OF AMERICA, Indian Territory,
Western   DISTRICT.

acquainted with
I, Dave Proctor , a acquaintance , on oath state that I was ~~attended on~~ Mrs. Era Edna Reynolds , wife of John R Reynolds on or about the 9" day of June , 1902 ; that

Applications for Enrollment of Creek Newborn
Act of 1905   Volume IV

there was born to her on said date a male child; that said child was living March 4, 1905, and is said to have been named Arthur Leroy Reynolds

Dave Proctor

Witnesses To Mark:
{

Subscribed and sworn to before me this the 27 day of June , 1905.

T. T. Caves
Notary Public.

BIRTH AFFIDAVIT.

DEPARTMENT OF THE INTERIOR.
COMMISSION TO THE FIVE CIVILIZED TRIBES.

IN RE APPLICATION FOR ENROLLMENT, as a citizen of the Creek Nation, of Arthur Leroy Reynolds, born on the 9 day of June , 1902

Name of Father: John R Reynolds   a citizen of the United States Nation.
Name of Mother: Era Edna Reynolds   a citizen of the   Creek   Nation.

Postoffice   Hanna, Ind.Ter.

AFFIDAVIT OF MOTHER.

UNITED STATES OF AMERICA, Indian Territory, }
Western   DISTRICT.

I, Era Edna Reynolds , on oath state that I am 29 years of age and a citizen by blood , of the Creek Nation; that I am the lawful wife of John R. Reynolds , who is a citizen, ~~by~~ *(blank)* of the United States Nation; that a male child was born to me on 9 day of June , 1902 , that said child has been named Arthur Leroy Reynolds , and was living March 4, 1905.

Era Edna x Reynolds
mark

Witnesses To Mark:
{ Alex Posey
  DC Skaggs

Subscribed and sworn to before me this 20 day of March , 1905.

Drennan C Skaggs
Notary Public.

Applications for Enrollment of Creek Newborn
Act of 1905 Volume IV

AFFIDAVIT OF ATTENDING PHYSICIAN OR MID-WIFE.

UNITED STATES OF AMERICA, Indian Territory,
Western DISTRICT.

my wife
I, John R. Reynolds , ~~a~~, on oath state that I attended on ^ Mrs. Era Edna Reynolds , wife of *(blank)* on the 9 day of June , 1902 ; that there was born to her on said date a *(blank)* child; that said child was living March 4, 1905, and is said to have been named Arthur Leroy Reynolds

John R. Reynolds

Witnesses To Mark:

Subscribed and sworn to before me this 20 day of March , 1905.

Drennan C Skaggs
Notary Public.

Cr NC-338

Muskogee, Indian Territory, June 8, 1905.

Eva Edna Reynolds,
Hanna, Indian Territory.

Dear Madam:

In the matter of the application for the enrollment of your minor children, Arthur LeRoy and Lizzie Reynolds, as citizens of the Creek Nation, you are advised that it will be necessary that you and the father of said children appear before the Commission, at its office, in Muskogee, Indian Territory, at an early date, for the purpose of being examined under oath.

Respectfully,

Chairman.

Index

ADAMS
  Martha 38
ALLAN
  Robert 64
ALLEN
  George 272
  R C....28,29,30,286,287,288,290, 291, 292, 293
ASBURY
  Davis 50
  Eliza 136,137,138,139
  Francis 17,206,207,208,209
  George 136,137,138,139,140
  Jennetta 205,206,207,208,209
  Joseph 134,135,136
  Joshua 134,135,136
  Mrs Joshua 135,136
  Mrs Miley 136
  Sarah ... 136,137,138,139,140,141,142
  Sippie 205,206,207,208,209
ASHUNT
  J H 115,117

BAKER
  Billie 210,215
  Billy 211,212,213,214,216,217
  Enverett M 201
  Everett M ... 200,201,202,203,204,205
  Evereyy M 205
  Inez E 211
  Inez W 210,211,214,215,217
  Kinkeha M 200
  Kinkehee M 204
  Kinkehee N 202,203,205
  Luther I 200,201,202,203,204
  Pauline E 210,212,213,214,215, 216,217
  Rebeca J 204,205
  Rebecca J ... 200,201,202,203,205,211
  Susie 204,205,210,211,212,213, 214,215,216,217
  Susie A 204,205
BANTOU
  R 54,55
BARKER
  H H 34,35,36,37,38
BARNETT
  Dick 140
  Jensie 55
  Melvina 258
BEALL
  Wm O 217,280
BEMO
  Charlie 25,26,27
  Dora 25,26
  Louis 25,27
  Maggie 26,27
BEMORE
  Charlie 27,28,29,30,31
  Dora 29,30,31
  Lewis 27,28,30,31
  Maggie 27,28,29,30,31
BERRYHILL
  Andrew J 66,67,68
  Charles Percy 66,67,68
  Charley 167
  Charlie 166,167
  Clent 167,168
  Lula 66,67,68
  Sam 166,167
  Sophia 166,167,168
  Sophuma E 301
BIGPOND
  D 54,55
BIXBY
  Tams ... 3,4,6,18,25,31,97,99,102,105, 120,126,151,152,161,176,191,202, 215,221,247,261,268,270,281,295, 296,313
  Thams 283
BOUDINOT
  Cornelius 85
BOYLE
  J P 305,306
BREWER
  Joseph 80,81,82
BRIGHAM
  W A 6,7,8,10,21,84,85,91,92,94
BROOKS
  Bettie 239
  John 239
  Thomas Clifford 239
BROWN
  Ada 235,236

325

Index

Annie 53,54,55,56,57
Cilla 129
Fortyfour 53
Forty-four 54,55,57
Forty-fur 57
Hannah 53,56
Joe 235,236,237,238
Lizzie 235,236,237,238
Sandy 235,236,237,238
Thomas 53,54,55,56,57
BRUCE
   J L 170
BRUNER
   Mary 84,85
   Paul 273
   Pauline 273
   Robert 243,245
BUCK
   Rozella 113
   Sarah 273
BURNETT
   Herford 273
BURTON
   Charles Checotah 130,131,132
   Jesse 130,131,132,133
   Mary 130,131,132,133
   Rufus Cheestell 130,132,133
BUSEY
   J C F 154
BYRD
   Lucy Ann 253
   Miss Lucy Ann 252

CAKOCHEE 231
CALLAHAN
   J O 116
CANARD
   Jeff T 154
CARDER
   A E, MD 91
CARR
   Ada 57,58,59,60
   Thomas 58,59,60,61
   Vera Vinita 58
   Verna Vinita 58,59,60
CARVER
   Illegible M 49

CASITKA
   Miss 95,97
CAVES
   T T 320,322
CEASAR
   Calley 273
CHALAKEE
   Jimmy 209
   Nancy 209
CHEALAKE
   James 206
   Nancy 206
CHERRY
   Colona Blanche 162,165,166
   Francis Doyle 162,163,164
   Jennie 162,163,164,165,166
   Jennie Pitman 162
   Joe 162,163,164,165,166
   Lee 165
CHILDERS
   Anderson J 218,219
   Annie 285,289
   Annie B 286,287,288,289,290,291,292,293
   Ben 285,286,287,288,289,290,291,292,293
   Liddia 218,219
   Liddie 219
   Lydia 218,219
   Mose 286,289,290,291,292,293
   Ruthie 287,288
   Ruthis 285,286,288
   Sousa 288,293
   Stella 218,219
CHISHOLM
   Bettie 239
   Mattie 239
CHUPCO
   Letka 232
CLAWSON
   L L 123,124
   W R 123,124
CLINTON
   Fred S 39
   Vera 38,39
COACHMAN
   Chas 135,136

COBB
   Addie 283,284
   Almeda 223
   Almetie 224
   Eddie 283
   John 284
   Johnnie 283,284
CO-DEN-NY 53,55,56,57
CO-LAH-YAH
   Bank Chief 175,180
COLLIER
   H C 212,213
   Lavonia 213
   Thos M 213
COLLINS
   Eliza 59
COMBS
   Eli 195
COSA
   Mary 188
COX
   Annie 28
   Maggie 25,27
COYNE
   P E 39
CRAWFORD
   D M 252
CROWDER
   Paul 195
CUE
   Mrs Grace 41

DARRSAW
   Toche 283
DAVES
   T T 323
DAVIDSON
   Charles A 63
   Chas 62
   Chas A 63
DAVIS
   Barney 155,156
   Cooper 3,4,5,6
   Eli 3,5
   Eliza 156,167
   Ella 259,261,262,263,264,266, 267,268,269,273

Ella S 264,265
Eugene 261,262,264,267,268,269
G W 115
Georgia 273
Jess 261,262,263,264,266,267,268, 269,273
Jesse 260
Jesse E 264,265
Lewis 259,260,261,262,263,264, 265,267,268,269,270,271,272,274
Lizzie 155,156
Ollie 3
Ross 264,266,267,268,269
Susie 150,153,154,155,156
DAWS
   Hon 175,178,180
DE GRAFFENRIED
   R P 50
DEAN
   Josie A 62
DEER
   Ellen 49,50,51,52,53
   Nancy 49,50,51,52,277,280
   Silas 49,50,51,52
DEERBACK
   Ralph 114
DEGRAFFENRIED
   R P 50
DICKSON
   Lottie 273
DILL
   M E 146
   R D 167
   R H 152,153,156
   W H 146
DITZLER
   James Albert 255,256,257,258,259
   Melvina 255,256,257,258,259
   W H 257
   Will 256,258,259
   Wm H 256,257
DODGE
   Emma 273
DONOVAN
   Irwin 26,27
   Orwin 132,133
DREBACK

Index

Ralph 114
DRESBACK
  Ralph 51,295
DU BOIS
  B R 115,116
  Elizabeth C 115,116
  Elizabeth Gladys........... 115,116
DUBOIS
  B R 114
  Elizabeth Gladys................. 114
DUNN
  Tupper 150,152,153,156,158,159, 163,166,167,168,169,198

EASLEY
  R M................................ 6,7,10
EDWARDS
  Henry................................ 272
ENRIGUES
  Jesus 48
  Lizzie 48
  William............................... 48

FAIRFIELD
  H L 240
FARRIS
  G W 8
FAULKNER
  J D 60
FENNELL
  Joe 29,288,292,293
FIFE
  George 277
FIPPS
  Alice M........................ 172,173
  Eva.............................. 173,174
  Myrta May 172
  Nancy 173,174
  Sam 173
FISH
  Melia................................ 249
FISHER
  Eunice........................ 288,293
  Rosie........................... 256,258
FIXICO
  California 169,170
  Cano 169,170
  Hulbutta............................ 143
  Kano 170,171
  Lucy 169,170,171
  Quagus 95
  Throtho...................... 136,139
FIXICO, ... 171
FLYNN
  Tom W 65
FOSTER
  Bessie 170
  David......................192,193,194
  Jimmie 193,194
  Melanie..................192,193,194
  Mesaley 194
  Oceola 192
FRANCIS
  Minkey 43,45
  Minky 44,45,46,47
  Nellie 45,47
  Roly 43,44,45,47
  Sam................................ 45,47
  Samuel 46,47
  William.................43,44,45,46,47
  Wm 43,45
FRANK
  Barney 168,169
  Illegible J............................ 265
  Leah 168,169
  Lidda 159,168,169
  Liddie 158
  Lydia 157

GA?NTT
  W L 115
GARDNER
  Mandy 284
GARRIGUES
  Anna 53,54,96,100,123,137,139, 143,150,275
GATLIN
  C C 253,254,255
  Helen 253,254,255
  Hellen 252,253
  Lucile 253,254
  Lucy Ann...................253,254,255
  Mrs C C 252
GENTRY

Index

Joshua 273
GIBSON
  Thelma Maud 273
GILLIAM
  Dr W C 79
  W C 77,78,79
GOODEN
  Lizzie 48
  Sordie 48
GOUGE
  Sallie 83
GRAYSON
  Betty 49,51
  Louiza 83
  Luiza 82
  Nancy 135
  Robert 82,83
  Samson 82,83
GREENLEAF
  Sarah 107,110,111
GRIESEL
  E C 1,2,26,65,66,113,117,118,
    132,133,134,210
  Edw 2
  Edw C 1,4,5,14,16,26,27,52,54,56,
    63,66,68,70,72,73,86,90,108,109,112,
    113,117,118,121,126,131,132,133,134,
    143,157,201,207,210,220,226,230,
    231,282,285,289,294,319
  Lucy 126
GROSS
  Ben D 283

HADFIELD
  S L 219
  Signa L 218,219
HAINES
  Martha 302,303
HAINS
  H G 93,99,100,134,208,275
  Henry G 50,101,123,137,139,232
HAMILTON
  J O 250,251
HARJO
  Albert 197,198
  Arney 157,158,159,160,161,169
  A E 156,157,158,159,160,161

Hulbutta 274
Huntie 197,198,199
Joseph 149,150,153,154
Josie 149
Ladia 171
Lilley 149,153,154
Lillie 150,231
Lilly 150,154
Lizzie 23,24
Louis 232
Lucy 274,275,276,277,278,279,
  281,296
Mahala 150
Mahaley 150
Mehaley 153,154
Melissa 21,22,24
Millie 295,296,297,298
Mollie 21,22,23,24
Mollie (Yahola) 24
Mord 158,159,160,161
Nord 156,157
Peter 123
Roman 156,157,158,160,161
Sallie 274,275,276,277,278,279,
  280,281
Sarah 196,197,198,199,200
Sousa 296
Sukie 231
Susie 123,274,295,296,297,298
Thulwar 149
Tom 295,296,298
Tommache 296
Tulsa 21,22,23
Yahola 274,275,276,277,278,279,
  280,281,313
HARLAN
  J 60
  John 99
HARLINGS
  Tony 272
HARMAN
  B T 92
  Ben T 93,94
  Lonie 93,94
  Mary J 93,94
HARMON
  B T 91

Index

Ben T 90,91
Lonie 90,91
Mary J 90
HARRIS
  E B 49,195,196
HARRISON
  Geo H 164,165
  R P 61,98,99
  Robert P 60,98
HARRY
  Aggie 32,33
  Henry 32
  Micey 35,36
  Micy 34
  Nicy 32
HATCH
  A A 258
HAWKINS
  Gabriel 273
HAYNES
  J M 224
  Martha 305,307,308,310
  S J 22,23,24
HAYNIE
  Felix 83,84,85,86
HAY-NIE
  Mar ch 84
HAYNIE
  Mar ch 84
  Mary 83,84,85,86
HENAHA
  Roy 143
HENEHA
  Artus 142,143
  Lucy 144,145,146,147,148
  Michiley 145,146
  Mitchell 143,145,146,147,148
  Mitchelly 147,148
  Ralph 142,143,144,145,146,147
  Roy 142,143,144,148
HENRY
  Allen 66,67
  Hillibe Micco 251,252
  Hugh 251,252
  Luella 250
  Mintie 251,252
HEPSIE 96

HERRING
  Fannie 170
HILDEBRAND
  Lizzie 96
HILDERBRAND
  Lizzie 103
HILL
  Arney 161
  Jesse 143
  Jim 305
  Lucy 143,145
HOLT
  Coburn 273
HOWARD
  Laura 257
HUBBARD
  T A 54,55
HUGHES
  B F 288,292,293
HUNTER
  R C 92
HUTTON
  Annie 225,226,227
  Henry 225,226,227
  Iola 225,226,227

INGRAM
  J R 265

JACK
  Lena 311,312,314
JANIE 274
JEFFRIES
  Mattie 273
  Tom 273
JENELY 232
JIMBOY
  W W 154
JOHN 232
  Albert 233,234
  Short 233,234
  Winey 233,234
JOHNSON 232
  Ella 227,228
  Hannah 227,228,229
  Leora 228,229
  Paro 227,228,229

Index

S D 227
JONES
  M C 265
JOSIE
  Jennie 311,312,313,314,315,316, 317
  Lena 311,312,313,314,315,317
  Sofley 311,312,313,314,315,316, 317
KELLEY
  Ned 6,7,8,10
KELLY
  Elizabeth 195,196
  Ferdinand 194,195,196
  Lizzie Moore 194,195,196
  Ned 8,11,12
  Roland E 194,195
KERNELLS
  Lucy 170
KEY
  Hugh Benjamin 250,251
  John E 250,251
  John S 250
  Luella 250
KILLINGSWORTH
  M Y 82,83
KIND
  Ludie 181
KING
  Amos 313
  Falba 34,38
  Harlothoyar 138
  Ludie 178,179,181
KNIGHT
  Jackson 145,146

LARRABEE
  C F 272
LEADER 95
LEETKA
  Jenely 232
LENA
  Lucinda 262,263,265,266
LEVI
  Eddie 273
LINDSEY 96

LITTLEHEAD
  La-sa-wee 65
  Whiteman 65
  Yar-la-wee 65
LONDON
  Betsey 192
LONG
  Jesse ... 302,304,305,306,308,309,310
  Jessie 303,307,308
  Lola 302
  Lolie 305,310
  Roley 302,303,304,306,307,308, 309,310,311
  Wiggie 302,303,304,305,306,307, 308,309,310
LOONEY
  Josiah 135,136,137,138,140,141
LOWE
  Losanna 231
  Louie 231
LUCAS
  W W 188
LUCINDA 231
LUCY 150
LUCY ANNA 142
LUMPKIN
  R W 207
LUMPKINS
  R W 209
LUSK
  A M 63
LYNCH
  Robert E 39
  Yanah 8,10,21
  Yarnah 11
  Yarnar 12,15

MCBIRNEY
  Dorothy V 39
  Dorothy Vera 38
  James H 38,39
  Lea 39
  Robert A 39
  Vera 38,39
MCBRIDE
  B A 49,50,51,52
  Nancy 50

Index

MCCAN
　Mrs T E 252,254,255
MCCOY
　Henry 128,129
　Ollie 128,129
　Sallie Clinton 128,129
MCCOZO
　Bennie 118,119
MCDERMOTT
　J 2,16,44,46,96,99,100,113,117,
　　118,122,151,210,240,241,275,303
　Jesse 11,13,17,56,95,99,100,136,
　　139,149,156,200,260,302
MCDONALD
　Edward Ray 87,88
　Martin J 87,88
　Mattie B 87
　Mattie B Dryden 88
MCGIRT
　Katy 228,229
　Solomon 242,244
MCGUIRE
　Geo W 282
MCINTOSH
　Josiah 272
　Nelson 273
MCKENNON
　A S 182,183,186
MCKINNON
　A S 187
MCQUEEN
　W E 303,306,307,308
MALAT
　H G 178,181
MALOT
　H G 265
　Harve 260
MARLIN
　W M 61
MARS
　F L 41,42,43
　James J 71,73,75,76
MEACHAM
　Olin W 252
MEADERS
　Illegible 154
MERIWETHER

A L J 107,110,112
MERRICK
　Edward 40,42
　Lona 14,16,208,319
MERRIWETHER
　A L J 106,110,111
MICCO
　Chisse 178,181
　Sissie 178,181
MICHILEY 142,143
　Ralph 143
　Roy 143
MICKEY 118
　Palmer 119
MILES
　E D 158,159,167,168,169
MILLER
　Benjamin 39,40,41
　Benjamin F 40,41,42,43
　George Thomas 40,41,42
　J Y 1,157,201,303
　James Franklin 39,40,42,43
　Maggie 76
　Maggie M 71,74,75,76
　Margaret A 39,40,41,42,43
　Mrs Maggie M 43
MITCHELL
　Addie 283
　Albert 220,221,222,223,224
　J 240
　Joseph 240,241,242,243,244,245,
　　246,247,248
　Mrs Sam 245
　Nellie 240,241,242,243,244,245,
　　246,247,248
　P S 196
　P S, MD 196
　Peggie 220,222,223
　Peggy 221,224
　Sam 240,241,242,243,244,245,
　　246,247,248
　William 188
　Willie 220,221,222,223,224
MOFFIT 150
MOORE
　Albert 76,77,78,79
　Leah 76,77,78,79

Index

Susie 76,77,78,79
MORTON
   Ellis M 64
   Ellis N 62
   Josie A 62,64
   Mossie 62,64
   Mossie M 62
MOTT
   M L 270
MURPHY
   Joseph 151,152,153
   Lilley 152,153
   Lillie 149,150
   Lilly 150,151,152
   Mahala 150,151,152,153
   May 94
MURRELL
   Calhoun 230
   Lucy 230
   Wiley 230
MUSGROVE
   George 172
   Herold D 172
   Myrta May 172

NEWBERRY
   Buford 281,282
   Jennetta 281,282
   John 281,282
NOON
   Louisa 117,118,119
   Lucinda 117,118,119,120
   Wiley 117,118,119,120
NORMAN
   H T 255

OPRY
   Luther 206
OWEN
   Dr J P 252
OWNBY
   Noel C 17

PARKS
   Dora Ellen 133,134
   Margaret Atkins 133,134
   Margret Atkins 134

Wm 133
PARRISH
   Zera E 66,209
   Zera Ellen 4,26,121
PATTERSON
   John B 140
PEA
   Maggie 219
PERRYMAN
   Benjamin 293,294
   E N 287,290,291
   Illegible C 48,49
   Mary 293,294
   Montie 293,294
   Willie 273
PHILLIPS
   John H 22,23,24,198,199
PITMAN
   Jennie 162,163,165,166
PITTMAN
   Jennie 164
   Lewis 79
PLUMMER
   Lizzie 89
POE
   Magie Nola 273
POSEY
   Alex 44,45,46,47,122,125,147,148,
171,174,184,185,189,192,193,194,223,
228,229,231,233,234,236,238,239,24
1,249,258,260,262,263,266,274,275,2
76,284,296,297,298,304,309,311,312,
313,314,315,317,321,323
PROCTOR
   Dave 322,323
PRYOR
   M R 29
PURSLEY
   George A, MD 88
PURSLY
   George A, MD 88

REDDING
   William P 79
REYNOLDS
   Arthur 318
   Arthur Leroy 322,323,324

Index

Era Edna 319,320,321,322,324
John R 318,319,320,321,322,324
Lizzie 318,319,320,321,324
William 318
RICKETS
   Charles Francis 72
   Clarence Francis 71,73
   Dora Ardell 70
   Ethel J 70,72
   Robert J 72,73
   Robt J 70,72
RICKETTS
   Clarence F 74,75
   Ethel J 68,69,70,71,73,74,75,76
   Goldie A 70,71,73,74
   Goldie Ardell 69,73,75,76
   Joseph C 137,138,141
   Robert J 70,71,73,74,75
   Robt J 69
   Robwer J 76
RIDER
   Chas 118,119
RILEY
   Bonney 283
   Louisa 233
   Sarah 233
ROBINSON
   Geo B 106,107,110,111,112
   Geo L 227
ROBISON
   Barney C 242,243,244,245
ROGERS
   John 1,2
   Lecus 1
   Legus 1
   Louie 1,2,3
   Melvina 1,2
ROOSEVELT
   President 318
ROSS
   Joshua 88
ROTHHAMMER
   Ernest Ralph 113,114
   Joseph 113,114
   Louisa J 113,114
ROWELL
   D R 92

RUNYAN
   Chas F 98

SALLIE 302
SANDY
   Jacob 249
   Sophia 249
   Stella 249
SARFARTCHA 154
SARHOSA 23
SARHOSKA 22
SARTY
   Jasper 8,15,20,21
SCHARNAGEL
   Belle C 251
   Charles E 250,252
   Charles E, MD 252
   Chas E, MD 251
SCHOENECKE
   Amalie 164
SCOTT
   James .. 121,122,123,124,125,126,127
   Jas 145,146
   Lillian 121,122,123,124,125,126
   Lillians 127
   Lucinda 234
   Lucy 121,122,123,124,125,127
   Marguerite 273
   Robert 273
   Wicey 150
SELIE 137,139
SEWIKIE 136,139
SHALLENBERGER
   W D 257,258
SHELBY
   David 56
SHEPHERD
   K H 82,83
SHERRILL
   Chas M 68
SIMBALY 274
SIMMONS
   John 136,139,140,141
   Samuel 136,139,140,141,142
   Sarah 140
SIMON
   Sophia 29

Index

SKAGGA
  D C 47
  Drennan C 47
SKAGGS
  D C 44,45,46,63,93,122,125,147,
    148,171,174,184,185,189,192,193,194,
    223,228,229,233,234,236,238,239,24
    1,249,258,262,263,266,276,284,296,2
    97,298,304,309,311,313,314,315,321,
    323
  Drennan C 44,45,46,64,65,89,125,
    147,148,149,171,172,173,174,184,185,
    186,189,192,193,194,200,204,205,
    211,212,213,214,223,228,229,232,233,
    234,236,237,238,239,240,241,242,
    249,250,253,258,259,260,262,263,266,
    267,276,284,285,298,299,300,304,
    309,315,321,322,323,324
SLAWSON
  Alcy 320
  Mrs 319
SLOAN
  Lillie 231
  Lodie 231
  Peter 231
SMITH
  Belcher 198,199
  Estella 196,197,198,199
  Ester 299,300,301
  Eurania 299,300,301
  Frank J 165
  Jep 165
  Joe 322
  John 299
  John F 300,301
  Lucinda A 114
  M T 295
  Phyllis 195
  T H 188
SNAKE 231
SOLOMON
  Wisey 197
SPENCER
  Echoille 183
  Lamsey 178,181
  Lanah
    174,175,176,177,178,179,180,181,18
    2,184,186,187
  Loma 174,175,176,177,179,180,
    181,183,185,186
  Lomah 178,179,181,182
  Ludie 177,178,179,181,182,183,
    186,187
  Nancy 183
  Ramsey 174,175,176,177,178,179,
    180,181,182,183,184,185,186,187
  Rhoda
    174,175,176,178,179,180,181,182,18
    4,185
SQUIRE
  Annie 112,113
  John 112,113
  Sarah 112,113
STEWART
  Chas E 48,49
STIDHAM
  Eliza 240
  Mahala 187
  Tim 242,243,244,245
  Timmy 240
SUKEY
  Martha 230
SUVIER
  Martha 32
SWOFFORD
  J S 242,244

TARYE 149
TATUM
  B S 50,51
TAYLOR
  Dennis 273
TEMARHESEH 150
THOMAS
  Lucy 3,5
THOMPSON
  Alex 17
TIGER
  Charles 273
  James
    .6,7,8,9,10,11,12,13,14,15,17,18,19
  Jas 8,20,21
  Jefferson 232
  Jim 18

Index

Joanna 7,8,9,10,11,12,13,14,15,16,17,18,19
Lilly 232,233
Lily 7
Lucinda 232,233
Mary 14,19,20,21,132,133
Moty 17
Nancy ...6,7,8,9,10,11,12,13,16,18,19
Nicey 13,14,19,20,21
Philip 9,11
Phillip 6,7,9,11,14
Thomas 12,15,16,19,20,21
TONEY
  Foley 231
  Lijah 231
TRENT
  Chaney A 134
TULMOCHUSEE
  John 317
TULMOCHUSSEE
  John 311
TURK
  N G 59

UPTON
  Dan 277,278,304,306,307,308

WAINWRIGHT
  W H 116
WALKER
  Rhoda 272
WAREN
  S E 320
WASH
  Austin 95
  Goerge 95
  Lizzie ...94,95,96,99,100,101,102,103
  Mrs 95
  Peter 95,99,100,101,102,103
  Rhoda 95
  Wesley 95
WASHINGTON
  Aggie 32,35,36
  Dixon 32,33,34,35,36,37,38
  George 31,32,33,34,35
  Lizzie 96,97,102,103
  Maggie 31,32,33,34,37,38

Peter 95,96,97,102,103
Sadie 31,32,33,36,37,38
WATSON
  S A 277
  Sandy 237
WEAVER
  Amos 105,106,107
  Bert Leo 81
  Bert W 80,81
  Billie 104,105,109
  Billy 110
  Edward 104,105,106,107,108,
    109,110,111
  L J 80
  L P 81
  Lizzie 104,105,106,107,108,
    109,110,111
  Lois Alleen 80
  May 104,105,108,111
  Mrs L J 81
  Rena 80,81
WESLEY
  Charley 303,306,307,308
WHITFIELD
  A W 227
WIGGIE 303
WILLIAMS
  Ada Bell 61
WILLINGHAM
  Minnie 170
WILLIOR
  Peggy 220,221
WILLIYA
  Peggie 222
WILLMOTT
  Jno W 183,186,187
  John W 182,183,186,187
WILSON
  Horace 305
  Jesse E 273
WINE
  Miss 319
WINN
  Lizzie 236
WINSTON
  James A 92,93
  Jas A 93

336

Index

L A 62
WISEMAN
    Charley 88
    Charlie 89
    Charly 90
    Harry 88,89,90
    Hepsey 89,90
    Hepsie 88,89
WOLF
    Nancie 191
    Nancy 187,188,189,190,191
    Seaner 188,189,190,191
    Senar 187,188,189
    Wallace 187,188,189,190,191
WOOD
    Eliza 212,213
    Mary 92
    Zigler 212,213
WOODS
    Cora 67
WRIGHT
    Fannie 224
WYNN
    Earl 237

YAHALA
    Chapley 150
    Wicey 150
YAHDIHKA
    Cinda 231
    Joe 231
YAHOLA
    Mollie 24
YARHOLA
    Mollie 24
YAS-TA-KO-THLA-NAN 65
YOU-CON-CO-CON -THLA-NAY .. 57
YOU-CON-CO-CON-THLA,NAY 57
YOU-CON-CO-CON-THLA-NAY
    53,55,56

www.ingramcontent.com/pod-product-compliance
Lightning Source LLC
Chambersburg PA
CBHW020244030426
42336CB00010B/602